KT-502-444

Healthcare Library H05
Tom Rudd Unit
Moorgreen Hospital
Southampton SO30 3JB
Tel: 023 8047 5154
www.hantshealthcarelibrary.nhs.uk
library.moorgreen@southernhealth.nhs.uk

To be renewed returned on or before the date marked below

-3 JAN 2007   19 FEB 2013

- 7 FEB 2008   15 APR 2013
1 6 APR 2008   -9 SEP 2013

29/4/09

2 4 JUL 2009

1 1 FEB 2010   - 8 JUL 2015

1 9 NOV 2010   2 1 UEU 2016

1 1 JAN 2011   1 3 MAR 2017

19 FEB 2013   1 9 APR 2022

Author   GROICH, C

Title   Qualitative data analysis.

SWNHS

C20303781

Qualitative Data Analysis
An Introduction

Carol Grbich

Healthcare Library
Hawthorn Lodge
Moorgreen Hospital
Southampton
SO30 3JB

 **SAGE Publications**

London • Thousand Oaks • New Delhi

© Carol Grbich 2007

First published 2007

Apart from any fair dealing for the purposes of research or
private study, or criticism or review, as permitted under the
Copyright, Designs and Patents Act, 1988, this publication
may be reproduced, stored or transmitted in any form, or
by any means, only with the prior permission in writing
of the publishers, or in the case of reprographic
reproduction, in accordance with the terms of licences
issued by the Copyright Licensing Agency. Inquiries
concerning reproduction outside those terms should be
sent to the publishers.

 SAGE Publications Ltd
1 Oliver's Yard
55 City Road
London EC1Y 1SP

SAGE Publications Inc.
2455 Teller Road
Thousand Oaks, California 91320

SAGE Publications India Pvt Ltd
B-42, Panchsheel Enclave
Post Box 4109
New Delhi 110 017

British Library Cataloguing in Publication data

A catalogue record for this book is available
from the British Library

ISBN 978 1 4129 2142 8
ISBN 978 1 4129 2143 0 (pbk)

Library of Congress Control Number 2006927822

Typeset by C&M Digitals (P) Ltd, Chennai, India
Printed on paper from sustainable resources
Printed in Great Britain by The Cromwell Press Ltd,Trowbridge, Wiltshire

Healthcare Library
Hawthorn Lodge
Moorgreen Hospital
Southampton
SO30 3JE

Contents

Part One

The State of the Art

These first two chapters clarify some of the theoretical and practical issues which underpin qualitative research and about which you as researcher need to be informed prior to making decisions regarding the design and analysis of your study. If you decide to go down one particular path and choose say an ethnography as your preferred research design, you will need to understand and to be able to articulate which knowledge tradition (epistemology) together with its claim to understanding (ontology) your choice will fit into and how this may influence your data collection and data analysis.

One of the most important things to note with regard to qualitative research is its flexibility. This flexibility does allow very considerable deviation and adaptation of design to occur and – taking the ethnographic example further – would provide several options for you to choose amongst, including classical, critical and feminist ethnographies, autoethnography, ethno drama and cyber ethnography (see Chapters 3, 4, 7 and 13). In making your choice, it is important to understand that these approaches all come from very different knowledge traditions with different theories and principles underpinning them and with potentially quite different outcomes in terms of the type of knowledge to be gained. Understanding these differences will put you in a better position to clarify, justify and further adapt your choices.

Chapter 1 identifies the major knowledge traditions and indicates the impact of these epistemologies on the design you might choose. The inclusion of a hypothetical research question should help to illustrate how you might go about applying each different tradition.

Chapter 2 examines the key issues which you will need to consider in deciding how you will design and analyse your study and explains the broad analytic groups that are available for you to choose from. In particular you will be shown how to undertake the two most useful forms of data analysis: preliminary data analysis and thematic analysis.

1

Epistemological Changes and their Impact on the Field

This chapter identifies the knowledge traditions (called epistemologies) which you as qualitative researcher will need to be familiar with in choosing the approach you will take in your own research study, As you can see, each tradition is still surrounded by very considerable debate both for and against. The most recent epistemology – postmodernism – is explored in some detail, in particular the impact it has had across the field of qualitative research on research design, on the positions of the author and reader, and on data display.

Key points

- What constitutes truth (and acceptable knowledge) has been a source of considerable argument over the last 200 years.
- There are four broad epistemological traditions impacting upon qualitative research within which claims for 'truth' have been made:

  - positivism/empiricism
  - critical emancipatory positions
  - constructivism/interpretivism
  - postmodern and poststructural positions.

- The advent of postmodernism and poststructuralism within the past four decades has had considerable impact on:

  - what now constitutes knowledge
  - research design
  - the positions of the author and the reader
  - data display.

Epistemological and ontological positions

The term 'epistemology' comes from the Greek language, with *episteme* meaning knowledge and *logos* meaning theory. Epistemologies deal with questions about 'truth': what do we accept as truth? And how has this been constructed? Our claims to knowledge about the nature of being and reality (ontology) are also questioned: what do we know? And how can we know this?

In choosing your research design and analytical processes, it is essential to be able to identify which of the following epistemological traditions you have chosen to work within. A brief history of the major epistemologies from positivism to postmodern and poststructural positions will help you to clarify and contextualise the terminology and will provide for you a more in-depth perspective of their influences on qualitative research as you seek to justify your research choice. At the end of each tradition, a quick insight is provided into how the research question *What can we do about youth homelessness?* could be dealt with by that particular approach. The advent of postmodernism and poststructuralism has had considerable impact on qualitative research in general and the forms of this impact will also be clarified for you.

Positivism/empiricism

The eighteenth century in Europe was an era, termed the Enlightenment, where positivism (the school of philosophy that asserts that reality lies only in things which can be seen with the eye), optimism, reason and progress became the dominant discourses (ways of thinking, speaking and writing) and all knowledge was believed to be accessible through processes of reason. The 'rational man' was believed to have the capacity to uncover a singular knowable reality through pure understanding and rigorous intellectual reasoning. These processes of broader reason, needed to gain knowledge, included a focus on observation in order to gain 'facts' via scientific deduction. Scientific knowledge gained from observation and based in logical thought processes was seen as having the potential to displace ignorance and superstition which were the tools of power of the Church. Scientific knowledge was seen as having the capacity to facilitate freedom from religious influences and to lead the way to a new world built on the notion of a universal foundation of knowledge.

In more detail, positivism views truth as absolute and values the original and unique aspects of scientific research such as realistic descriptions, truthful depiction, studies with clear aims, objectives and properly measured outcomes, a focus on neutrality, objectivity (knowledge of reality gained by a neutral and distant researcher utilising reason, logic and a range of carefully pre-tested research tools) and theory testing that can distinguish between facts and values.

Major characteristics

- Knowledge is viewed as being able to be deduced from careful processes of hypothesising, variable identification and measurement within experimental designs, resulting in the identification of causality and allowing predictions to be made about 'facts' which have been properly evaluated by mathematical logic.

- Dominant features include scientific principles, regularity, order, deductive logic, 'laws' of nature, observation and experience (reason), causality, linearity (along a one-dimensional line), logical determinism (everything is caused by something else in a long line of causation) and statistical analytical approaches based on 'true facts'.
- Classification, order and hierarchy, prediction and the universality of findings are emphasised and the central authority of the learned, published author is paramount.
- Knowledge lies in the grand theories and the master narratives of progress reinforced through processes of scientific measurement and rationalist thought. This knowledge is stored in specialist disciplines with defined boundaries, which are carefully protected and maintained.

Despite the fact that most of our best scientific advances occur within this tradition, debates regarding positivism/empiricism have been very active. Around the turn of the twentieth century, changes in scientific knowledge led critics to query the probability that science could provide all the answers. Researchers' ability to provide predictable and replicable outcomes and to control variables came under debate as Einstein's theory of relativity and later Heisenberg's theory of uncertainty were highlighted. These new theories challenged the assumption that a world, which could be precisely measured and documented, exists independently, just waiting for us to gain sufficiently sophisticated tools to discover it. The belief that absolute, knowable truth existed became sidelined and provisional truths became a more likely outcome. The ultimate essence of external reality was also challenged by Sigmund Freud's (1900/1913) exploration of the unconscious mind as a source of reality construction. He suggested that 'reality' was not only constructed from internal as well as external sources but also changed continually in interaction with the environment, especially in interaction with others, and that what had previously been considered as externally and objectively 'real' was also closely linked to the maintenance of power.

Ongoing issues of contention

- Difficulties with verification of hypotheses, and problems with both analysis and the exact replication of data over time.
- The argument that knowledge is not limited to sense experiences alone and that intuition and other thought processes are also important contributors.
- How objective is objectivity?
- There is an over-focus on causal explanation.
- Positivism tends to impose a particular world view without investigating, describing and understanding phenomena.
- The more static views of rationalism, reason, order and logic have limitations when compared with the newer and more flexible theories of chaos and complexity.

Types of research

Quantitative: experimental or survey.

With regard to the research question *What can we do about youth homelessness?*, your design could involve a survey of a random sample of the population or groups of the population. The results could then be analysed with descriptive or inferential statistics depending, in the latter case, on the capacity of the questionnaire to isolate and measure the relationships between relevant variables within questions. Or, and perhaps even subsequently, you could develop an experimental design where various solutions are trialled with a large group of homeless youth who have been randomly sampled either into different trial programmes, or into a control group who remain in a homeless situation. You could then use statistical analyses to compare the different outcomes.

Although quantitative experimental research is not considered qualitative, descriptive surveys with open-ended questions are often used as one form of data collection, particularly when a broad overview of a population is required (see Chapter 15 for combining quantitative and qualitative data).

More recently within *postpositivism* it has been argued that scientists are inherently biased by their education and life experiences and that their observations are value laden and fallible, making errors likely. Our ability to know reality with certainty is thus problematic and no findings can be viewed as absolute or universally generalisable. This has led some positivists to the modfied epistemology of realism. *Realism* asserts that structures creating the world cannot always be directly observed (as in positivism), and when and if they are observable their genesis is not always clear; thus we also need our creative minds to clarify their existence and then to identify explanatory mechanisms. For example, we can't see gravity but we know it exists, and it requires a mixture of intuition, various intellectual processes and the laws of physics in order to clarify the workings of this force. The focus for research in a realist approach involves the identification of the linking of different realisms: for example, in nursing the biological and psychosocial models of nursing can be linked to a biopsychosocial model which has bridging links to our interpretations of biological mechanisms and to the empirical world as well as our influences on these.

Critical emancipatory positions

Changes in the economic system through industrialisation around the turn of the twentieth century led to increased recognition of Karl Marx's critique of capitalist exploitation, profit, power and class conflict. The outcomes of such economic change became viewed as resulting in societal fragmentation. During the 1960s and 1970s social critics such as feminists identified power imbalances and pointed to the long term oppression of women by men, while others pointed to inequalities in social justice. Reality was now being viewed as power directed and multiply constructed. The origins of 'truth' were seen as lying in obscure history and/or layered aspects of the present and access required a range of approaches including those beyond the scientific. The simplicity of such notions as the integration of the individual, the power of the author, the universality of knowledge and concepts of uniqueness and originality came under question.

In research, critical positions view reality not as existing 'out there' but as being produced by particular exploitative social and political systems comprising competing interests where knowledge is controlled to serve those in power. Issues of race, gender, poverty, politics and culture are seen to shape individual identity. Researchers attempt to identify those who are powerless (usually exploited by those in powerful positions) in order to document their unequal situation and to bring about change through an active process of emancipation involving knowledge sharing or the transformation of society.

Major characteristics

- A focus on questions of identity and how these have been shaped by such dominant cultural institutions as the media, science and religion.
- Documentation of clashes between those in power and those with limited power, be it economic or political.
- Emancipation of oppressed individuals and groups through social transformation is seen as a desirable outcome.

Ongoing issues of contention

- The issue of emancipation: who is in a position to emancipate whom? Are emancipators any better than religious zealots colonising the lives of others, assuming not only that they have all the right answers but that others are lacking in some way?
- How realistic is it to expect researchers to promote social transformation? Even if this could be achieved, what would an ideal democracy look like in terms of equality, justice and freedom?

These problems continue to be subject to fairly considerable debate.

Types of research

Qualitative: including grounded theory, phenomenology, ethnomethodology, ethnography, hermeneutics, socio-linguistics, narratives and feminist research (see later chapters for more on these) and any other qualitative approach which has taken a critical stance. Interviewing, field notes, observation, thick contextualised description and textual perusal using discourse analysis or deconstruction are the most commonly used tools here.

With regard to the question *What can we do about youth homelessness?*, the underlying assumption would be that the current political and economic systems in many developed countries are based in capitalism, whereby profit is the driving force and fewer and fewer workers are forced to produce more and more surplus labour (where the value of producing is less than the value of the product) in order to enable higher profit margins to be gained. This means that those workers with limited qualifications or variations in style, gender, age, race, levels of mental health etc. may be considered unemployable in certain areas. As researcher, you could gather data through interviewing and observation of a range of key people, including people who are homeless, and undertake a discourse analysis of policy documents. These data should clarify the problem and show if and where marginalisation and exclusion are occurring. Data analytic tools you might choose would probably include preliminary data analysis and thematic analysis (see Chapter 2) as well as any other approaches of relevance to your research question. From the information gained, you could suggest solutions to the problem of youth homelessness or you could conduct focus groups with key figures in the welfare industry in order to develop possible solutions. Close interaction with participants, particularly those who are homeless, in order to feed back information and solutions would be assumed to go some way in supporting an emancipatory stance, but you could also choose to become involved in action research (where you work either with people who are homeless to further their agendas and help them to facilitate collective action, or with the government to implement solutions).

Constructivism/interpretivism

These positions assume that there is no objective knowledge independent of thinking. Reality is viewed as socially and societally embedded and existing within the mind. This reality is fluid and changing and knowledge is constructed jointly in interaction by the researcher and the researched through consensus. Knowledge is subjective, constructed and based on the shared signs and symbols which are recognised by members of a culture. Multiple realities are presumed, with different people experiencing these differently.

Major characteristics

- The research focus is on exploration of the way people interpret and make sense of their experiences in the worlds in which they live, and how the contexts of events and situations and the placement of these within wider social environments have impacted on constructed understandings.
- The understandings that researchers construct and impose through interpretation are seen as limited by the frames derived from their own life experiences.
- Subjectivity (the researcher's own views and how they have been constructed) and intersubjectivity (reconstruction of views through interaction with others via oral language and written texts) are of interest here.

Ongoing issues of contention

- The problem of intersubjectivity: how do we know when we have accessed other people's minds?

- An over-focus on the micro as opposed to the macro approach, with the production of a superficial understanding of individual action which takes insufficient account of the structures that produced this.
- The lack of exploration of the interpretive processes which provide the key to the views of both researcher and researched.

Types of research

Qualitative: including grounded theory, phenomenology, ethnomethodology, ethnography, hermeneutics, socio-linguistics, narratives and feminist research (see later chapters for more on these). Interviewing, field notes, observation, thick contextualised description and textual perusal using discourse analysis or deconstruction are the most commonly used data collection tools here.

In the study *What can we do about youth homelessness?*, you would seek patterns of meaning, understandings and definitions of the situation from a range of people including those who are unemployed. It is assumed that interaction between you and those researched will serve to produce a constructed reality and, in order that your interpretations do not dominate, the voices of the researched are usually given fairly substantial displays. You would seek common patterns of meaning through preliminary data analysis and thematic analysis. The major focus would be on in-depth understanding of the problem and identifying related issues, although solutions and recommendations for change are often suggested.

Postmodernism

As we moved toward the last decades of the twentieth century, unified, powerful, centred individuals with an authoritative point of view became rejected in favour of anti-heroes and complex multidimensional individuals. Literature began to mirror the changes in the economy, science, art and architecture by portraying reality as shifting and uncertain rather than set, and by incorporating multiple perspectives from a range of disciplines such as music, philosophy, psychology, sociology and drama as well as including visual possibilities.

Postmodernism views the world as complex and chaotic and reality as multiply constructed and transitional – unable to be explained solely by grand narratives or metanarratives (such as Marxism and Buddhism which make universal claims to truth). Postmodernism is very sceptical of such narratives, viewing them as containing power-laden discourses developed specifically for the maintenance of dominant ideas or the power of individuals. The search for reality 'out there' is qualified by the understanding that society, laws, policies, language, discipline borders, data collection and interpretation are all socially and culturally constructed. In recognition of this socially constructed nature of the world, disruption, challenge and a multiplicity of forms are essential in order to pull these constructions apart and to expose them for what they are. Meaning rather than knowledge is sought because knowledge is limited by 'desire' (lack of knowledge or the imperative to being about change) and constrained by the discourses developed to protect powerful interests and to control the population's access to other explanations. Truth is multifaceted and subjectivity is paramount.

The assumptions from positivism, that the universe is ordered and completely knowable by observation and that an objective reality exists, give way to a view that the universe is chaotic and unknowable. As social constructions and questionable discourses are increasingly seen to dominate knowledge, meanings become recognised as individual creations which require interpretation, negotiation and deconstruction. Interactive communication becomes the context in which knowledge is clarified. If all we can be sure we know are individual and situational constructions, then absolute knowledge becomes unattainable, and all knowledge becomes relative and subject to negotiation. Considerable scepticism should now be observed, particularly toward the metanarratives of social organisation, religion and economic theory, which are seen as having the capacity to provide neither privileged discourses nor universal explanations. Deconstruction of these narratives is viewed as one important way of removing their power.

Major characteristics

- Postmodernism favours 'mini-narratives', which provide explanations for small scale situations located within particular contexts where no pretensions of abstract theory, universality or generalisability are involved.
- The emphasis on the explanatory power of metanarratives has been downplayed in favour of descriptive documentation of specific processes.
- Individual interpretation is paramount; there is no objective reality, and truth and reality lie in the meanings we construe regarding our own subjective perceptions of our life experiences. These narratives must then be considered as providing only a narrow illumination of the chosen topic – a constructed reflection which is time and context bound, a momentary impression of 'truth', a truth limited by the constructions and interpretations of both researcher and researched, a truth which is fluid in its capacity to shift and change with further time and other contexts.
- Reflexive subjectivity (the constantly reflective and self-critical processes undergone by the researcher at all stages of the research process, both here and in constructivism/interpretivism) replaces objectivity. Self-reflexivity involves a heightened awareness of the self in the process of knowledge creation, a clarification of how one's beliefs have been socially constructed and how these values are impacting on interaction, data collection and data analysis in the research setting.
- Truth, reason and logic are seen as being constructed within particular societies and cultures, providing illumination only of meanings within specific cultural understandings.
- Realities are multiple. All are subject to endless formation, reformation, construction and reconstruction, including those of the self, the family and the groups we are aligned to.

- The terminology of 'validity' and 'reliability' gives way to indicating how individually constructed views, which are relative to time and context, match or vary from others in the cultural/social group under investigation. No one view or group of views can be privileged over any others. All are 'valid'. Subjectivity becomes paramount, multiple identities are accepted, and it is assumed that any individual will comprise multiple subjectivities and that these may shift, form and reform in unpredictable ways. Different contexts with different situations and different people allow different identities to be constructed or foregrounded. The researcher and the researched are no longer identifiably separate; they interweave their constructed meanings in a delicate dance of recognition and interpretation as the same narratives are told and retold, presented and re-presented for the reader to hook into.

- Postmodernist forms of display characteristically seek and incorporate irony, playfulness, illusion, pastiche and parody; an emphasis on improvisation and satire targeted to others as well as the self; and the use of a variety of visual, textual and other genres. Multiple narrators and voices as well as fragmented and open and closed forms are used to break open the boundaries and to encourage the audience to see and see through, to participate in events and to interpret experiences gained at (almost) first hand.

- Montages (collages) of sound, text and music and an emphasis on fragmentary images invite readers to participate, to contribute from their own experiences and to take away challenging images for integration with their own life experiences. Complex individuals displaying different aspects of their personae are favoured over simple two-dimensional characters. There is an emphasis on multiple voices providing multiple perspectives but offering no finite answers. (For more on innovative forms of display which have been incorporated into the mainstream of qualitative research, see Chapter 16.)

Ongoing issues of contention

- The pulling apart of language and the deconstruction of discourses may lead to nihilism (or nothingness) and the collapse of knowledge.
- The rejection of objectivity and a lack of certainty make it too difficult for a researcher or the readers to come to any solid conclusion.
- Montages of social reality are too limited to provide information upon which policy decisions can be made.
- The rejection of grand narratives and logic and rationality lead to very limited theoretical explanations.
- Privileging and marginalising, although rejected as an approach, are also tools of postmodernists, and the rejection of truth has not stopped postmodernists seeking their own versions of truth.

Types of research

Most forms of qualitative research now have an established postmodern position: ethnography, grounded theory, action and evaluation research, phenomenology and feminist research in particular (see later chapters). Poststructuralism is also a form of postmodernism.

If you were attempting a postmodern approach to the question *What can we do about youth homelessness?*, you would adopt a small scale, in-depth focused project with multiple data sources and individual narratives. Your study would probably take a specific geographical area where young homeless people were evident, and gain their perspectives through interview or by giving them video cameras to record their own lives and concerns. Other perspectives to be gained might include those of residents living in the areas where people who are homeless congregate, social workers, staff from shelter houses, policy makers and local shopkeepers. You might collect further data from observations of people who are homeless in order to clarify the steps that might successfully be taken to improve their situation at that time. You would display all views – and many are needed to shed light on such a complex situation. If data were collected over time then each set would serve to enhance the overall picture; no one set of data and views would be privileged as being more relevant than any other, including yours and those of the reader. All views are seen as being transitional, time limited, context bound and liable to change with the advent of winter, the withdrawal of support services, the 'clearing' of certain public spaces so that young people who are homeless are forced to withdraw to new locations and adapt new ways of surviving, or the shifts in the views of all parties as other issues take precedence.

The impact of postmodernism on qualitative research

There are three major areas of impact that you now need to consider regardless of whether you undertake a postmodern inquiry or some other qualitative approach. These are the author's position, and the positions of the researchers and the participants (see Chapter 2 for more information). As well as providing new options for these positions, postmodernism has also introduced new and innovative forms of display which have impacted across the whole field regardless of the epistemological tradition or the approach chosen. The following sections demonstrate the variety in choice that is now available to you as researcher regarding positioning.

The position of the author/researcher

As researcher you can choose one position along the continuum from *centred* to *decentred* for the whole study or you can move flexibly between these two polarised positions. Certain techniques are available in order to enable you to achieve decentring: presenting views through the eyes of others who speak directly to the audience, or incorporating the views of others with your views which are represented through your own lens but with transparency of process. As authority slips away, the dominant voice of the researcher is replaced by the voices of participants, voices from other texts, or your own 'I/eye' speaking in your own right. You can highlight both your biases and the sources of information which have influenced your textual construction by bringing the footnotes and secondary sources up into appropriate places in the body of the text. Quotes can be hyperlinked to the original interview (which can also be viewed as a hard copy appendix) so the reader can view the broader content and the intertextual nature of the document. In postmodern approaches, deconstruction (the pulling apart) of previously accepted maxims, overt recycling of ideas and a strong resistance to closure are also evident in the decentring process.

The position of the reader

The reader used to be perceived to have only a passive role and some research still maintains this assumption, presenting information for the reader in such a way s/he either accepts the authority of the researcher or challenges it if sufficiently well informed. In general, it is now assumed that your reader has a more active role and is encouraged to use the text produced by the researcher as one of many sources in the construction of a response to this information. The reader is seen as having the capacity to participate, to interact, to interpret and to respond to the information displayed. To encourage the widest possible reading of your text and to ensure that your reader's role is an active one, you as author can include open reading approaches such as gaps in the text (to be filled in by the reader), paradox (apparently true yet contradictory statements to prompt responses) and complexity (the inclusion of many different layers of voices). It is assumed that each reader will take away something different from your text and that further interpretations and deconstructions will occur in an ongoing manner. The formal incorporation of readers' comments within new editions of previously published books serves to emphasise active participation in the generation of new meanings and this is part of the ongoing transformation of the text.

Poststructuralism

Poststructuralism, with its emphasis on language, forms an important subset of postmodernism. It developed as a reaction to structuralism which sought to describe the world in terms of systems of centralised logic and formal structures. In the creation and communication of meaning, language was seen as a key process. Patterns provided meaning and all words were seen as having recognised meanings which could be learned. In viewing language as a system of signs and codes, the rules and conventions – the deep structures which enable a language to operate within a cultural system – were sought.

Within structuralism and poststructuralism, two data analytic approaches have become popular and are available for use by qualitative researchers. In *discourse analysis*, the dominant ways of writing and speaking about a particular topic are set in place over time and require historical tracking back to identify who has benefited from one particular discourse and how other competing discourses have been marginalised (see more on this in Chapter 11). *Deconstruction* involves textual unravelling via the use of binary opposites and an acceptance of the multiple meanings of words in order to break the boundaries before putting the text back together in another transitional form (see more on this in Chapter 13).

Summary

The epistemologies of positivism, critical theory, constructivism/interpretivism and postmodernism and poststructuralism provide a complex field for you to navigate. Although each epistemology has achieved dominance at particular times, all are still contentious and all are available for you to consider for your own studies. You need to choose the one which best reflects your research question and preferred orientation, or you can choose to blend different traditions. In both cases, you will need to be familiar with the epistemological traditions on offer so you can adequately justify the choices you have made.

FURTHER READING

Alvesson, M. (2002) *Postmodernism and Social Research.* Buckingham: Open University Press. This book provides an overview of postmodern themes and indicates how they might be applied in social research, in particular in interviewing, writing and dealing with language.

Crotty, M. (1998) *The Foundations of Social Research: Meaning and Perspective in the Research Process.* Sydney: Allen and Unwin. A detailed and accessible discussion of positivism, constructivism, interpretivism, hermeneutics, feminism, critical inquiry and postmodernism is provided here.

Denzin, N. and Lincoln, Y. (eds) (2003) *The Landscape of Qualitative Research: Theories and Issues,* 2nd edn. Thousand Oaks, CA: Sage. Part II looks at competing epistemologies (positivist, postpositivist, constructivist, critical theory) as well as specific interpretive perspectives, feminisms, racial discourses, cultural studies, sexualities and queer theory.

Fox, N. (1993) *Postmodernism, Sociology and Health.* Buckingham: Open University Press. Fox shows clearly and simply how the philosophical aspects of postmodernism and poststructuralism can be applied to an individual discipline – here the area of health.

Grbich, C. (2004) *New Approaches in Social Research.* London: Sage. This book explores the implications of postmodernist and poststructuralist ideas on research and in particular on qualitative research. It includes a number of case studies and practical examples to clarify the impact on the researcher, the reader and the participants.

Guba, E. and Lincoln, Y. (1994) Competing paradigms in qualitative research. In N.K. Denzin and Y.S. Lincoln (eds), *Handbook of Qualitative Research*. Thousand Oaks, CA: Sage. This book by Denzin and Lincoln is a collection of readings with authors selected from many disciplines. The chapter by Guba and Lincoln examines various knowledge traditions which are relevant to qualitative research.

Wainwright, S. (1997) A new paradigm for nursing: the potential of realism. *Journal of Advanced Nursing* 26: 1262–71. This article provides an explanation of the potential of realism and its practical application to nursing research.

2

General Approaches to Designing and Analysing Data

Prior issues which you as researcher need to consider as part of your research design are discussed and the four broad traditions of inquiry used in qualitative research are identified. Two generic and widely used approaches to the analysis of qualitative data as they are collected will be illustrated in depth through preliminary data analysis and thematic analysis.

Key points

- In undertaking qualitative research, apart from deciding on your research question and identifying your preferred epistemology, three further aspects need to be dealt with early in the process:

  - frames and framing
  - the positions of the researcher, the participants and the reader
  - research design approaches.

- Within design approaches there are four broad traditions of inquiry:

  - iterative
  - subjective
  - investigative
  - enumerative.

  Each of these has links to one or several epistemological traditions and has a particular focus.

- Preliminary data analysis is a technique which can be undertaken on most data as each segment is collected. It serves to summarise issues emerging and to identify further questions which need to be asked in order to gain holistic data.

- Thematic analysis is commonly used in qualitative research and occurs when all the data are in. It is a process of segmentation, categorisation and relinking of aspects of the database prior to the final interpretation.

Clarification of terminology

The epistemological orientations indicated in Chapter 1 are not concretised into particular time spans; elements of all can be identified throughout the twentieth century, although postmodernism and poststructuralism were largely limited to the latter part of that century. In addition, the traditions of inquiry used to gain data are also very flexible. For example, quasi-statistical approaches from the enumerative tradition can be combined with pure observational ethnographic approaches from the iterative tradition, and may be used in the same study but for different purposes, e.g. the former could be used to identify priorities in policy documents and the latter could enable the understanding of cultural rituals. Thus you can vary your approach to research design depending on your research question and the purposes of data collection.

There are many research designs/approaches in qualitative research, e.g. ethnography, grounded theory, phenomenology. Some have specific sets of guidelines (rather than mandatory steps) including the principles and procedures of inquiry used to collect and analyse information, while others allow you considerable choice in how data will be gathered and managed in order to explore the research question posed. Terminology is somewhat loose here: *methodology* usually involves specific guidelines based on particular principles, while *method* is the technique used for collecting and/or analysing data. In this text *approaches* will be used to cover the former, while the latter will be specified under particular forms of data collection and analysis.

Prior issues for consideration in research design

Once you have decided on your research question and have refined it to a manageable project, clarified your epistemological location and undertaken your review of the literature (although the timing of this is contentious in grounded theory), it is necessary for you to identify and address the following issues, all of which will impact on your chosen design:

- frames and framing
- the position and power of the researcher
- the position of the reader
- research design approaches.

Frames and framing

Every researcher is subject to the influences of their own life experiences and these will frame both your choice of design and more importantly your individual interpretation of the data. The notions of frames and framing came originally from Erving Goffman's frame analysis in which frames 'are the principles of organization which govern social events and the actors' subjective involvement in them' (1974: 10). In other words – how have we come to see the world the way we do and how has this influenced our participation in and understandings of this world? Framing is not just an unconscious process of viewing situations through the frames we have gathered in our lives to date; it is also an active process of the selection of aspects of reality and the application of specific frames to them for clearer comprehension or better communication purposes. For example, an untidy man muttering incoherently and staggering into an emergency ward of a hospital may evoke the initial frame 'drunk' until further examination might lead to a reframing such as 'experiencing a neurological disorder'. Or, you may select and highlight aspects of data in order to apply a frame pertinent to your discipline in the process of presenting results to a particular audience, e.g. the frame 'locus of control' will have particular meaning to psychologists.

So what constitutes a frame? The specialist disciplines we are attached to provide their own set of frames in terms of the theories, concepts and models which have gained explanatory dominance. The particular research approaches we choose have their own framing devices: so if we are undertaking grounded theory (Strauss's version) we would treat the data differently than if we were undertaking a postmodern ethnography, with the former undergoing data fragmentation and the latter maintaining the data largely intact and contextualised. Gender is also a frame where particular world views such as masculinism or feminism may dominate, and membership of a particular ethnic group may also provide its own set of frames based on the religious and moral principles underpinning that group. Adoption of particular frames often blinds you to other possibilities. Class and age differences between you and those you are researching, with their accompanying language and attitude differences, may present similar problems – as may your own particular leanings such as heterosexuality, homosexuality, political viewpoint or preferred theoretical orientation.

Gale McLachlan and Ian Reid (1994) have identified four areas of framing which you need to be aware of:

- *extratextual frames* – the accumulated knowledge which you have obtained and through which you view the world
- *intratextual* frames – your internal framing devices of age, sex, class etc.
- *intertextual frames* – the interpretive frames which you are partial to or dominated by from your discipline/s
- *circumtextual frames* – involving contextual construction and your interpretation of the immediate situation or event.

Recognition, acknowledgement and exposure of the frames that are dominating both your view of reality and your interpretation of texts are clearly necessary, as is an awareness that the act of framing part of the text will disturb and distort existing frames as well as decontextualise the segment. Decontextualisation is further complicated by the likelihood that the social context may well have been significantly constructed through interaction between you and those who you are researching; so you have to be mindful not only of your existing frames and the framing process but also of the level of contribution of the frames of those being researched to your interpretation of the actual data collected.

The position and power of the researcher

Your position as researcher will depend on the approach chosen or adapted together with your frames and the anticipated audience to be addressed. For example, a phenomenological approach would require you to get as close as possible to the essence of the experience being studied while displaying the comments of those being researched in their own voices; an autoethnography (researching the self) would require you to take a position of intensely reflexive subjectivity in order to document your own emotions and experiences; and a postmodern position (except where a highly subjective orientation was being pursued) would decentre your voice in favour of a polyphonic display of the voices of the researched, where your voice will only be one of many.

Depending on the design approach chosen and your frames, decisions will have to be made regarding what is to be done with the data for purposes of analysis. Will the data be rigorously segmented in order to track all possible elements, themes and codes? Or will they be viewed as a complex construction requiring considerable deconstruction or discourse analyses to identify the shifts in power reflected in the ways of writing, speaking and acting which have been tracked historically? Or will you respect the data collected and leave them largely intact to be reconstructed and re-presented in some form of verse, as a dramatic performance or as a pastiche (quilt) of voices to bring the reader closer to the views and events under study? Again the design approach chosen provides guidelines, but these are flexible and can be changed (with justification) by you to suit the needs of the investigation at hand.

The position of the reader

What role will your readers be encouraged to take? Will your strong authoritative voice encourage these people to take a passive position along the lines of: 'As the expert researcher I went out into the field, this is what I found, this is my analysis and interpretation of the situation: take it or challenge it if you dare'? Or will your readers be encouraged to interact in a more dynamic way with the text by virtue of the gaps you provide (for the reader to seek hidden meanings or to fill from their own experience) or through your considerable exposure to the voices of the participants whose stories, artfully woven, bring your readers close to their experiences, their pain, their longings and their understandings, allowing your readers to come to their own interpretations?

Research design approaches

The particular approach which you have chosen may have its own set of guidelines which will indicate not only the type of data to be gathered but also the forms of analysis which may be most useful. The flexibility of qualitative approaches means that these guidelines can be treated either as stage by stage steps not to be deviated from or as indicators of direction enabling you to incorporate other approaches. For example, Anselm Strauss's grounded theory approach, if followed meticulously, would involve you in the precision of a three-stage coding technique with memos and data integration of a graphical as well as a written nature. However, if you wanted to undertake modified data collection or coding approaches you could change this to a 'quasi' grounded theory approach where you could modify these processes or include other approaches, e.g. a phenomenological data set. Justification of these changes by you in relation to your research question will be very important here.

Some approaches encourage creativity by their very general guidelines: for example, using a *basic hermeneutic approach* (interpretive inquiry seeking to understand the meanings of parts within a whole) could give you almost total freedom to decide how to undertake the study, what design aspects to incorporate, which techniques of data collection and analytical tools to employ and what perspectives to call on to provide an interpretation. The older term *field research* also provides the same flexibility, indicating only that you are going out into the research field (however defined) in order to explore it using what you perceive as the best tools available for the job.

Traditions of inquiry and design approaches

There are four major traditions of inquiry: iterative, subjective, investigative and enumerative (Table 2.1). Within each of these fall general design types which can be used flexibly; some design types occur in more than one tradition, while combinations of design approaches and traditions of inquiry can occur in the same study.

The following is a summary of the four broad types of qualitative inquiry. Most of the design approaches listed in the table will be described in greater detail in later chapters.

Iterative (hermeneutic) inquiry

Iterative approaches involve seeking meaning and developing interpretive explanations through processes of feedback. An iterative design is defined as one involving a series of actions of data collection which are repeated until the accumulated findings indicate that nothing new is likely to emerge and that the research question has

TABLE 2.1   Traditions of inquiry and design approaches

Iterative (hermeneutic)	Subjective	Investigative (semiotic)	Enumerative
Grounded theory	Autoethnographic	Structural	Quasi-statistical
Phenomenology	Heuristic phenomenology	Poststructural	Transcendental realism
Ethnography	Postmodern versions of iterative approaches	Discourse analysis	Matrix analysis
Oral history		Content analysis	
Action evaluation		Conversation analysis	
Feminist research and memory work	Feminist Research		
Narratives – socio-cultural		Narratives – socio-linguistic	

been answered. In more detail, this involves you going out into the field, collecting data, and subjecting these data to a critically reflective process of preliminary data analysis to determine 'what is going on' in order to build up a picture of the data emerging and to guide you in the next set of data collection. This cycle is then repeated until the research question is answered and no new data are apparent. There is recognition within this process that both you and those whom you are researching inevitably construct meaning and that you will attempt to minimise both your impact on the setting and your possible over-interpretation of the situation in favour of highlighting the views of those researched. Post data collection, thematic analysis often occurs. This is also a process where data are segregated, grouped, regrouped and relinked in order to consolidate meaning and explanation prior to display. Iterative approaches include the *basic hermeneutic approach* as well as more defined approaches such as *grounded theory, phenomenology, ethnography, oral history, action, evaluation, socio-cultural narratives, feminist versions* of all of the above and *memory work.*

Example
Consider the research question *What is the experience of mature aged women returning to university/college?* An iterative approach within the basic hermeneutic tradition of inquiry would just go backwards and forwards to and from the field (in this case involving interviews with mature aged women, sampled for diversity of age, situation and years in study) using preliminary data analysis as a guide (see later in this chapter), resampling to include unforseen groups/situations, rethinking aspects of the question, and collecting and cross-questioning all the data until no

new data emerge. A phenomenological approach would examine the experiences of six women over time, and in-depth information would be gained through going back several times to ask the same question: 'What is the experience of returning to university/college like for you now?' A Straussian grounded theory approach would use the three-stage coding process to identify and to open up all the sub-questions relating to the major research question, to cross-question and critique information in order to track the experiences of 15–30 women. An ethnographic approach would meticulously observe and record over time how experiences changed as individuals changed and became more confident within their new contexts. An oral history or narrative might explore in depth only one or a few life stories, while an evaluation might carry out a broad survey of many women plus individual case studies selected for diversity. Feminist/action researchers or critical ethnographers might seek to emancipate those women whose experiences indicated that oppression had been an issue.

As you can see, in all of these designs the common element involves the *recursive spiral*: define the question, go out into the field, examine the data collected, adjust the various tools of questioning, sampling approach, design aspect and data collection in light of emerging issues, and go back into the field to find out more. You repeat this process until no new data emerge and all possible aspects of the question appear to have been answered.

Subjective inquiry

Subjective approaches are defined as those where there is a focus on you the researcher and on what takes place within your own mind, recognising that this is limited by your own biases and judgements. Data collection approaches will be different when the focus of the research includes your experiences. Here you will need to maintain a critically reflective diary record and be prepared to subject yourself to regular periods of debriefing with a colleague or supervisor. The process involves a rigorous assessment of both your emotions and experiences and your impact on the research process. When your experiences are the sole or partial target of the research you will occupy a dual role – that of researcher and researched. Preliminary data analysis is again a key analytic technique, with thematic analysis being a further option depending on how much decontextualising and segmenting you regard as appropriate or desirable. Subjective approaches include *autoethnography, heuristic phenomenology* and *some postmodern versions of ethnography, grounded theory, feminist, evaluation* and *action research* where the researcher has chosen to include a significant segment of subjective data.

Example
Carolyn Ellis has been instrumental in developing subjective approaches. Her personal and emotive story of her relationship with her husband Gene (Ellis, 1995)

demonstrates the tracing of the impact of change on herself as she moves from a situation of being part of a couple, very much in love, to becoming a caretaker for a husband dying from emphysema. The documentation of this process led her to accumulate considerable data including: detailed field notes of the relationship and the illness processes from eight months prior to his death; interviews with family and friends; medical case notes; personal diaries and travel logs. Carolyn was the object, subject and researcher and also wrote the final version in the first person as she attempted to move from realist ethnography to literary narrative in her search for the right 'voice' to clarify her personal experiences and understandings as well as the sociological significance of these events (the process is documented in more detail in Tierney and Lincoln, 1997: 127–31). Ellis focused on emotions and feelings (narrative truth rather than historical facts), moving from past to future, incorporating alternative versions and her own multiple voices in an open text which emphasises ambivalence and contradiction as outcomes.

You can see from this example that although subjective inquiry provides the opportunity for a focus on the self it is also possible to use the general iterative inquiry approach in order to achieve this.

Investigative (semiotic) inquiry

Investigative semiotic approaches involve the uncovering of previously hidden information relating to languages within their cultural contexts. The understanding of signs and symbols is central to this approach, in particular their mythical strength and the embedded power of particular discourses, which you will need to disentangle to reveal the original elements as well as to identify arguments which have been marginalised. There is considerable variety amongst the continuum of possibilities relating to analysis of documentation, visuals and body language, varying from the looser ethnographic content analysis approach which attempts to contextualise the document and to identify and describe the values and attitudes evident, to the precision of some forms of discourse and semiotic analysis. But again the flexibility and the ever changing nature of qualitative approaches allow you considerable variation, especially when you provide adequate justification. Investigative approaches include *structural, poststructural, content analysis and feminist research,* as well as *discourse analysis, conversation analysis* and *narratives of the socio-linguistic* type.

Example
Julie Hepworth (1999) undertook an investigative, feminist, discourse analytic approach to explore medical documentation on anorexia nervosa from the late nineteenth century over a period of 100 years in order to identify the major discourses present. She also interviewed current health professionals. From these two sources of information she was able to expose five discourses in the medicalisation of anorexia nervosa: *femininity* (women as emotional and deviant psychological,

mental and reproductive entities); *medical* (the search for scientific organic causes); *clinical* (prescriptive treatment and the (moral) quality of relationships); *discovery* (link between medicine and psychiatry); and *hysteria* (link between femininity and the psycho-medical framework through the notion of hysteria). The power of medicine in the maintenance of the enduring discourse of *femininity* (irrational female behaviour) was exposed.

Enumerative inquiry

This involves the listing or classifying of items by percentages, frequencies, ranked order or whatever is useful to the research question. These approaches involve you in the production of 'objective' accounts of the content of verbal, written or visual texts, the development of codes and categories often prior to analysis, and the definition and measurement of units of analysis. Tools include flow charts, logical reasoning processes, the seeking of links between causes and antecedents, and the frequency of occurrences through identification of word frequency, ordered (ranked) word frequency, key words in context and incidence counting. Replication of outcomes, particularly when specific documents are used, is also sought in the enhancement of validity.

The development of previously decided codes can also be seen in the imposition of 'matrices' (conceptual frames of interlinking variables from which propositions with causal implications have been derived) where you apply this to one case and then further apply it to other cases to develop cross-case analysis (Miles and Huberman, 1994). There is an underlying assumption in this process that fully pre-designed instrumentation will enhance validity and generalisability. Enumerative approaches are often questioned because of their tendency to atomise and decontextualise the data and the fact that connection does not necessarily equal causation. Approaches include *quasi-statistical, transcendental realism* and *matrix analysis*.

Example
Clive Seale (2002) undertook a content analysis of reports of people with cancer from a range of worldwide English speaking newspapers to compare portrayals of males and females. From the original sample of 2419 he chose a subsample of 358 where there was significant coverage of the life or death of a person with cancer. The computer management program for qualitative data NVivo was used to help extract and code segments and identify linguistic themes relating to people with cancer. The program Concordance (used for proximity of certain words, counting word frequency and key words, and available at no cost at http://www.concordancesoftware.co.uk, accessed 16 April 2006) was also used for further examination of these themes for word concordance (location and similarities). Seale discovered that women's emotions of fear and anxiety were reported much more often than men's and that 10 metaphors relating to 'the journey' of cancer were used for women but only three for men. 'Courage' and 'inspiring to others' formed

the dominant portrayal of women while 'hardworking' and 'altruistic' dominated for men.

During data collection: preliminary data analysis

For many of the above design approaches, the initial stage of analysis involves preliminary data analysis. This applies in particular to the iterative approach – apart from Strauss's version of grounded theory (which has its own more developed version of this, open coding) – and to subjective approaches, as well as to some of the investigative approaches. Preliminary data analysis is an ongoing process which is undertaken every time data are collected. It involves a simple process of checking and tracking the data to see what is coming out of them, identifying areas which require follow-up and actively questioning where the information collected is leading or should lead the researcher. It is a process of engagement with the text, not so much as to critique it – although this is one possibility, especially where existing documentation is concerned – but more to gain a deeper understanding of the values and meanings which lie therein.

Regardless of whether the data collected come from written observations, transcriptions of interviews or the perusal of existing documents, you should undertake this process in order to highlight emerging issues, to allow all relevant data to be identified and to provide directions for the seeking of further data.

The process with regard to interview data is demonstrated below.

Process

The following is a segment of an interview conducted in 1990 by Robert Couteau with the author Ray Bradbury. The segment has been treated as if it were a research interview and the process of preliminary data analysis is displayed.

Following the completion of this process, you then undertake collation and summary of the major points gained from the interview, observation or document. I find a face sheet containing the following information to be effective.

Firstly, identifiers for the data set:

- Who is this interview/observation with/of (pseudonym/code is usual to maintain anonymity)?
- When and where was it conducted and for how long?
- What special circumstances or contextual issues might have impacted on the data?

Secondly, examination of what is going on in this text:

- What are the major issues emerging?
- What issues need to be followed up (with this person/setting or the next interviewee/setting/document)?

25

'The Romance of Places': an interview with Ray Bradbury

Interview segment	Preliminary data analysis
Couteau: My first question concerns the actual process of writing. Do you have any sort of daily ritual that serves as a preparation to writing, or do you just sit down every day at a certain time and begin?	
Bradbury: Well, the ritual is waking up, number one, and then lying in bed and listening to my voices. Then, over a period of years ... I call it my morning theater; inside my head. And my characters talk to one another, and when it reaches a certain pitch of excitement I jump out of bed and run and trap them before they are gone. So I never have to worry about routine; they're always in there talking.	*'Morning theater': how long does this process take? What does he do if he forgets what they have said or is distracted before he can complete writing down what they have said?*
Couteau: How long do you write for?	
Bradbury: Oh, a couple of hours. You can do three or four thousand words and that's more than enough for one day.	*Do all authors write this fast: 3000 to 4000 words in a couple of hours?*
Couteau: How has the use of the computer affected your writing?	
Bradbury: Not at all, because I don't use it.	
Couteau: You never use a computer?	
Bradbury: I can write faster on a typewriter than you can on a computer. I do 120 words a minute and you can't do that on a computer. So I don't need anything ... That's plenty fast.	*Efficient typing appears to be the key to high productivity here.*
Couteau: So you're saying that the technology still hasn't caught up with you?	

(Continued)	
Interview segment	Preliminary data analysis
Bradbury: Well, if it won't be any more efficient than my IBM Selectric, why should I buy it? It's for corrections, you know? Then I give it to my daughter and she has a computer and she puts [it] in, and she then corrects it in the computer. And we have a record so we have [the best of] both worlds at the same time. Couteau: How about the imaginative process itself, the building of a story? How do characters and plots first arise? (You've maybe covered this a little just now.) Do they appear spontaneously or do they first originate in a carefully planned, conscious construct?	*Is this process similar to that undertaken by other authors who started writing in a pre-computer age?*
Bradbury: Any carefully planned thing destroys the creativity. You can't think your way through a story; you have to live it. So you don't build a story; you allow it to explode. Couteau: Do you, for instance, use people and places out of the past, out of your own life? Bradbury: Very rarely. More recently [yes,] in my two murder mysteries, *Death Is a Lonely Business* and the sequel, which just came out, *A Graveyard for Lunatics*. Events in my past life are in there; some people that I knew. But most of my stories are ideas in action. In other words, I get a concept, and I let it run away. I find a character to act out the idea. And then the story takes care of itself.	*The 'exploding' story is creative but unplanned. Does it always work like this?* *Does increasing age lead authors into their memories of people and events – what happens to other writers?* *Process involves getting a concept then finding a character to act this out.*

(Continued)

(Continued)	
Interview segment	Preliminary data analysis
Couteau: Certain modern writers such as William Burroughs have used characters and settings first observed in dream states as the basis for fictional experiments. Others such as Henry Miller have often spoken of being dictated to by the unconscious …	
Bradbury: That sounds more like my cup of tea …	*Is the unconscious the only place his characters come from?*
Couteau: Have you had similar experiences with what might be termed non-ego influences on the creative imagination? I mean there are others: drugs or meditation or whatever. Or dreams.	
Bradbury: No, dreams don't work. And I don't know of anyone that ever wrote anything based on dreams constantly. You may get inspiration once every ten years. But dreams are supposed to function to cure you of some problem that you have, so you leave those alone. That's a different process. But the morning process when you're waking up, and you're half-asleep and half-awake: that's the perfect time. Because then you're relaxed and the brain is floating between your ears. It's not attached. Or getting in the shower first thing in the morning, when your body is totally relaxed and mind is totally relaxed. You're not thinking; you're *intuiting*. And then the little explosions, the little revelations come. Or taking a nap in the afternoon. It's the same state. But you can't force things. People try to force things. It's disastrous. Just leave your mind alone; your intuition knows what it wants to write, so get out of the way.	*Not from dreams. Drugs?* *'Intuiting' in a relaxed state may have links to phenomenology and the intuiting of the essences of an emotion or a situation. Would he agree?* *This process sounds almost automatic; did it always happen like this? Does he ever experience writer's block?*

Source: the complete text of this interview – this segment reprinted with permission – is located at http://www.tygersofwrath.com/bradbury.htm, accessed 26 April 2006, copyright © Rob Couteau, 1990

The face sheet from the above interview segment would then look as shown.

Face sheet: interview with Ray Bradbury

Data identifiers

- *Location*: public domain interview with the author Ray Bradbury conducted by Robert Couteau in Paris in the lobby of the Hotel Normandy during the summer of 1990.
- *Date and time*: unrecorded.
- *Length of interview*: approximately one hour.
- *Special circumstances*: none recorded.

Major issues emerging

- For Ray Bradbury his style of text creation, which he views as intuitive, lies in early morning and shower or nap time 'explosions' of the 'voices' of his characters which come via the unconscious when the body is in a relaxed state.
- His style of writing is by typewriter – intense writing of 3000–4000 words over a couple of hours which is then fed into a computer program for correction (by his daughter).

Issues to be followed up

- Has this process always happened like this for Ray Bradbury? What other processes have occurred?
- Would he see this process of intuiting stories via the relaxed consciousness as phenomenological in style?
- How do other writers create text and write?

There is some diversity within the literature as to how this process of preliminary data analysis might occur, but given that it is idiosyncratic, each researcher must decide what works for them. Examples of what other researchers do can be found in the text by Ian Dey (1993: 83–8) who identified the techniques for early interactive reading of data segments as: free association, that is writing freely regarding words, phrases and topics in order to avoid and release fixed researcher assumptions; comparing interviews with own experiences; identifying aspects of the research map, namely the self, the situated activities, the emergent meanings, understandings and definitions, the aspects impacting on the contextual setting as well as the interactions, history, events, strategies, processes and consequences; shifting the focus among the levels of data to highlight other areas; reading the data in different sequences; critiquing the data by asking 'Who?', 'What?', 'Why?', 'When?', 'So what?'; and transposing the data by asking 'What if?' in order to seek new perspectives.

Michele Bellavita (quoted in Ely et al. 1997: 181) has a similar but looser approach. She allows herself to go over the data segment initially, noting ideas and then trying to create names for chunks of data; listing topics, grouping them, noting exceptions and brainstorming; playing with metaphors, analysing specific words and employing the 'flip flop' technique (looking at aspects from different perspectives, asking 'Why?' and 'What if?'); and perhaps attempting to re-present some of the data in the form of a poem or vignette which may form part of a later display of the overall database.

Summaries of issues emerging

You will find it helpful during data collection to start accumulating emerging issues into potential themes. You do this by summarising supportive data for a particular aspect every three to five sessions of interviewing or observation. The advantage of this is that by the end of data collection the twin processes of preliminary data analysis and judicial summaries mean that you have remained close to the data and have plugged any obvious gaps in information. The following is a summary of issues which were starting to become obvious as data were collected in a study on the impact of a government policy to integrate young people with severe to profound disabilities who had previously attended 'special' schools into 'normal' school settings.

'Perceptions of integration': researcher's observations, parents' and teachers' views (from six interviews)

One of the central issues emerging so far is how different people view the integration of special school students into regular schools (maximum of one half to 2 days per week). Parents (of X, Y and Z) all favour this, seeing it as a glimmer of hope, an indication of 'improvement' and a move across the great divide from 'special' to 'regular' schools with accompanying connotations of normality. All are very anxious their son/daughter should remain in the integration program despite 'fitting' (epileptic fits) experienced on regular school days by X, isolation and perceived loneliness of Y when his mate was withdrawn from the program (teacher's perception). X seems to be settling down over time – he likes the pop music in practical classes and although he can't speak he can sing along to the radio/ cassette player and the girls think he is 'cute' and encourage him to sing. Y is ignored (nonverbal and almost blind) and Z has full aide support and a home room to retreat to (for all the special students being integrated in this setting) one where regular students are encouraged to come in and play cards (with students with disabilities – very popular on wet days as it beats standing around in the windswept

---

(Continued)

covered ways which is the only other option). Z seems calm and settled but the presence of an aide may be preventing interaction with regular students in the classroom setting. The environment and support/lack of support appear to impact on the students' experiences. Teachers in special settings fear integration seeing it as leading to a loss of students with the potential of job loss for them – they feel that if the students are starting to move to regular settings they should go too, as they could provide expertise to support regular teachers. The latter view integration is ideologically sound but pointless in practice unless there is full aide support so they don't have to worry about the presence of X, Y and Z or adjust their curricula (and none have so far). X and Y's regular teachers express concerns about what X and Y are gaining from the experience, viewing it as negative and stressful for them (and also for themselves?). It seems clear that schools that are more academically oriented (like the ones X and Y attend) are more resistant to any disturbance caused by integrating students whereas less academically oriented schools, such as the one where Z is located, express less hostility and are more oriented to 'giving it a go'.

Source: data summary for Grbich and Sykes (1989)

The usefulness of preliminary data analysis in filling the gaps and completing the holistic view of the research area becomes obvious here. By the end of data collection you should be 'on top' of the data as opposed to being buried under them. If this process has not been undertaken, you are likely to end up with a room full of data with which you have largely lost contact, and further analysis then exposes the holes and unpursued signposts which may require further sampling and additional data collection to complete.

Following preliminary data analysis, you have a choice either to move directly to interpretation and display or to undertake more formal processes of thematic analysis and coding. Smaller databases can usually be managed with preliminary data analysis alone but larger ones benefit from thematic analysis.

Post data collection: thematic analysis

This is a process of data reduction and is one of the major data analytic options. By the time preliminary data analysis has been completed and all the data are in, it is likely that you will have a fairly clear idea what the database contains in terms of issues that are becoming evident and you will have had the opportunity to explore aspects which initially may not have been considered central to the research question/s.

Thematic analysis is particularly idiosyncratic and can involve a focus on repeated words or phrases, case studies or evidence of answers to the research question/s which have been devised. Metaphors can also be sought on the assumption that all language comprises metaphors but that the choice of particular metaphors by participants can often clarify emotive meanings. Themes may come from previous relevant research which you have reviewed, from myths/evidence within the area being studied, or from your gut feelings, as well as from the views of those being observed or interviewed. This approach to qualitative research insists that the data should speak for themselves initially before any predesigned themes are imposed.

Process

The process of reducing the data into meaningful groupings which are easier to manage can be carried out by a *block and file* approach, by *conceptual mapping*, or by a combination of the two.

The *advantage* of a block and file approach is that you can keep fairly large chunks of data intact; the *disadvantage* is that you end up with huge columns of data which can become unwieldy. The *advantage* of the conceptual mapping approach is that you have a neat and brief summary of the issues which are emerging; the *disadvantage* is that these brief words and phrases tend to oversimplify and decontextualise issues and you need to keep going back to the database to get the fuller story.

To demonstrate this for you, the following example shows how two responses to a question addressed to parents of children with severe intellectual disability were managed. The question was: 'What was the process of gaining an initial diagnosis for your child?' (Grbich and Sykes, 1989).

Block and file approach

Here data can be either <u>underlined</u>, italicised or colour coded to keep them within the context of the overall interview data, or to maintain cases as separate entities.

Responses to: 'What was the process of gaining an initial diagnosis for your child?'

Response 1

<u>He was 14 months old and my husband virtually had to threaten the doctor at X hospital to tell us what was wrong.</u> We knew <u>there was no sign of him [child] trying to sit up at the time. Very quiet, didn't move a lot, hardly cried – more a sort of a whine.</u> <u>The doctor was very evasive</u> and <u>my husband said 'We're not leaving until you tell us and you're not leaving until you tell us.'</u> Then he called another doctor behind a screen and they had a whispered conversation. Then he came

---

(Continued)

back. He felt 'there was a certain degree of retardation but no specific reason why' He told me to continue on with what I was doing and he told me that once a month for four and a half years.

Response 2

*It took me 12 months to convince anyone that there was something wrong. She didn't move, she didn't cry, she slept. The hospital paediatrician said 'No problem'. At three years we took her to another paediatrician because she wasn't walking, wasn't showing any reaction to anyone, she verged on the autistic, used to sit as though terrified. All we wanted at the time was a label. The doctor spent a long time analysing which parent she looked like, we got a bit sick of this. We asked about autism, she went right off. 'There's nothing autistic about your child, you wouldn't want one of those, if she was I wouldn't have her in the place.' We were sent back later to a psychiatrist, she gets this book out – an English book with a picture of a shoe. She said to [child], 'Point to the plimsoll'. Of course [child] sits there and I said, 'Do us a favour, ask her which is the runner'. So she did and [child] pointed, but she still got zero because she didn't know what a plimsoll was. When she was about 8 we found a book on Dyspraxia at the local library which seemed to fit her, we rushed to our local doctor and he sent us back to the hospital. The paediatricians were not impressed. 'I've heard you make **your own diagnosis'** [emphasis in interview] they said looking unamused. But our diagnosis was correct.*

The segments are then grouped and placed in a table with headings added to clarify and categorise the contents of each column (Table 2.2). As you can see, some aspects occur in several columns. In this example the data have been repeated in order to avoid decontextualisation.

Conceptual mapping

You can see the detail available through the block and file approach. Conceptual mapping (Figure 2.1) provides a simpler, more flexible (although potentially more decontextualising) picture of issues emerging from the same two responses. However, a combination of the two approaches can help to minimise the disadvantages.

Both these approaches face the issue that columns and maps can become very heavy with accumulated data. The advantages of both styles are that the data are now in a form from which early writing up can be contemplated. You could take the outcomes of each approach and attempt to summarise or to re-present the data in poetic, narrative or case study format in order to excite your reader.

TABLE 2.2 *Thematic analysis, block and file approach: creating columns*

Length of time to gain diagnosis	Child's symptoms	Responses of health professionals to parents	Parents' responses to health professionals
Response 1 He [child] was 14 months old. He [doctor] told me to continue on with what I was doing and he told me that once a month for four and a half years was correct.	there was no sign of him [child] trying to sit up at the time. Very quiet, didn't move a lot, hardly cried – more a sort of a whine.	The doctor was very evasive. He felt 'there was a certain degree of retardation but no specific reason why'. He told me to continue on with what I was doing and he told me that once a month for four and a half years.	My husband virtually had to threaten the doctor at X hospital to tell us what was wrong. My husband said 'We're not leaving until you tell us and you're not leaving until you tell us.'
Response 2 It took me 12 months to convince anyone that there was something wrong.	She didn't move, she didn't cry, she slept. The hospital paediatrician said No problem'.	The doctor spent a long time analysing which parent she looked like, we got a bit sick of this. We asked about autism, she went right off. 'There's nothing autistic about your child, you wouldn't want one of those, if she was I wouldn't have her in the place.'	The doctor spent a long time analysing which parent she looked like, we got a bit sick of this. We asked about autism, …
When she was about 8 we found a book on Dyspraxia at the local library which seemed to fit her, we rushed to our local doctor and he sent us back to the hospital. The paediatricians were not impressed. 'I've heard you make **your own diagnosis**' they said looking unamused. But our diagnosis was correct.	At three years we took her to another paediatrician because she wasn't walking, wasn't showing any reaction to anyone, she verged on the autistic, used to sit as though terrified.	We were sent back later to a psychiatrist, she gets this book out – an English book with a picture of a shoe. She said to [child], 'Point to the plimsoll.' Of course [child] sits there and I said, 'Do us a favour, ask her which is the runner.' So she did and [child] pointed, but she still got zero because she didn't know what a plimsoll was. When she was about 8 we found a book on Dyspraxia at the local library which seemed to fit her, we rushed to our local doctor and he sent us back to the hospital. The paediatricians were not impressed. 'I've heard you make **your own diagnosis**' they said looking unamused. But our diagnosis was correct.	We were sent back later to a psychiatrist, she gets this book out – an English book with a picture of a shoe. She said to [child], 'Point to the plimsoll.' Of course [child] sits there and I said, 'Do us a favour,' ask her which is the runner.' So she did and [child] pointed, but she still got zero because she didn't know what a plimsoll was.

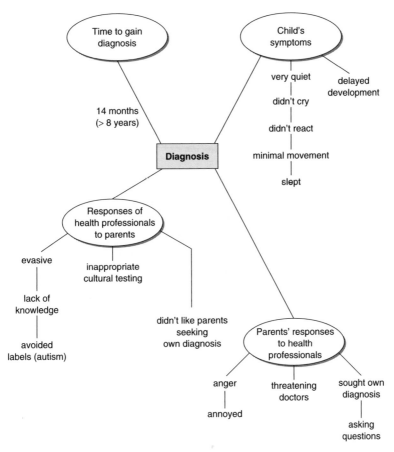

FIGURE 2.1 Thematic analysis, conceptual mapping approach

Summary

In deciding on your design you need to consider who you are and where you are coming from in terms of ideas and life experiences, in terms of your position in the study and in terms of the positions in which you plan to place both your participants and your future readers, as all of these decisions will impact on your design and the collection and analysis of qualitative data. The four broad design types of iterative, subjective, investigative and enumerative link to epistemological traditions: iterative and subjective tend to fall within the constructivist/interpretivist or postmodern traditions, while investigative and enumerative can fit either in the same places or into positivism and postpositivism. To confuse things further, most design approaches have a postmodern version and a critical emancipatory version and some designs will pick up a mixture of versions depending on the question to be researched. The two most useful and most widely used analytic tools are preliminary data analysis and thematic analysis, so it is worth coming to grips with these early.

FURTHER READING

Cresswell, D. (2002) *Research Design*. Thousand Oaks, CA: Sage.
This book provides a focus on theoretical traditions and is accessible to students through the use of exercises and examples.

Kumar, R. (2005) *Research Methodology: A Step by Step Guide for Beginners*, 2nd edn. London: Sage. This book is designed for beginners; it covers the major research traditions as well as general data collection, analysis and interpretation.

Miles, M. and Huberman, A. (1994) *Qualitative Data Analysis: An Expanded Sourcebook*, 2nd edn. Thousand Oaks, CA: Sage. This update of the 1984 edition is a how-to regarding cross-case and matrix analysis.

Minichiello, V., Aroni, R., Timewell, E. and Alexander, L. (1995) *In-Depth Interviewing: Principles, Techniques, Analysis,* 2nd edn. Australia: Longman. This is one of the few books which provide useful detail on the iterative processes of data analysis (preliminary and thematic) as well as the general processes of undertaking a research project.

Part Two

Specific Analytical Approaches

In the following 11 chapters we will examine the tools and analytic procedures which have developed within particular approaches. Although these procedures have a strong historical attachment to the design approaches within which they originated, they are flexible entities and can be lifted out, used and adapted to suit the needs of individual researchers in order to illuminate particular aspects of a research question. The evolutionary nature of qualitative research means that it is most appropriate that you hunt through the tools and procedures available to find the best one for the job at hand and, where none quite fits, to adapt several in order to provide answers to your research question.

However, as most analytical approaches have been strongly linked to particular forms of data collection and may also be underpinned by specific epistemological and conceptual or theoretical underpinnings, you will need to know what it is you are adapting in order to see more clearly what limitations and advantages may eventuate. For example, what happens when a particular approach, underpinned by the concepts of symbolic interactionism and designed primarily for observational data, such as grounded theory, is applied to documentation or to interview data? In another situation, say you have determined that the grounded theory approach (Strauss's version) is the most appropriate for your data analysis but you also want to bring your own voice into the analysis in a subjective manner. The original grounded theory approach you have chosen has embedded in it a neutral researcher position and a third-person voice, so some adaptation of the original method and a justification for the insertion and analysis of your own voice would be necessary. Your approach might then be named subjective grounded theory, or quasi-grounded theory, or postmodern grounded theory, depending on how the adaptation was made and how you have justified this. You need to investigate the advantages and disadvantages of any approach, to trial new ways of proceeding when disadvantages are found, then to publish the outcomes for other researchers to add to their list of possible choices. In this way the field continues to move forward.

Chapters in this part cover

- classical ethnographic approaches
- newer ethnographic approaches
- grounded theory
- phenomenology
- feminist research.

3

Classical Ethnographic Approaches

In this chapter, traditional ethnographic approaches such as classical and critical ethnographies which have their origins in anthropology will be discussed. The techniques of creating taxonomies, typologies, domain analysis, event analysis and social network analysis will be demonstrated for you.

Key points

Classical ethnography

- The design derives from anthropology.
- It has been adapted from large scale tribal to small scale urban settings (mini-ethnographies).
- Analytical tools which have been developed for classification of data in classical ethnographies include:

  - cultural domain analysis (the development and explanation of the interconnected groupings that make up a culture), in particular freelists (identifying what fits into a domain), pile sorts (identifying the internal structure of a domain) and triads (identifying the hierarchies within a domain)
  - taxonomies (organisation of knowledge into discrete categories)
  - typologies (classification within one group)
  - frame analysis (deliberate imposition of frames on the data)
  - social network analysis (identification of social relationships)
  - event analysis (intensive analysis of a key event).

Critical ethnography

- The foci are power location, inequalities and emancipation.

Classical ethnography: background and purpose

When to use: when you want to describe a culture and its operation, belief systems etc.

Types of question best suited: what is the culture of a particular hospital ward, a classroom, a street, a department, a family group, a tribe, a professional group etc.?

Strengths: detailed description of the belief systems, values, behaviours, interconnections of whatever has been defined as a 'culture' – a group of people usually with common elements of location, language, purpose etc.

Weaknesses: researcher neutrality is often difficult to maintain. Large amounts of observational data are time consuming and expensive to collect.

Classical ethnography has strong links with the anthropological tradition of observation of culture *in situ*. The theoretical underpinnings lean heavily on a combination of structural functionalism and interactive social networks. Structural functionalism focuses on the major structures of a society and how each part contributes via consensus and moves toward equilibrium in the orderly functioning of that society. Change and adaptation are possible with moves toward a new adjusted equilibrium as interactive social networks develop and the society becomes more complex.

The purpose of the classical ethnography is to describe the whole culture (however it has been defined), be it a tribal group or a group of young people living by their wits on the street. Key informants are sought and their voices highlighted. Your role as a researcher is traditionally that of a 'neutral' distant reflective observer (dialoguing between the research process and the product), meticulously documenting observational and visual images, and asking questions in both informal conversation and formal interviews, in order to identify, confirm and cross-check an understanding of the societal structures, the social linkages and the behaviour patterns, beliefs and understandings of people within the culture. This will usually involve you participating for several years in the setting, learning the language and collecting data. It is usual (where possible) to return to the culture after a period of time (and after the original data have been analysed and written up) to see that nothing has changed and that your 'picture' of the culture is confirmed. This approach has been linked to colonialism and late nineteenth century imperialism and has also been criticised in that the 'cine shot' approach separates culture from its historical links.

The ethnographers of today have truncated the original process to the mini-ethnography characterised by a shorter time in the field and an eclectic use of data collection techniques, including: focus group and face to face interviewing, participant observation, surveys, and visual and written documentation, with options of preliminary, thematic, content, discourse, narrative and conversation analysis.

Data collection areas can include:

- the gathering of contextual information
- the delineation of economic, political and social organisation
- the documentation of language, customs and rituals, events, incidents, shared belief systems, attitudes and understandings of events, behaviours and actions.

Analysis of descriptive data is within the interactive tradition and is ongoing in the form of preliminary data analysis alone or in combination with thematic analysis (See Chapter 2 for details of these processes). Each set of data informs the next, providing feedback in a process of building up and confirming the holistic view of the 'culture' under examination.

Analytical tools used in classical ethnographies

Although preliminary data analysis and thematic analysis now tend to be the mainstay of much of the data collected in classical ethnographies, a number of classificatory tools have been used in the past and are exposed below. These can be used in addition to or in place of thematic analysis depending on the types of data collected.

Cultural domain analysis

There is a presupposition within this approach that domains are structures to which items/entities (symbols of importance as defined by participants) belong and within which there are meaningful links, e.g. kinship terminology, animals, colours, illnesses, types of knowledge, emotions etc. According to Spradley (1980) the overall process for domain analysis involves:

1 initial data collection
2 the identification of the major domains of data which might include the structures and rituals which serve to support, maintain and provide uniqueness to the particular culture under study
3 further data collection to elicit more detail or to clarify the types/parts of these domains.

The undertaking of a taxonomic analysis of these domains will serve to identify groupings of subsets and hierarchies. In using further forms of analysis such as typologising or thematic analysis, selected dimensions of contrast will be used for identified groupings to arrive at componential analysis (the display of a model documenting the result of a systematic search for the units of meaning that people assign to cultural categories). In order of hierarchy amongst the classificatory tools, domain analysis tends to provide the big picture, followed by taxonomies and typologies.

For example, say a domain was defined by indigenous people as 'indigenous knowledge'. This domain is likely to demonstrate webs of strong internal relationships regarding the types of knowledge regarded as particular to the group. Similarities of what is considered cultural knowledge by the group are likely to be found together with some agreement on the language to be used regarding particular aspects or events within this knowledge. Differences are also likely and may lead to the development of separate domains or subdomains.

The process of further identifying whether or not we have a domain involves:

1 finding out which items fit into the domain
2 identifying commonalities and relationships
3 locating where items fit within the hierarchical structure of the domain
4 contrasting one domain with another, e.g. influences and outcomes.

The processes which are available to you for identification, eliciting data and developing matrices to support domain analysis are freelists, pile sorts and triads.

Freelists

This approach is used to identify which aspects fit into the proposed domain. It involves asking semi-structured questions in group or face to face interviews, such as 'What belongs to indigenous knowledge?', 'What doesn't?', 'When is it used?', 'When is it not used?', 'What is it used for?' The views of 20–30 randomly sampled members of the group (more if needed) are sought in order to attempt to gain consensus (identified through frequency of responses) about what is salient (most important) to the domain in terms of indigenous knowledge, what should be put into a subdomain or excluded and what level of consensus there is regarding these items. Data are tabulated for order of individual responses (related items tend to be mentioned close to each other), for frequency of responses overall, which can also be rank ordered and checked against gender, age and status in the group, as well as for co-occurrences of different aspects of responses by individuals.

Table 3.1 shows the freelist results of 14 undergraduate student responses to a request, 'List all the animals you can think of' (Borgatti, 1999). The number of items identified by each student averaged 22.

Pile sorts

This technique is used to identify the internal structure of the domain – the similarities between and among items and the commonalities and relationships therein. Up to 100 cards (or fewer) are developed from the freelist with relevant pictures/statements – one card for each item/aspect of the domain.

In a *single pile sort*, the cards are put in random order and the participants are asked to 'sort' the pile into a number of relevant (to them) piles. For example, a pile of 20 cards with pictures and names of various 'drugs' from heroin to milk were given to groups of students who had undergone drug education programmes in schools (Garrard and Northfield, 1987). In order to ascertain what they had retained from the programme they were asked to sort the cards into one pile of 'most to least' harmful drugs to the community (see Table 3.2) and their conversations were audio recorded as they carried out this process. It is useful to ask participants why they have sorted particular items into particular piles in order to gain greater insight as to where the links are seen to lie and also how relevant to the domain under consideration the process of sorting items actually is.

TABLE 3.1   *Top 20 animals mentioned, ordered by frequency*

Rank	Item name	Frequency	Response (%)
1	Cat	13	93
2	Dog	13	93
3	Elephant	10	71
4	Zebra	9	64
5	Squirrel	8	57
6	Tiger	8	57
7	Cow	7	50
8	Fish	7	50
9	Bear	7	50
10	Whale	7	50
11	Deer	7	50
12	Monkey	7	50
13	Giraffe	6	43
14	Gorilla	6	43
15	Mouse	6	43
16	Snake	6	43
17	Lion	5	36
18	Antelope	5	36
19	Leopard	5	36
20	Turtle	5	36

Source: adapted from Borgatti (1999)

In a *successive pile sort* items are sorted into piles, as in the single sort method, but participants are limited as to the number of piles they can sort into. They may also be required to subdivide these piles until further subdivision is impossible. Responses from the single sort are fed into a matrix showing which item went into which pile to identify the percentages of participants who connected items together. Responses from successive sorts are used to identify a matrix of individual responses and to compare this with others.

The limitation of both freelisting and pile sorting is that important aspects may be missed if they are only mentioned by a few people or one person, when this response may represent an important subgroup within the culture.

Triads

You can use the triads approach to tease out similarities and identify hierarchies for items in the domain. Combinations of triads (three items) are developed and, where all items are involved, randomised. The items are presented to the participants as triads and their task is *either* to identify the item which differs most from the other two, *or* to order the three items from most to least in terms of an identified aspect. For example:

TABLE 3.2 *Ranked most to least dangerous drugs for the individual user*

Substance	All students (20 groups × 6 = 120)		Students 10–13 years (60 students)		Students 14–18 years (60 students)	
	Mean	SD	Mean	SD	Mean	SD
Crack[a]	16.6	0.9	16.2	1.2	17.0	0.0
Heroin	15.9	0.6	15.8	0.9	16.0	0.0
Cocaine	14.7	1.5	15.2	1.4	14.2	1.5
LSD	14.2	0.5	14.1	0.5	14.4	0.5
Marijuana	11.9	0.9	13.6	1.3	10.3	3.1
Sedatives	9.8	2.7	9.0	2.7	10.5	2.6
Pep pills	9.2	2.6	8.7	2.6	9.6	2.6
Cigarettes[b]	9.0	2.9	9.8	3.2	8.2	2.4
Beer[c]	8.9	2.4	8.6	1.9	9.3	2.9
Glue	8.2	3.8	7.4	3.9	9.0	3.7
Wine coolers[c]	7.8	2.9	6.4	2.6	9.1	2.5
OTCs	7.7	2.0	7.7	2.4	7.6	1.5
Analgesics	6.4	2.1	6.7	2.2	6.0	2.0
Vitamins	5.3	2.6	6.6	2.1	4.0	2.5
Coffee	4.3	1.8	3.9	1.9	4.6	1.6
Salad roll	1.7	0.6	1.6	0.5	1.7	0.7
Milk	1.6	0.6	1.6	0.7	1.5	0.5

[a] At the time of this study crack was not available but students had seen a television documentary indicating that it was very dangerous. Illicit drugs all gained the highest ratings.

[b] Tobacco, which causes the most deaths, was rated 8th.

[c] Beer and wine coolers were rated 9th and 11th respectively, although wine coolers have higher alcohol content than beer.

Source: (Garrard and Northfield 1987)

Order this list from most to least dangerous:

cocaine   crack   heroin

Identify the item which differs most from the other two:

marijuana   glue   cigarettes

Rank ordered data can be tabulated and matrices of similarities can be developed for each individual as well as for the overall group so that comparisons can be made. Hierarchical clustering and multidimensional scaling are other options. Triads are most useful in clarifying the similarities in small domains where the items are close in kind or meaning, where the strength of individual connections is unclear, or where a proposition needs to be tested. Again, it is essential to clarify and contextualise participants' thought processes and the decisions they have made.

Taxonomies

This form of classification of data involves the organising of knowledge into discrete categories in a logical manner. Examples of this are the Dewey system of classifying books in libraries, various directories and the Yahoo web-based system. For example, Bloom et al.'s (1994) taxonomy of the cognitive domain involves the following hierarchy of possibilities:

1 knowledge
2 comprehension
3 application
4 analysis
5 synthesis
6 evaluation.

In research, you might choose the taxonomic approach to provide categories so that you can compare data across interviews or observations. These categories can either be developed by you or borrowed from some existing source and then applied to the data, or they may come naturally from the data as in the example below. Apart from applying existing taxonomies it is possible to develop a taxonomy early in data collection and to apply it like a matrix over the database, but it is more usual to mine the data in order to identify and clarify the categories that the data present.

Example: taxonomy

The following taxonomy was developed from data gathered in order to classify the activities undertaken in a typical day of one father at home, and this framework was then loosely applied to the situations of other at-home fathers for comparison (Grbich, 1997, data consolidation).

Before school

- Helps wife make breakfast for selves and three children.
- Organises school-aged children and walks them to school.

Morning after 9 a.m.

- Organises youngest preschool child – painting, reading stories, sandpit.
- Undertakes housekeeping tasks – often shared with child:
  - breakfast dishes
  - beds

- washing
- sweeping
- vacuuming.

- Takes youngest to playgroup and stays with her there.
- Home for lunch.

Afternoon

- Organises youngest child into play activities.
- Shopping/continues with housework from morning.
- Picks up school-aged children and walks them home.
- Organises play/homework for all children.
- Starts to prepare tea.

Typologies

A typology involves classification into one particular group or class. It tends to be used for smaller scale data than a taxonomy and involves processes of grouping information of particular relevance to the research question.

One guideline to typology formation involves:

1 collating all data relating to the particular issue
2 identifying variations, layers and dimensions
3 classifying into a type/types (subgroups)
4 presenting/re-presenting these to the reader.

For example, I developed a typology of terminology of the language which primary caregiver males used to define their at-home roles (Grbich, 1987). These were first listed, then classified into groupings relating to the context in which the terminology was used (Table 3.3).

From this typology of the role definition of fathers at home, a *proposition* can be developed which could form the basis of writing up and the re-presentation of this data:

> *That this group of primary caregiver men mostly define their role as child carers or house/home persons, with a few seeing the role as achieving equality with their partners or as having a work focus.*

Frame analysis

The basis of frame analysis lies in the writings of Erving Goffman (1974) and Gregory Bateson (1972). They were interested in how, during social interactions, individuals classify, using metacognitive devices or mental short cuts to set

TABLE 3.3   Role definition

Child focus	House/home focus	Egalitarian focus	Work focus
Caregiver (× 5)	Housewife (slave to house)	Helpmate (to partner)	My job
Child nurturer		Planned equality (× 3)	My career
Full-time daytime nurturer of child	House cleaner		
	Father at home (× 2)		
Mate (to child)	Person at home		
Child minder (× 2)	Parent at home (× 2)		
Child looker afterer	Parent in charge at home		

parameters in order to understand information, the conversations, narratives, rituals, and behaviours and situational encounters with which they are presented.

Frame analysis is a useful tool which you can consider in order to answer the following questions with regard both to yourself and to those whom you are researching:

- What sorts of conceptual and contextual interpretive frames do we place around situations and what sense do we make of them?
- How are meaning and understanding constructed?
- What classifications do we use to frame different kinds of communication/situations and to shape our social lives?

Frames structure our realities: they can be fixed or emergent, and they are not so much consciously as unconsciously applied to situations and can be revealed during interaction and communication.

In order to see how this works, you may find the following process useful:

1 Draw frames around transcripted conversation (a frame is the smallest coherent group of words, but frames can also be very broad).
2 Group frames into categories and name these.
3 Develop larger groupings, often termed galleries (if useful).
4 Interpret and display.

Example: frame analysis

Taking some extracts from interviews with female partners of at-home fathers recalling their decision to change parenting roles (Grbich, 1997) a broad framing approach can be applied as follows.

Interview 1

Well I suppose it happened fairly naturally for us and I don't feel we really planned beforehand for a very long period of time. Because I think we'd gone along for many years thinking that we were going to have children and it didn't happen and when the endocrinologist finally said after about seven years he didn't think we were likely to have children without quite a bit of intervention I decided, well I'll do something. So I got myself into a couple of training programs, sat exams and then I got pregnant. Then I really had to take stock and I really didn't particularly want to stay at home and by that time T had tended to work through a lot of things he wanted to do with his work and we discussed it and he said well perhaps he should stay home and it just fell into place like that.

Interview 2

I suppose it was to do with the pressure on John that started the whole thing in his mind. We were talking about it once and he said 'What would you think if I gave up work?' and I said 'Well if you want to you must do that' and he was travelling a lot and trying to study part-time and trying to be a parent as well. There was a lot of pressure there and I found that being at home, although it was quite relaxing being your own boss, but it was still quite restricting and I'd wanted to do something else and I started doing a course but found that having the alternative of going to work and knowing that our child would be well cared for was a good option so I was quite happy to change over.

Interview 3

Just happened. It's complicated because D came from England and couldn't get a work permit and couldn't get permanent residency so that I took over the breadwinner role and I became pregnant and he became very excited about that and he wanted to be with the baby and it didn't worry me because my job is very convenient and I enjoy doing it. We just stayed as we were. I could just get six months' leave of absence not 12 months because I hadn't been employed long enough full-time, so I went back to work when G was only four months of age. But I was able to come home at lunchtimes. So it was really financial and political reasons why we swapped roles.

In terms of frame analysis there are two aspects here:

1 the frames indicated by the participants
2 the frames imposed by the researcher.

In terms of responses to the question 'How did you come to change roles?', *participants' frames* appeared to be:

- *natural progression of events over time* (interview 1)
- *work pressure* (interview 2)
- *wife's dissatisfaction with the limits of the at-home role* (interview 2)
- *financial and political reasons* (interview 3).

In terms of later data interpretation, *researcher's frames* appeared to be:

- interview 1, two frames: *convenience* and *values regarding equal childrearing* (drawing from other data provided by this couple)

- interview 2: *work pressure leading to a sea change*
- interview 3, two frames: *political/financial* and *convenience*.

In all cases there was perceived to be an underlying frame of *fathers' preparedness to participate in childcare*. This could be substantiated by 'and he said well perhaps he should stay home' (interview 1); 'What would you think if I gave up work?' (interview 2); and 'I became pregnant and he became very excited about that and he wanted to be with the baby' (interview 3), and was further substantiated by additional data from the interviews with the fathers themselves.

How does the process of frame analysis differ from thematic analysis? It has a great deal of similarities. The essential difference is that the framing process is a natural one that occurs within the participants' and the researcher's minds even as the data are being collected and tend to frame what is being said and what is being received. The danger on both counts is that these frames may be applied in such a way that they become inflexible and prevent the participants and researcher from identifying other aspects. For example, my desire to frame in terms of *fathers' preparedness to participate in childcare* may deflect my attention from the fact that financial and work pressures might be a more important frame (from these three families' perspectives). Overall, frame analysis is particularly useful to you in its capacity to clarify your imposition of cognitive frames and the degree to which these are shared between individuals and among groups regarding communications and events they have experienced.

Social network analysis

Moving from the more formalised approaches of classificatory schemes and identifying and confirming domains and frames, another approach involves the illumination of social structure in groups, systems and organisations through the identification of the webs of social networks evident in the culture under study. This approach allows for greater flexibility in viewing the formation, dynamics, linkages, context and changing nature of such networks. Social network analysis is particularly useful when the identification of linkages is important – how these operate in terms of patterns of interaction and how individual and group behaviours change over time.

Process

1 Identify the people who constitute the group.
2 Assess the relationships in terms of the focus of the research, e.g. lines of power, decision making etc.
3 Produce a graphical analysis; show any changes over time.
4 Confirm with the collection of other data over time.

Figure 3.1, taken from William Whyte's (1955) study on a group of street males, indicates the results of such an analysis. You can see that the most powerfully networked male in the group is Doc.

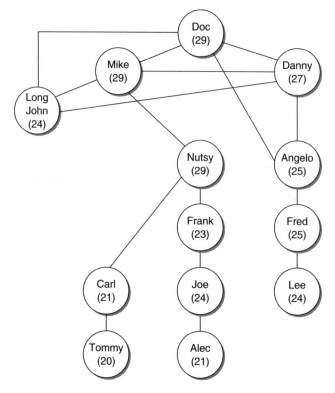

FIGURE 3.1 Relationships in the organisation of a street corner group: **the Nortons, spring and summer 1937 (**Figure 2.2 in W. Whyte, *Street Corner Society,* 1955: 13, copyright 1943 and 1955 by the University of Chicago Press, reprinted with permission)

[*Note*: Numbers in brackets give the ages of the group]

Event analysis

When you identify a particular event within a larger base of data collection which requires more detailed explication than is provided by preliminary data analysis or thematic analysis, this can be undertaken by employing event analysis.

Process

1 Describe the event. What actually happened? Here the 'voices' presented will be important. Whose perspective is represented? Is it only that of the researcher? What about the people actually involved in the event as well as bystanders and any relevant others?
2 What are the structural aspects of the event? Time, space, location, context, culture – again there are a range of perspectives possible here.

3   What meanings and actions can be interpreted in the context? How can what went on be explained?

4   What is the wider impact of the event (historical links, future potential, or just the impact on those immediately involved)?

5   Classify the event/s – either broadly, or break them down into separate parts and place them in related groupings for more intense scrutiny, theory development and writing up.

6   How has the researcher's representation of the event been affected by the fieldwork situation? By their limited access to people? Or by their own views developed within their own cultural grouping?

The breadth of classical ethnography

It must be becoming clear to you from the above examples that there is considerable variation in classical ethnography, ranging from the precisely organised classifications and interpretations represented in this chapter to broader, less defined or more imprecise multiple presentations of data reflecting many views. William Whyte has indicated that for him the experience of data analysis in classical ethnography is a very imprecise process of immersion in the field, muddling around to see what emerges, juggling ideas and waiting for an 'Aha!' or eureka moment where some of the items, issues and behaviours may start to make sense:

> The ideas that we have in research are only in part a logical product growing out of a careful weighing of evidence. We do not generally think the problems through in a straight line. Often we have the experience of being immersed in a mass of confusing data. We study the data carefully, we bring all our powers of logical analysis to bear upon them. We come up with an idea or two. But still the data do not fall in any coherent pattern. Then we go on living with the data – and with the people – until perhaps some chance occurrence casts a totally different light upon the data, and we begin to see a pattern that we have not seen before. This pattern is not purely an artistic creation. Once we think we see it, we must reexamine our notes and perhaps set out to gather new data in order to determine whether the pattern adequately represents the life we are observing or is simply a product of our imagination. (1984: 3–4)

This more intuitive approach to analysis of classical ethnographic data, utilising only preliminary data analysis and some loose thematic analysis, clarifies the breadth of approaches available.

Critical ethnographic approaches

Critical ethnographic approaches are particularly useful when you are concerned about issues of power in society. Who has power? How is it distributed? And how are those who are powerless managing to have their needs heard? This approach grew out of dissatisfaction that classical ethnographic approaches were ignoring the elements of power within social constructions. So rather than just describing what is apparent in observation and interviewing, you as researcher need to go beyond this to elicit the whys and wherefores and then perhaps move even further into action to correct power imbalances by alerting participants to the previously unrecognised inequalities they are subject to. Another move would be to approach institutional groups in order to alert them to the inequalities they are perpetrating so that steps can be taken to improve the situation. In the move toward critical ethnography, the notion of the 'value neutrality' of the classical ethnographer was also questioned. In critical ethnography, the researcher moves from the fairly static position of 'observer' of the classical ethnographer to a more active analytical position where terminology such as 'location of power', 'ideology', 'hegemony', 'alienation', 'domination', 'oppression', 'hierarchy', 'exploitation under capitalism', 'empowerment' and 'transformation' become important. History, politics and the economics of a situation dominate, as do explanatory links from within the Marx–Habermas tradition of critical theory and the principles of feminism.

When to use: when you want to identify the power dimensions within a defined culture particularly in relation to gender, race, politics or socio-economic differences.

Types of question best suited: where does power lie in this situation? How can power relations be equalised?

Strengths: identification of power location and the possibility of improving the lot of the powerless.

Weaknesses: see Chapter 1 p. 7. Ongoing issues of contention.

Criteria

It has been suggested that a critical ethnography should meet the following criteria:

- Power and the location of power must be a key issue.
- Emancipation and social transformation of inequality and oppression suffered by participants needs to be addressed by some form of action.
- Who the author is and how he/she are influencing the data collection, design and analysis needs to be addressed.

Example: critical ethnography

Both health and education research have been important sources of critical ethnographies. One example (Bennett, 1991) investigated the relationship between students' Appalachian cultural background and their grade 1 classroom reading programme which was supposed to meet the written goal of being culturally sensitive to this background. Data were collected by observation and formal and informal interviews within the classroom setting, including audiotaping of small group reading sessions, staff meetings and district education meetings, and these data were analysed thematically. Analysis of student report cards, district curriculum guides, absentee records, achievement scores and criterion referenced test scores was also undertaken. Bennett found that the reading programme did not meet the goal of cultural appropriateness and in fact was in conflict with the Appalachian culture by presenting only a white middle class curriculum. There was no place for the use of children's natural language patterns or life experiences in the process of learning to read. In addition, teachers' autonomy was hindered by large class sizes, rigid district policies and insufficient funding as well as the beliefs they had been taught about how children learn. Lack of success in learning to read was the outcome for two-thirds of the Appalachian children involved. The identification of inequality and the reporting of such to the Appalachian people as well as to the education authorities should have begun to raise the awareness of both sufficiently to start the process of change.

The majority of research which has been undertaken within critical ethnography has occurred in situations where socio-economic inequality and oppression are likely to be found, in particular within the institutional structures of workplaces, schools and hospitals and in underdeveloped countries. The production of reports with recommendations for change can often be very effective if targeted to the right audiences.

Summary

Classical and critical ethnographic approaches are particularly useful for the meticulous documentation of whole cultures – however these are defined. Data collection occurs within the iterative approach, and epistemologically two traditions tend to be drawn on: postpositivism with its emphasis on realism and the tracking back to locate the genesis of current situations, and interpretivism/constructivism. The data analytic tools available reflect this diversity and vary from a light intuitive approach, the utilisation of preliminary data and thematic analysis, through to the more structured frame, event and social network analyses, and ending with the classificatory analytic processes of identification of domains, taxonomies and typologies. Critical ethnographies tend to favour the more intuitive analytic end of the scale, with preliminary data and thematic analysis dominating; here, issues of power and the problem of how to correct unequal situations and empower participants are key foci.

FURTHER READING

Atkinson, P. (1990) *The Ethnographic Imagination: Textual Construction of Reality.* London: Routledge. Atkinson exposes the textual descriptive strategies used in more traditional forms of ethnographic writing.

Becker, H. (1998) *Tricks of the Trade*. Chicago: University of Chicago Press. Becker is full of tactics for problem solving the issues that arise in research from design to analysis. His colloquial style is very readable and he draws upon many years of expertise as an ethnographer.

Bernard, R. (ed.) (2000) *Handbook of Methods in Cultural Anthropology*. Oxford: AltaMira. Here 27 authors describe anthropological fieldwork in practice, providing a comprehensive description of the methods that anthropologists use, the logic behind them, and the complex problems that field research with humans entails.

Myers, M. and Young, L. (1997) Hidden agendas, power, and managerial assumptions in information systems development: an ethnographic study. *Information Technology & People* 10 (3): 224–40. Using critical ethnography, this paper discusses the development of an information system in mental health, revealing otherwise hidden agendas, power and managerial assumptions to be deeply embedded in the project. This study raises broader questions about the extent to which information systems can be seen as 'colonising mechanisms'.

Schensul, J., Le Compte, M. and associates (1999) *The Ethnographer's Toolkit*, 7 vols. Oxford: AltaMira. This book provides a range of tools from research design to data collection techniques and analytical strategies for the novice ethnographer.

Wolf, M. (1992) *A Thrice Told Tale: Feminism, Postmodernism and Ethnographic Responsibility*. Stanford, CA: Stanford University Press. Margery Wolf has taken classical ethnographic data collected 30 years previously of an event which occurred in a village and has re-presented it in different ways: as her journal record of the event, as the record of her Asian research assistant who has cultural insight into the complexities of the event, and as an article for an anthropological journal.

http://www.npi.ucla.edu/qualquant/bibliography.htm, accessed April 2006, 'Complete annotated bibliography'. Try this for a lengthy but earlier list of texts and examples of ethnographic approaches.

4

Newer Ethnographic Approaches

Current moves in ethnographic practice have been away from the extreme realist position of researchers as neutral observers, sometimes seen in classical and critical ethnographies, where you stand apart from the setting and meticulously document the culture in an 'objective' manner through observations, interviews and the examination of existing documentation. This chapter follows more recent orientations in ethnography such as ethno drama, crafted for its political and social impacts, as well as autoethnography and cyber ethnography where either you as researcher or other individuals become the major focus of data collection within particular cultural contexts.

Key points

Autoethnography

- You are the focus of the research study.
- An in-depth analysis of your activities, feelings and emotions within particular cultural contexts is provided by this approach.
- You need a well developed capacity for critical reflexivity in order to avoid the pitfalls of self-indulgence.
- Your capacity to present data innovatively and to create an impact on the reader by bringing them in close to your experiences is very important.

Ethno drama

- Involves you in the use of ethnographic data to present political and social issues in dramatic form.
- Your primary objective is to educate and/or to bring about change in your audience.

Cyber ethnography

- Allows you to study online communication and interaction from an overt or a covert position.

Background to the newer ethnographic approaches

There has been a major shift away from the centre stage position of the classical ethnographer as the key authoritative voice to one which affords the participants' voices greater space and allows the reader to take a more prominent role in interacting with data and coming to their own individual conclusions regarding the data displayed. This shift has also allowed for a greater focus on the written/performed text, which then becomes 'a multidimensional space, in which a variety of writings, none of them original, blend and clash' (Barthes, 1977: 146). Your power as the writer then lies in your capacity to mix writings, to play with ideas from a variety of perspectives, to become an actor in your own right and to display information and voices in such a way as to encourage many interpretations. You become the eye of the text – the facilitator of the display of voices, including your own, and the illuminator of the text through reflexive/reflective/refractive critique.

This shift has involved recognition that you, as researcher, are a complex and constructed historical entity with multiple personae that shape both the data collected and their interpretation and presentation. These personae shift among those of author, academic, student, storyteller, pillager, recycler of ideas, and cyborg – the crossing of boundaries among person, nature and machines. Reflexivity is now essential and you must view your role and the processes of data collection and interpretation in a critical and detached manner through close scrutiny of what you know and how you know it in your development of knowledge claims. You become the focus, and there is an assumption that reflection on the self (looking and relooking) is essential in understanding the self and the identification of the discourses which have impacted on the lenses through which you view the world. This self-referential interrogatory process is both inward and outwardly reflected/refracted to the reader and is usually recorded in diary form and then re-presented in poetry, drama or narrative. The audience then has access to your real-life experience.

Autoethnography

When to use: when the focus is the self in various contexts.

Types of research question best suited: the exploration of your own subjective life experiences.

Strengths: very powerful data which if carefully re-presented allow the reader to get close to individual experiences.

Weaknesses: potential for you to become over-subjective and self-indulgent and to lose the capacity for critical self-reflection.

Definition:

> autoethnography: auto (self) ethno (culture) graphy (presentation of the self within the culture)

Autoethnography is an autobiographical genre of writing and research that displays multiple layers of consciousness, connecting the personal to the cultural. Back and forth ethnographers gaze, first through an ethnographic wide-angle lens, focussing outward on social and cultural aspects of their personal experience; then, they look inward, exposing a vulnerable self that is moved by and may move through, refract, and resist cultural interpretations. (Ellis and Bochner, 2000: 739)

The link between autobiography and ethnography is evident as you move from an internal examination of yourself including emotions and feelings to an external view of yourself within a sometimes conflictual cultural context where your performances need to be deconstructed. Carolyn Ellis and Art Bochner (2000) have used the image of a camera shifting from a wide-angle approach to zooming in and out of situations in order to examine and critique them more closely. This movement with its accompanying analytical reflective critique is what distinguishes autoethnography from narrative (a story with a beginning, a middle and an end).

You tend to focus on the self in interaction with others in situations where there are conflicting emotions or cultures. A dialogue between you as researcher and you as the focus of the research is often exposed as you move from insider to outsider position. Voiceovers, third-person voice or the subjective 'I' are often used to indicate the position you are taking. This source of the self as the major focus of data collection has been criticised as being self-indulgent, but these criticisms are usually based on judging autoethnography with the criteria of earlier, more traditional forms of qualitative research.

Varieties of autoethnography

Autoethnographies aim to create dual experiences of individual and cultural activity both for you as the researched and for your readership. Below is an example demonstrating the outside-looking-in approach fostered by the use of the third-person voice to provide distance while clarifying emotions and cultural context.

First story: third-person approach

It's 1969. She's on her high school senior trip to Florida. She's a white girl from a small, rural, southern town, attracted to Jesse, one of only two African American males on the journey. Prior to lights out the first night, students go for a walk on the beach. Immersed in talking about being Black in a White world, she and Jesse wander away from the others.

'You always remember you're Black,' Jesse says. 'People's responses remind you.'
'What was it like growing up?' she asks.

(Continued)

(Continued)

'We had no money. My father left when I was a baby, so I was raised by my ma and grandma. Then my mother remarried. Once I woke up and my step-daddy had a butcher knife to my throat.'

'Oh, my God. What did you do?'

'I ran outside. In the freezing cold, with no shoes, in my underwear. I got frost-bite on my toes.'

'What had you done to make him so angry?'

'Nothin'. He was drunk. And he was always jealous that my mother loved me more than him. That's all. Just jealous.'

'We better go back in,' she says, noting that everyone else has disappeared. She wonders what people will think about their being out in the dark . . . together . . . alone.

She leads the way into the room where the other students have gathered. She feels she has nothing to be embarrassed about since her time with Jesse was so innocent. What she feels does not matter when all eyes turn on her and she experiences the deadly silence of all voices stopping – at precisely the same time. She has never felt such hostile attention before. Jesse, who has, hesitates before walking into the same treatment a few minutes later. In those few silent, enraged moments, she knows viscerally a little of what it feels like to be Black in a White world – just a little.

Source: excerpted from Ellis (1995a: 152–3), reprinted with permission

The use of the first person, although often harder to write because of your own emotional involvement, presents a different experience and is demonstrated below from one of my own life experiences.

Second story: first-person approach

I got up as usual at 7ish that morning and headed upstairs towards the bathroom. As I neared the single bedroom where my mother, who had been staying with us for a couple of weeks, was sleeping I heard a strange noise – deep breathy sounds with a rattling sound at the end. I stopped dead and with one tentative finger pushed open the unlatched door of my mother's room. My eighty-year-old mother was lying flat on her back with her mouth open and it was from here that strange sounds were emerging. I paused in horror, frozen, aware of what I was potentially seeing and for a few seconds unable to do anything. I felt like a small child who

(Continued)

had opened a door on something too terrible to actually think about. Here it was the possibility that my mother might be dying. I took a deep breath and walked towards the bed, her eyes were open and they flickered towards me as I got close. There was entreaty in them. I reached forward and touched her hand reassuringly though I didn't feel at all reassured myself. She made a series of grunting noises that I couldn't begin to decipher. 'I'll be back in a moment,' I said and quickly left the room in a daze. My normal practical skills of mother and career woman had deserted me – I didn't want to take responsibility for this. I wanted to curl up in a corner, put my hands over my ears and not open my eyes until it was safe to do so. At the door, my mother-in-law and her husband appeared from the room next door. They had also been staying over for a short period of time. 'Is something wrong?' said my mother-in-law, looking concerned. I noticed that my father-in-law had stepped back into their room and was avoiding eye contact with me. I felt he didn't really want to be involved – not because he didn't care but because he was afraid. He too was in his 80s and had experienced a severe heart attack many years before. My mother-in-law pushed her way past me and into the room. She seemed to understand what was happening and glanced at me briefly. I rallied momentarily. 'I'll go and phone the doctor,' I said quietly so that only she could hear. I went to the phone but I couldn't think clearly, my fingers seemed to not know how to use the telephone directory and my brain refused to function. Who would be the best person to ring at this hour of the morning? Eventually I remembered the number of my general practitioner who was not in at this hour but his practice manager was and when I explained my mother's behaviour she said ring for an ambulance and gave me the number. The ambulance arrived within five minutes and during that time I raced downstairs put on some clothes cleaned my teeth and stood close to the front door. For some reason I could not go back to my mother's room and I waited for a couple of minutes willing the ambulance to arrive – it did almost immediately with a female paramedic and her male offsider. I showed them to my mother's room where my mother-in-law had interpreted my mother's strange grunting noises as needing her false teeth – she still had a sense of needing to present herself well and my mother-in-law was trying with some difficulty to insert my mother's false teeth into her mouth. I stifled a hysterical desire to laugh. The paramedics waited patiently until this procedure was completed, examined my mother and headed off with her to the hospital with me following close behind in my car.

In both of the above examples, changes in position from insider to outsider in the critical reflexive process can be observed.

Approaches to data collection and analysis

Although there no rules for undertaking autoethnography, some writers have clarified their approaches. In a study of anorexia (Ellis, Kiesinger and Tillman-Healy, 1997), where the last two named academics were or had been bulimic, they document, review and critique their thoughts and feelings as they interview each other. They interweave their thoughts with their mutual interview data, together with documentation written by each of the three authors after a dinner together (a clearly complicated form of interaction for all three). This process not only clarifies the previously hidden world of each researcher's mind in the reflexive process but also reveals to the reader much more starkly the insider views of the issues and contexts of bulimia as experienced by two sufferers. The contrasts provided within the spaces between Carolyn (as the non-bulimic researcher) and Christine and Lisa (as the bulimic researchers/interviewees) provide considerable insight. Carolyn Ellis points out the interesting dilemmas and risks of exposure of this process, in particular that the need to protect self-image may well lead researchers in the public domain, such as academics, to release limited or sanitised information.

If you start data analysis of a preliminary type early with this kind of data, you will be able to develop and identify concepts, themes and propositions, but the richness of the data will depend on the extent to which you as both researcher and researched are prepared to engage with the text both emotionally and intellectually through journal keeping. The opportunity to debrief with supervisors and colleagues or partners is also important. One approach to troubling the text during analysis involves identifying the level of analysis at which you are working and then applying a theory which operates at a different level. For example, you could view your individual interpersonal data through system-based theories such as feminism or Marxism to clarify the impact of structural influences on the constructed nature of your behaviour.

Examples: autoethnography

Autoethnography can also be an outcome of a study previously oriented in the more classical tradition. In a documentation of the life of a Mexican woman, Esperanza, Ruth Behar (1993) moves to a critical self-reflective tale exposing the typical researcher – herself – on whom she reflects and whom she criticises for her attempts to impose, categorise and interpret the life of a woman from another culture to fit into her ways of seeing (or at least the academic ways of the American anthropological culture). Behar started off attempting to gain information which she had been trained to believe was desirable in a 'proper' life story – in this case information about intimate and sexual relations. Her move to autoethnography exposed this imposed orientation and revealed a challenge by the participant who wanted to talk about her areas of priority: 'physical suffering, martyrdom, rage, salvation' (1993: 273). This book provides a biography with a shadow autoethnography which refract and interact with each other.

In a similar situation but with a different outcome, Karen Brown's (1991) study of Mama Lola, a voodoo priestess in Brooklyn, led to Brown eventually deciding to undergo initiation into voodoo practice herself. This shifted the study from classical to autoethnography as she became part of the group under study, enabling the documentation of observations of herself as community member and herself as researcher in this setting. Brown started to write herself into the story of Mama Lola so that in the final book she appears in two voices, one a fairly accessible academic voice and the other a more personal reflective voice.

The use of autoethnographic process can help to clarify whether you have achieved sufficient distance from the setting to gain the outside view. Susan Kreiger (1985) used autoethnography to expose the difficulties she had in researching in the live-in community of lesbian academics of which she had been a prior member. In order to separate herself from the community she underwent a 'process of re-engagement' which involved step by step self-reflexivity of her entry, personal and sexual involvement, key events, emotional responses and experiences of leaving this group. Kreiger concluded that: 'The great danger of doing injustice to the reality of the "other" does not come about through use of the self, but through lack of use of a full enough sense of self which, concomitantly, produces a stifled, artificial, limited and unreal knowledge of others' (1985: 320).

Autoethnography of the self as the primary phenomenon under study can be seen in Carol Ronai's (1992) experiences of the difficulties she faced in becoming an erotic dancer (age, feminist views, body changes post motherhood etc.) in order to study other erotic dancers in a strip bar. Her twin roles as researcher/dancer allowed her to move with ease from one role to the other and to layer her observations with a critical analysis of her experiences. Carolyn Ellis and Art Bochner (1992) go further and provide dual autoethnographies of the emotions and ambiguities each experienced in discovering their pregnancy and undergoing the decision and the procedure to terminate this. These experiences were re-produced as a dual-voiced dramatic production and presented at a conference to provide reflections on their own streams of consciousness and to explore the link between 'emotional, cognitive and physical experiences' (1992: 5) in an attempt to understand internal subjectivity through response and resistance to external social discourses. The text enters very personal territory where many researchers would fear to tread, preferring to remain silent regarding their participation in matters formerly regarded as private.

Writing autoethnography

The process of collecting data for autoethnographies is often very time consuming and emotionally complex and may involve you in years of writing and rewriting in order to gain distance from or to get closer to the data. Susan Kreiger, Karen Brown and Ruth Behar all spent up to 12 years collecting and writing their data and Carolyn Ellis took nine years to come to terms with a lost relationship and to find the right voice to do justice to her feelings. Ellis (1995b) indicated that the story of her relationship with her husband who had died of emphysema was interspersed with the horror of her brother being killed in a plane crash at around the same time. This double tragedy led her to a need 'to understand and cope with the intense emotion I felt about the sudden loss of my brother and the excruciating pain I experienced as Gene deteriorated. I wanted to tell my stories to others because it would be therapeutic for me and evocative for them' (1997: 126). She found it necessary to keep notes of the process of writing, as did Kreiger, in order to readdress the voices of participants and find a comfortable way of communicating.

The documentation of this process led Ellis to accumulate considerable data including:

- field notes of the relationship both during and up to two years after her husband's death
- field notes of the illness processes from eight months prior to his death
- interviews with family and friends
- medical case notes
- personal diaries
- travel logs.

The final integration of all this data was presented in the first person, in order to give her feelings an appropriate voice. See Tierney and Lincoln (1997: 127–131) for details of the process of writing.

The process of writing autoethnography can be further seen in Nicholas Holt's (2003) article where he presents a personal account of the tensions he experienced in trying to articulate and integrate his pedagogical approach as a new graduate student within the mandates of a university teaching programme and his need to get this experience published. He presents an analysis of a dialogue between two reviewers, each of whom comprises an amalgam of the seven sympathetic and seven unsympathetic reviews received regarding an article he submitted for publication, in order to demonstrate the conflicting views apparent in the field regarding the autoethnographic approach. The notion of methodological rigour, when the researcher provides the major 'voice', is at the core of the problem, along with reviewer discomfort at the perceived self-indulgence of the public expression of a researcher's emotions.

Data presentation

You can see a presentation of an autoethnography in a three-voiced dialogic, multi-vocal dramatic form in Loreen Olson's (2004) reconstruction of the identity of a battered woman (herself). This is performed on stage with two women sitting on stools behind a translucent white curtain. The first voice is provided by the narrator who in a voiceover provides the literary and statistical context of abuse for women and the theoretical and methodological framework for the study. The stage light then focuses on the first woman – the author as woman next door – who presents her story of her experience of abuse and her journey to reconstruct herself as an independent being. As she does this she uses the second woman – the author as academic voice – to critically reflect her experiences and to locate these within existing literature. The three women – narrator, author as woman next door and author as academic – speak sometimes in unison, sometimes over each other and sometimes alone or alternating, providing reflection and refraction on the content. In the final scene the three women appear on stage, move together, overlap and become one.

You can find presentation of a largely dialogical interaction in Carolyn Ellis's (2003) description of reluctant grave tending with her mother. This is written in the 'I' of the author interspersed with reflections on the people whose graves are being tended and quotes from other writers on this topic. Ellis links this experience to her mother's death a year later and notes how the ritual of grave tending was continued on in this family, through the female members, and how this ritual of love helped to give meaning to their loss.

A briefer form of display using poetic representation can be seen in Jeannie Chiu's (2004: 4) reported autoethnographies of the Hmong people. The example below exposes some of the difficulties of assimilation:

they are deaf when I speak
they clothe me in the old ways that I cannot understand
traditions that have become too heavy
I have worn them on my back for too long
As woman and as child
I know I cannot stay
Buried Voiceless

Assessment of autoethnographies

It has been suggested that criteria for assessing autoethnographic writing might include the following (adapted from Richardson, 2000: 15–16):

- How has the writing contributed to our increased knowledge of social life?
- The style of presentation – is it satisfyingly complex?
- Reflexivity – has the author been able to move between inside and outside subjectivities?
- What emotional/intellectual impact has this had on me as the reader and how close has this text drawn me into it?

Criticisms of autoethnographies

- Too indulgent, self-absorbed and introspective (insufficiently 'objective').
- Is exposing the emotions of the self and others 'real' research?
- How authentic is the voice of the researcher/researched? In centring oneself, one highlights one's own role and marginalises those of others: doesn't this lead to a lack of perspective balance? Or worse still, colonising? So that others' narratives are of lesser value.

Ethno drama and performance texts

When to use: when you have data which can be presented in dramatic form. The educative function of this performance is important.

Types of research question best suited: those with wider political and social ramifications where information dissemination or behaviour change are important.

Strengths: powerful stories which impact on the audience, often challenging long held beliefs and leading to change.

Weaknesses: the researcher also needs the skills of a playwright and stage director (or needs to co-opt these) in order to develop the data into a successful performance.

The move toward presentation of data in staged performances is one option in autoethnography which you can consider, but performance texts can also be seen in the form of *ethno drama* – the presentation of ethnographically gained data in dramatic form. The performance of texts has been described by Denzin (2003: 187) as something which 'can contribute to radical social change, to economic justice, to a cultural politics that extends critical race theory' leading to radical democracy. The anticipated outcomes of ethno dramatic presentations are somewhat different from those of autoethnography, where the purpose is to share and connect with the audience in a situation where the boundaries between the actor and the audience become blurred. In ethno drama the performances are vivid and dramatic and seek to educate by creating an emotional catharsis in the audience. Situations are presented with the view of confronting the audience and challenging their positions in such a way as to lead to an epiphany – an acute realisation with the potential for empowerment. Following the performance, open discussions between the actors and the audience often occur in order to consolidate the impact, to lead forward into action and to provide further data. Support counsellors and further information are usually available for those who may need this. In health, this approach has been used to display the powerlessness experienced by people with traumatic brain injury (Mienczakowski et al., 1996), the process of undergoing detoxification (Mienczakowski, 1996) and the experience of schizophrenic illness (Mienczakowski, 1992).

In more detail, the ethno drama which highlighted the experiences of people undergoing detoxification, written largely for health professionals (Mienczakowski and Morgan, 1993), opens with a scene derived from an informant's description of herself at a night beach party. A teenage girl stands alone drinking bourbon. An adjacent slide show echoes her drinking posture, showing images of this girl and other women drinking alone and in a range of drinking contexts. The girl then dances alone to music and is approached by an intoxicated male who offers her a bottle and tries to have forced intercourse with her. His advanced drunken state and her vomiting prevent this occurring.

In an ethno drama you collect data through the usual processes of observation and interviewing and the actors may be people who themselves have experienced the situations and emotions they are portraying. Denzin (2001: 24) has referred to the reflexive interview or performative interview as a useful tool for consideration in ethno drama. This is not so much an interview of the traditional data gathering type but a 'dialogic conversation that connects all of us' to the wider moral community – an interpretive relationship of the text by the audience via its performance. He sees it as a useful technique in the development of a performance text. The scripts which are produced in ethno drama derive from a compilation of interviews, observations and documentation gathered in the field which you then put together in a narrative collage. This is interspersed with your voice. The whole is amalgamated in such a way that the audience is drawn in, given that we are all 'co-performers in each other's lives' (Mienczakowski, 2000: 2). Time and space shift and change in the collage. The overall process of writing an ethno drama involves you in developing the plot around which the 'play' will evolve, working on the characterisation and development of the personae of the actors, and scripting the dialogue and the stage movements. It is clear that in many cases the average ethnographer may not have sufficient stagecraft skills to develop such a performance and may seek to work with people already skilled in these areas.

Examples: ethno drama

One ethno drama where collaboration between playwright and academic did occur, and which sought to create a provocative account in order to 'provide a level of insight and understanding into human social life', was *Finding my Place* (Saldana and Woolcott, 2001: 5). This is a double-edged title involving a situation where two actors both found 'places'. This drama is in three scenes. It portrays an academic who discovered that a cabin situated at the edge of his 20 acre property was inhabited by a 19-year-old unemployed male, and tracks the relationship between the two. The academic, Harry (Woolcott), interviews the young male, Brad, for a case study and develops his life history, later becoming sexually involved with him. Brad is diagnosed as a paranoid schizophrenic, and institutionalised for two years. Following this, he returns to Harry's house, trashes and burns it, and is caught, tried and imprisoned. Brad indicates that he hates the older man and goes to prison still threatening him. The overall purpose of the ending of this dramatic performance is to forefront the contentious notion of validity. This notion is taken up and thoroughly critiqued by Schreiber et al. (2001) who assert that Woolcott's behaviour was unethical in having sex with a research participant, particularly one who is dependent on the researcher for his survival. The portrayal of Woolcott as the victim and Brad as the predator in this power-laden performance is seen as extremely divisive in terms of audience impact.

In another example of an ethno dramatic performance the purpose was to 'challenge the way young audiences and student participants felt about substance abuse'. In particular, gendered drinking cultures were examined along with the implications of peer pressure in drug related settings. The following piece of data provided insight into the relevant cultural perspectives:

Voiceover/narrator:	You know. Women are the silent drinkers, especially in Australia. It's the male thing – drinking. It's accepted, you know? Aussie macho drinkers. Even the adverts. You know the one?
Friend:	I've got some bad news for you, your best mate has run off with the bride.
Bridegroom:	Oh shit!
Friend:	I've got some other bad news. He took the beer with him!
Bridegroom:	What! The bastard!!! (Mienczakowski, 1997: 368)

The quirky humour of the Australian male is used to demonstrate the cultural dependence on alcohol in social occasions and provides some insight into the basis of alcohol abuse in this culture.

Criticisms of ethno drama

- Without help or special playwriting skills, researchers may not be able to adequately translate their data into powerful dramatic presentations and may only achieve poor quality theatre.
- Bringing case studies to the public arena may provoke ethical dilemmas, especially if individuals can be identified.
- If individual characters (as non-actors) play themselves on stage, there may be complex psychological, behavioural and health outcomes for them.

Cyber ethnography

When to use: when internet interaction is to be examined.

Types of research question best suited: what are the forms of interaction and communication at a particular site or sites?

Strengths: can be done anonymously, picking up 'real' data.

Weaknesses: superficial presentations of participants and self may occur, so the dialogue is not representative and doesn't really reflect non-cyber situations.

Cyber ethnography is the study of the relationships between people within 'virtual' environments. Researchers often enter sites in their own right or anonymously, employing an observational role in order to minimise their impact. Once in, you can collect data on such aspects as: the numbers of monthly postings, message lengths, thread links and the gaps between the emergence of these and their being picked up and disappearing from the site, the numbers of members, any demographic details which are available, together with the content of messages. In these sites the anonymity factor operates, allowing people to disclose quite private information. Multiple links through hypertext mean that these sites are rhizomatic rather than linear and data collection can follow in any direction, running over into forms of analysis which may utilise internet-based quantitative tools. Presentation can also utilise multimedia and polyphonic juxtaposition of 'voices' together with different narratives from other sites.

Apart from the rhizomatic nature of the data, problems you may experience with researching on the internet include the lack of homogeneity of the population to be studied, the inability to determine the extent of its diversity, and the development of different cultures at each site which make comparisons difficult. Details of who the contributors are can often be inaccessible or non-existent, and it is problematic and time consuming to obtain participant consent for the quoting of comments or to gain the agreement of the group of individuals who may have assisted in the social construction of particular positions.

Data collection

The process of data collection involves you in identifying a transitional and changing community through textual postings and then making some sense of these postings by some form of thematic analysis or coding. More in-depth information, interviews, questionnaires and focus groups can be possible but these require you to reveal yourself and to move to a more 'visible' place.

Some basic guidelines which might be useful for you in the collection of data in cyber ethnography are (adapted from Miller and Slater, 2000: Chapter 1):

1   How do people engage with each other on the internet?
2   How do they engage with new media?
3   How do they transcend positions limited by internet media framing?

In a move to map emotions, Sade-Beck (2004) explored the expression of painful and difficult emotions expressed on the internet regarding loss and bereavement in Israeli communities. The study design involved three complementary observations: online observations (in person) focusing on particular issues such as the Holocaust and terrorist attacks as discussed over a period of one year; content analysis of press and internet databases; and a random sample of internet participants who were asked to participate in an interview offline.

Data analysis, examples and problems

Should you impose a frame and sequence the data in order to follow a particular thread? Or should you allow the generally chaotic nature of the data to follow their own patterns? Certainly the former is better in terms of the construction of a simple picture of communication at the site where certain foci of communication may be presented, but the latter presents a truer picture of some of the types of communication which occur. The tracking of discourses which develop at particular sites is another option

A study of a South Asian women's e-mail discussion list SAWNET (Gajjala, 2002) highlighted the problems of researching internet sites. Here the researcher sent out a questionnaire to a site where she was an active member. She also observed a second site for people of Indian culture where she acted as a 'lurker' and did not actively participate in the discussions. She sent her completed paper from her questionnaire and observations to the SAWNET site. The women members protested that they were unhappy about being researched and analysed, that permission would have to be gained from individual members to use their messages and that no generalised statements regarding group activity were to be made. These demands then prevented the research from continuing. Gajjala suggests that researchers need to find ways to disrupt their own authority as ethnographers by deconstruction to reveal partial truths and any betrayals and by exposure of bias; and that they need to address the issues of what or who constitutes such a community, how this is decided and who has control of the group, whether an e-mail list is a public or a private space, what the status of intellectual property is, how long a vote to prevent researchers entering and taking data can last, and what is to be the status of participants, as texts or as informants.

Further problematic issues were revealed in another study (Ward, 1999) which looked at two virtual communities – the Cybergirl Web Station and Women Halting Online Abuse (WHOA), both of which were 'read only'. She found that the notions of 'culture' and 'community' were very problematic on these sites. In addition, the dialogic process allowed participants considerable freedom to define their own reality and to pose questions to the researcher. This led to an open reflexive methodology with dual interpretation. She also discovered that a 'virtual community' was neither physical nor virtual but was illusionary and that participants' relationships with groups were short term and transitory.

Criticisms of cyber ethnography

- Ethical issues: there are difficulties in gaining permission at anonymous sites.
- How ethical is 'lurking'?
- Authoritative findings are difficult to gain when information is fragmented and follow-up cannot easily be undertaken.

Summary

The newer forms of ethnography which you might like to consider are: autoethnography, with its focus on the self as subject of the research; ethno drama, with its dramatic performances and political and social challenges; and cyber ethnography, with its observation and analysis of online communication. All these approaches require meticulous collection of data, careful interpretation and creative forms of display in order to impact on the reader or the audience.

FURTHER READING

Autoethnography

Bochner, A. and Ellis, C. (eds) (2002) *Ethnographically Speaking: Auto Ethnography, Literature and Aesthetics.* Walnut Creek, CA: Alta Mira. This is a collection of 27 papers from a conference in Florida held in 2000 and sponsored by the Society for Symbolic Interaction where research on personal life experiences provided the focus.

Buzzard, J. (2003) On auto-ethnographic authority. *The Yale Journal of Criticism* 16 (1): 61–91. This article provides a detailed critique on the perceived problems of autoethnographic texts.

Denzin, N.K. (1997) *Interpretative Ethnography:. Ethnographic Practices for the 21st Century.* Thousand Oaks, CA: Sage. Examines the prospects, problems and forms of ethnographic interpretive writing. Argues for postmodern ethnography and new forms of experimental texts. Sections include: on reading the crisis; experimental texts; whose truth?

Ellis, C. (2004) *The Ethnographic I: A Methodological Novel about Autoethnography.* Walnut Creek, CA: Alta Mira. This text captures the changing nature of this cross-disciplinary genre.

Ethno drama

Denzin, N. (2003) *Performance Ethnography: Critical Pedagogy and the Politics of Culture.* Thousand Oaks, CA: Sage. The focus is performance ethnography and autoethnography. Theory, the practical aspects and the ethics of these approaches are all discussed in detail.

Pelias, R. (2002) For father and son, an ethno drama with no catharsis. In A. Bochner and C. Ellis (eds), Ethnographically Speaking: *Auto Ethnography, Literature and Aesthetics*, pp. 35–43. Walnut Creek, CA: Alta Mira. An example of a less confronting ethno drama.

Saldana, J. (2003) Dramatizing data: a primer. *Qualitative Inquiry* 9 (2): 218–36. This is an accessible 'how-to' article by a theatre artist who later became an ethnographer and who offers this personal primer in playwriting with qualitative data. He presents information on such playwriting principles as plotting, characterisation, monologues, dialogue and staging. http://qix.sagepub.com/cgi/content/abstract/9/2/218, accessed 26 April 2006.

Saldana, J. (2005) *Ethnodrama: An Anthology of Reality Theater.* Walnut Creek, CA: Alta Mira. Seven ethno dramas are included here with foci on marginalised identities, abortion, street life and oppression.

Cyber ethnography http://webdb.lse.ac.uk/ethnobase/bibliography.asp, accessed 26 April 2006. Try this for 365 references to books and articles which have discussed cyber ethnography.

5

Grounded Theory

Grounded theory is an approach which was developed in the 1960s in order to generate theory from observations of real life as these were occurring. This chapter looks briefly at Barney Glaser's version of grounded theory, then clarifies the multiple processes inherent in the form of grounded theory, developed by Anselm Strauss.

Key points

- Grounded theory is a useful approach when the microcosm of interaction is the focus of the research question.
- There are two versions of grounded theory: Straussian, which has a focus on fragmentation of data through a three-stage coding process; and Glaserian, which is closer to field-based or hermeneutic qualitative research with a lesser emphasis on coding.
- Like all qualitative approaches, grounded theory has developed a number of other versions either through dilution of the original approach, or by combination with other approaches, or by the inclusion of a recent orientation such as postmodernism.

When to use: when there is little or no prior knowledge of an area; when the microcosm of interaction in particular settings is to be observed and all related aspects need to be explored; and when there is a need for new theoretical explanations built on previous knowledge to explain changes in the field.

Types of research question best suited: those relating to interaction between persons or among individuals and specific environments.

Strengths: can really tease out the elements of the operation of a setting or the depths of an experience.

Weaknesses: too much fragmentation of the data (Straussian version) may lead to loss of the bigger picture.

Grounded theory: underlying assumptions

The grounded theory perspective locates the phenomena of human experiences within the world of social interaction. The assumptions underpinning grounded theory come originally from symbolic interaction and presume that reality is a constructed and shifting entity and that social processes can be changed by interactions among people. There is a focus on the construction of self within the social processes of society, through interaction in the social world. 'Meaning' is constructed through the use of symbols, signs and language, and our ability to take the position of others and interpret our own actions from that position through the two phases of consciousness: the 'I' (the uninhibited self) and the 'me' (the societal controls reflected in the attitudes, values and behaviours of significant others). These symbolic interactionist underpinnings derive from George Mead as well as from the writings of John Dewey and Charles Peirce. These writers emphasised change, action and interaction in social settings and the construction of meaning within these settings through our reflections on both the phenomena and our own roles. The focus in grounded theory then becomes life as it is actually happening – the empirical, social world 'out there'. This world is viewed as comprising many different layers, as well as public and private views.

Grounded theory uses the inductive approach (which relies on observations to develop understandings, processes, laws and protocols) and ultimately aims for construction of substantive and formal theory. The grounded theory approach emerged in the mid 1960s and was the brainchild of two academics, Barney Glaser (a psychologist) and Anselm Strauss (a sociologist) (Glaser and Strauss, 1967; Glaser, 1978; Strauss, 1987). It was seen as a way of shifting researchers from theory directed to theory generating research using observations of reality to construct both meaning and theories which were relevant to the mid twentieth century rather than those which had been developed for the late nineteenth century. The primary focus then became the investigation of the context of the setting within which the day to day lives of people were occurring – their interactions, their behaviours and their constructions of reality which were further reconstructed through researchers' frames of reference. A secondary agenda of Glaser and Strauss involved exposure of the processes of qualitative data analysis in order to demonstrate that these were close in meticulous practice to those of the quantitative tradition and therefore as worthy of consideration.

The formal aims of grounded theory are to generate an analytic substantive schema (middle range) through processes of theoretical sensitivity which, after comparison with other substantive areas, can become formal theory (grand theory). The approach is best used for small scale environments and micro activity where little previous research has occurred. Analysis guides sampling. Although Glaser and Strauss jointly devised this approach they soon parted company and developed different emphases in their approaches to data analysis. These have firmed up into two very different approaches, a summary of which can be seen in Table 5.1.

TABLE 5.1   *Differences between Glaser and Strauss*

Characteristic	Glaser	Strauss
Style	Discovery	Verification
Question	Problem + variations	Dimensionalising and critiquing
Process	Emergent directions	Coding and hypothesis testing
Literature review	Ongoing from first category identification	When categories emerge – if desired
Coding	Constant comparison	Three levels of data fracturing
Open coding	Words, lines, sections	Words, lines, paragraphs
Axial coding	Unnecessary	Meticulous procedure
Selective coding	Core variables only	Core categories to other categories
Theory	Theory generation	Theory verification

The Glaserian approach to grounded theory

From Table 5.1 it becomes evident that Glaser is opposed to what he sees as 'fracturing' the data through the various stages of coding and prefers the constant comparison of incident to incident, and incident to emerging concept, in order to enable the development of new theoretical explanations rather than framing data with existing conceptual positions. Glaser indicates that through open coding, theoretical sampling and constant comparison, the answers will emerge. Glaser's approach would be closer to a more meticulous version of the form of preliminary data analysis previously described in Chapter 2, followed by a grouping of emerging categories derived from empirical data which are then combined with a close reading of relevant literature in order to facilitate the constant comparative process of indicator to concept. The researcher 'should simply code and analyze categories and properties with theoretical codes which will emerge and generate their complex theory of a complex world' (Glaser, 1992: 71). He sees the difference between grounded theory and the management of the data from field research not as the turning of a huge pile of data into themes and categories but as a looser process of generating connections and ideas and explaining them theoretically.

In more detail, the focus for Glaser is the substantive problem to be researched, its variations and its categories (those emerging and those it is linked to). He suggests you seek for the underlying patterns amid the many perspectives which participants present. These can be identified by adding an abstract layer of conceptualisation which helps to distance you from the data and should allow you to see these patterns more clearly. He rejects the constructivist orientation with its interacting interpretations between you and participant as inappropriate for grounded theory, seeing your role as researcher (although inevitably biased) as one of greater passivity in the receiving of data and one where there is minimal intrusion of your own predilections as you go about the constant comparative process (Glaser, 2002). Glaser avoids reviewing the literature until the first core variables or categories have been identified; then literature relating to these categories should be examined and any further categories should also be explored as they emerge.

Theoretical sensitivity is one area where Glaser has held stronger views than Strauss. According to Glaser, 'sensitivity is necessarily increased by being steeped in the literature that deals with both the kinds of variables and their associated general ideas that will be used' (1978: 3), and these ideas can be derived from a range of disciplines. The processes which help to enable this to occur are: *theoretical sampling* (the process whereby you concurrently collect, code and analyse data in an ongoing process); *memoing* (the development of theoretical and conceptual links and their relationships within the empirical data which serve to transcend these data and are made each time you move into coding of data collected); *saturation* (an awareness that no new information is emerging); and *substantive coding* (theoretical codes which conceptualise how substantive codes relate to each other and consolidate the story emerging from the data which will form the basis of the final written version).

Examples: Glaserian grounded theory

The outcomes of this approach can be seen more clearly in the write-up of a study of women, who are mothers, returning to college (West and Glaser, 1993). There is no formal consolidated literature review preceding the data display, and any literature mentioned is documented at appropriate places throughout the text. The explanatory theory developed is clearly indicated early in the article and comprises three interrelated core processes: *staying power, cumulative studenthood* and *recasting family performance.* Each of these goes through three stages: *cupellation* (probationary stage), *consolidation* (getting it all together) and *confirmation* (reaffirming and a search for a new focus). Considerable data are displayed to substantiate these core processes and stages.

Another example of the Glaserian approach attempted to identify the major concerns of health professionals working in interdisciplinary teams and to explain the processes used to resolve practice problems (McCallin, 2004). The approach was chosen as it was seen as a way of clarifying how individuals within groups make sense of chaotic environments and reveal common patterns of behaviour. An initial literature review was undertaken here to permit greater sensitivity to interprofessional issues. Data were collected from 44 participants in seven disciplines from three teams in two acute care teaching hospitals, and included 80 hours each of interviewing and participant observation. The researcher found that co-operative thinking and moving away from a discipline focus toward an emphasis on clients' needs had developed together with the establishment of dialogue groups, practice development and supported team learning. Pluralistic dialoguing (the framework of pluralism is one in which different groups show respect and tolerance toward each other, enabling peaceful coexistence) allowed the rethinking of professional responsibilities, leading to a reframing of team operations.

The Straussian approach to grounded theory

Anselm Strauss indicates that the first step is for you to raise generative questions from your insights in order to develop concepts and propositions and to explore their relationships. Provisional linkages can be made and verified on real-life data.

Dimensionalising and subdimensionalising

The earliest work occurs on the research question and this involves you in a basic operation of making distinctions in terms of dimensions and subdimensions, starting with the research question itself. For example, in the study question 'How does the use of machines in intensive care units affect interaction between staff and patients?' the dimension of mind–body connection was developed by Strauss. Such mind–body connections can be either internal or external to particular body parts and can be further subdimensionalised into levels of discomfort and safety issues. This process helps to open up the research question and to gain insights into the areas where data need to be collected.

Open coding

You must undertake this process every time data are collected. Open coding involves word by word, line by line analysis questioning the data in order to identify concepts and categories which can then be dimensionalised (broken apart further). Core to this process is the concept indicator model where analytical concepts are drawn from empirical indicators in the data by comparing indicator to indicator. A conceptual code is then developed and the indicators are further compared to this; changes may be made to these codes until a process of saturation is achieved and no new information is emerging regarding the properties of the category or code. The words 'code' and 'category' tend to be used interchangeably by Strauss but he does define category as a distinction emerging from the process of dimensionalising and indicates that codes surround a core category and strengthen it.

Strauss (1987: 30–2, adapted) has suggested that the following guidelines may be useful in undertaking open coding:

1 Look for *in vivo* (within the data) codes and attach existing concepts (from your own discipline) to these.
2 Name each code.
3 The application of the following questions will gain broader dimensions:

 (a) What is going on here?
 (b) Why is this being done?
 (c) What if – this or that changed?
 (d) What would be the outcomes of any change?
 (e) What category does this incident indicate?

4   Locate comparative cases.
5   Account for all data in the coding process.

This constant critiquing of data should enable you (the researcher) to break open the text and lead you to seek specific examples of this or that aspect (theoretical sampling) in a process of induction (inferences from observations), deduction (reasoning from general to particular instances) and verification (double checking or cross-checking against other data). Strauss has provided pages of his initial stream of conscious thought undertaken during open coding, a small part of which is shown in the following example to illuminate the process.

Open coding as a stream of thought

'She *changed* ...' This is a *task* [drawn from common experience].

'*She* changed ...' qua task she is doing the task by herself. This apparently does not require any immediate division of labour [a category drawn from technical literature]. However there is a division of labour involved in supplying the blood, an issue I will put aside for later consideration [raising a general question about that category].

'... *blood transfusion bag*' – 'Blood transfusion' tells that this is a piece of equipment, the bag and its holder require supplies [category]. Again, a fascinating issue, about which I can ask questions in a moment.

Let us look at the '*changed*' *qua* task. What are its properties or what questions can I ask about its properties? Is it visible to others (the dimension here being visible–invisible)? It seems like a simple task so it probably doesn't take much skill. It's a task that follows another (replace one bag with another). It seems routine – it doesn't take long to do. Is it boring or just routine? It isn't a strenuous task either and certainly it doesn't seem challenging. How often must she do this in a day's work? That is, how often does it take for the blood to get transfused into the patient? Or, perhaps, how much time is allowed to elapse before new blood is actually transfused into the patient between each bag? Or does that depend on her assessment of the patient's condition? What would happen if they temporarily ran out of the bags of blood? [Implication of safety for the patient which will be looked at later] I would hypothesize that if there is no immediate danger, then replacing it would have low salience. But if there were potential danger for certain kinds of patients, then there would be organisational mechanisms for preventing even a temporary lack of blood bags. Well I could go on with this focus on the task, but enough.

Source: Strauss (1987: 60), reprinted with permission

The activity of opening up the data, through the twin processes of constantly questioning the data and then comparing the data with other empirical data and linking to conceptual frameworks, can clearly be seen here.

Strauss also reproduces an example of faulty open coding undertaken by one of his students regarding the statement, 'Our society is so locked into the physical.' The following takes this student's analysis.

'Our society is so locked into the physical'

Open coding: version 1

	'Our society is so locked into the physical'... when you've got a major deviation you have got to come to terms with it, what's meaningful, what's bullshit. While someone else may be dealing with feeling too fat, for example, if your whole body is different, you've got to come to terms with it. It can be a liberating experience, a time for reassessment.
'Our society'	'Our society is so locked into the physical'... this implies a notion of some big 'Society', with a capital S, as opposed, perhaps, to what she or some others might think. Anyway I think it implies that there is another way of looking at things than 'our society' does. 'Our society' is a powerful, impersonal, abstract entity. Normative and impersonal.
'is so locked into'	*Locked* – this is a very strong word. It suggests a strong connection. Not just 'partial to' or 'accustomed to' but 'locked into'. Sounds permanent, restricting, involuntary, certain.
'the physical'	Physical – as opposed to psychological, emotional, spiritual. Notions of beauty, perfect bodies, magazine ads. Not various standards of beauty, but one. Does not imply being understanding and tolerant of physical differences, but being locked into one standard of physical perfection. Judging people physically.

Source: Strauss (1987: 153), reprinted with permission

Instead of this very descriptive and closed analysis you could attempt a more open approach to the phrase encompassing the critiquing and constant comparison techniques, as shown in the following.

'Our society is so locked into the physical'

Open coding: version 2

'Our society' contains an assumption that all those within a defined location or racial boundaries see themselves as one homogeneous group. But are they homogeneous? And are all views shared? Most societies are very diverse in terms of race, colour, age, gender roles, ability, disability and social and political views (I think *diversity* may be a key concept here). But what does diversity mean, particularly with regard to people with disabilities and their views? And how does any variety in views impact on policy? On funding? And on individuals, both abled and disabled? Is it different when the media portray the 'heroically disabled', or are they notably silent regarding disability?

'is so locked into the physical' reinforces the notion of a cohesive society? Have societies always favoured the physically perfect? What about the notion of 'special gifts' from higher beings, and the Paralympics – or are these viewed as imitations of the real heroes, the physically abled?

'Locked' links to 'unlocked'. But how 'locked' is locked? What does 'unlocked' look like? When has the physical been of lesser importance or unlocked? Or mental ability seen as a substitute for a lack of physical capacity? An example of this could be Stephen Hawking? What other forms of diversity or variety of approaches are evident?

Theoretical memos

You will need to write these up every time data are collected and open coded. Memos become a record of identification both of indicators and categories from the database and of the link with concepts (which may come from the literature or be imposed by you). They are a descriptive record of ideas, insights, hypothesis development and testing.

The purpose of memoing is to:

- follow the pathway from indicator to concept
- develop the properties of each category
- identify hypotheses relating to categories
- link categories and generate theory.

Memos emphasise conceptual and theoretical processes and are consolidated over time. The detail of the kind of observational and critical questioning of what is being observed and reflected on by you as researcher can be seen in the following example.

Spiritual care: theoretical memo

I observed nurse F. working with a woman who had locked in syndrome after having had a stroke. One week ago she was a healthy active 36 year old woman with two young children, now she could not communicate with her family at all. Visiting hours were a real trial to her, causing her and her family great sadness. Mrs C. was unable to move or speak, she could not even shed a tear when she cried. Nurse F. went into Mrs C.'s room before her husband arrived to visit. She gave Mrs C.'s hair a brush and washed her face and cleaned her teeth. She sat next to her and stroked her hair and talked soothingly with her. Informing her quietly about the day's weather, the latest news on what was happening while she stroked her. Nurse F. asked Mrs C. questions and looked carefully into her eyes for answers. She told Mrs C. she would find out how her family were coping at home and what support they could get while she was in hospital. She ended her time spent with Mrs C. by giving her a hug and quietly whispered a joke in her ear. Mrs C.'s eyes lit up. Nurse F. left the room, turning to Mrs C. and giving her a smile, a wink and a 'thumbs up' sign and then went about to her other tasks.

This raised many questions which were given hypothetical answers and checked out later with the nurse:

Q. what is the nurse aiming to achieve in stroking her hair?
A. care, concern?

Q. is the discussion about weather 'smalltalk' or is there a method in her action?
A. keeping patient in touch with world outside hospital walls?

Q. why joke? What is she trying to achieve?
A. rapport, relax, break tension, release?

Later that evening, over supper, I discussed the incident with nurse F. to find out the rationale for her actions … Nurse F. stated clearly that Mrs C. was 'worried about her family and how they were coping without her'. She felt 'isolated in her body' and 'frightened of what the future was going to be'. She needed to know 'she was supported and valued' because 'we all need to feel we belong'. She needed to know she was still 'a valued part of a wider world'. Nurse F. said touching Mrs C. in a caring way conveyed to her that she was not alone. Nurse F. would be there for her at all times. Nurse F. empathised with Mrs C. and wanted her to know that 'in my eyes she had not lost value as a person'. She hoped in this way to shore up the inner reserves she needed to 'face the family', and that Mrs C. would 'have a more hopeful outlook on living'. She wanted to help her 'create some sense out of the mess she was in, so she could 'get on with the job of healing'.

Source: Van Loon (1995: 79–80), reprinted with permission

Spiritual care
- Spiritual dimension and causal condition of spiritual needs
- Stating spiritual needs
- Nurse's assessment of the patient's spiritual needs
- Intervening conditions which affect nurse's decision to attend to the patient's spiritual needs
- Nurse's ways of being for/with the patient
- Nurse's ways of doing for/with the patient
- Nurse/patient relationships and their outcomes

FIGURE 5.1 Spiritual care: axial coding (Van Loon, 1995)

Axial coding

This involves you in taking one category which has emerged in open coding and linking it to all the subcategories which contribute to it, as seen in Figure 5.1.

Selective coding

Selective coding is where you validate the relationship between a nominated central core category such as spiritual care by the drawing together of additional categories of context, conditions, actions, interactions and outcomes together with the focusing of memos and the generation of theory regarding this category.

Integration

This involves you in the final putting together of the two major files, the empirical data and the theoretical memos, both of which have been building up along parallel lines and should now be ready to be put together within the conceptual sets which have been identified. In some cases a series of operational mapping diagrams are developed in the process of sorting data and moving them toward consolidation of memos and integration in preparation for writing up illustrative data and constructing case histories.

Examples: Straussian grounded theory

An example of Strauss's version of grounded theory (Strauss et al., 1985) looked at sentimental work in the technologised hospital. As in Glaser's work, no formal review of the literature in the field is presented. The abstract is largely a series of questions developed from dimensionalising and open coding (Are there different kinds of sentimental work? How is sentimental work carried out? When and where is it done? When is it not done? Who does it? What is its relation to other types of work? When is it likely to be a focus for the workers? When is it visible? Invisible? And to whom? What are its consequences for work, staff, clients and for the organisation?). Data collection is explained and the core category *trajectory work* is used to demonstrate related codes (clinical danger, work done by strangers, medical aspects prioritised, lengthy duration) and types of sentimental work are also identified (interactional work and moral rules, trust work, composure work, biographical work, identity work, awareness context work and rectification work). Each of these is substantiated with data. References are sprinkled throughout the text. As can be seen, this format is very similar to that of Glaser in terms of presentation except for the dimensions of the question identified in the abstract upon which the article is based and the presumed (but not demonstrated) greater process of fragmentation through the extra stages of coding.

Formal theory

This is a much later stage involving many years of research in a number of related fields. Glaser and Strauss (1971) identified the core category 'status passage' which they said was in the process of moving from substantive (empirical research) to formal theory through the ongoing process of theoretical sampling and selective coding of a range of status passages in literature and other documents. Examples such as single to married, defendant to prisoner, pregnant woman to mother, married man to divorced man, dying to death, all have an emphasis on the processes of transition.

Both Glaser (Burgess, 1982: 225–32) and Strauss (1987: 241–2) indicate that the process of developing a formal grounded theory is as follows:

- Identify the core category to be developed.
- Open code and write memos of an example of the data in which this category occurs.
- Theoretically sample in a range of different areas.
- Continue until a wide range of sources have been covered.

Criticisms of grounded theory

Anselm Strauss's version of grounded theory has received several criticisms:

- There is a focus on a quasi-objective centred researcher with an emphasis on hypotheses, variables, validity, reliability and replicability. This contrasts with the move away from this more quantitative form of terminology in recent qualitative research approaches.

- Existing theories cannot be ignored by avoiding a literature review. The researcher invariably comes to the research topic bowed under the weight of intellectual baggage from his/her own discipline.
- There is a focus on a complex method and confusing and overlapping terminology rather than data. The meticulous three-stage coding process with associated data fragmentation may lead the researcher to lose track of the overall picture which is emerging.
- Poorly integrated theoretical explanations tend to be the outcome where data are linked conceptually and early to existing frameworks. Concept generation rather than substantive or formal theory may be the best outcome.

What are the criteria for evaluating substantive/ formal theory?

In their earliest work, Glaser and Strauss (1967: 237, adapted) agreed that the following provided a guide for assessment:

1 *Fit*: the link between the theory and the arena where it will be used to provide insight needs to be clear.
2 *Understandability*: will the theory be meaningful to those who don't work in the area from which the data have been collected?
3 *Generalisability*: the theory needs to be meaningful in a large range of areas.
4 *Control*: does the theory empower users within the field with knowledge to improve their situation?

Method modification

Many new versions of grounded theory are now evident, including 'quasi' grounded theory where the approach itself has been modified so that perhaps only open coding or some form of this is incorporated. Grounded theory and Heideggerian hermeneutics (seen as interpretation of the understanding of in-depth human experiences gained via intuitive embodied knowledge of our culture) have been combined (Wilson and Hutchinson, 1991) to explore nursing practice. Here the Straussian approach has been added to the hermeneutic immersion in the data to clarify themes and include the reading of related scholarly documents – an outcome somewhat closer to the Glaserian tradition. Glaserian grounded theory and Husserlian phenomenology have also been combined (Baker et al., 1992). Here the participants' experiences of the world provide the major focus, and the process of intense reflection on experiences (bracketing) is followed by open coding from the emerging codes and categories which are linked to a conceptual framework.

A postmodern feminist orientation combined with Straussian grounded theory (Wuest, 1995) has been used to displace symbolic interactionism which initially underpinned the original grounded theory process. The feminist orientation provides an emphasis on multiple explanations of reality and a critical framework for exploring the shifting issues of power, knowledge, truth, gender, class, race, socio-economic location, education and sexual orientation. The processes of reflexivity, and the fluid nature of the conceptual framework utilised, are said to provide sufficient breadth in the constant comparative process. Postmodern and poststructural possibilities in grounded theory have further been explored by Starr (1991). Dimensional analysis has replaced coding (Schatzman, 1991) in order to bring the researcher's focus back from linear procedures (such as those suggested by Strauss) to the data themselves through the use of an explanatory matrix. Each story is subjected to a process of reflection regarding attributes, dimensions and consequences and all dimensions can influence analysis. The potential of grounded theory as an integrative mechanism, particularly through the use of the Straussian guidelines for the constant comparative process, the processes of axial coding and the notions of 'fit' (accurate representation of the experience) and generality (applicability to a range of situations) to bring together evidence from both qualitative and quantitative studies for health practitioners and policy makers, is also being explored (Dixon-Woods et al., 2004).

Summary

Grounded theory has proved very popular in qualitative research. Whether you undertake the meticulous three-stage coding approach or the more general hermeneutic approach with variations, this approach allows you to look in depth at interaction in particular contexts to see how people define and experience situations. In grounded theory, as in ethnographic approaches, the flexibility of the qualitative field allows you to be creative and to add aspects of other approaches in order to access the information you require and so to answer your research question.

FURTHER READING

Glaser, B. (2005) *The Grounded Theory Perspective III: Theoretical Coding*. Mill Valley, CA: Sociology Press. The focus here is on the processes of developing theoretical codes, sorting memos and making sense of developing theoretical perspectives.

Glaser, B. and Strauss, A. (1995) *Status Passage: A Formal Theory*. Mill Valley, CA: Sociology Press. This book provides a useful model for generating formal theory from substantive theory. It shows that many studies on diverse substantive areas can be theoretically sampled for their properties of status passage and comparatively analysed in order to develop formal theory.

Mead, G. (1934) *Mind, Self and Society*. Chicago: University of Chicago Press. Mead describes how the individual mind and self form as a result of communication and interaction within social processes.

Strauss, A. and Corbin, J. (1990) *Basics of Qualitative Research: Grounded Theory Procedures and Techniques.* Thousand Oaks, CA: Sage. Accessible introduction to grounded theory study with chapters on getting started; the uses of literature; various forms of coding processes; theoretical sampling; memos and diagrams; writing up; and criteria for judging a grounded theory study.

Strauss, A. and Corbin, J. (eds) (1997) *Grounded Theory in Practice.* Thousand Oaks, CA: Sage. Provides examples of the Straussian form of grounded theory method.

6

Phenomenology

Phenomenology is an approach which attempts to understand the hidden meanings and the essence of an experience together with how participants make sense of these. Essences are objects that do not necessarily exist in time and space like facts do, but can be known through essential or imaginative intuition involving interaction between researcher and respondents or between researcher and texts. This chapter attempts to expose the varieties of underpinnings in phenomenology and to clarify data collection and analytical procedures.

Key points

* Phenomenology involves exploring, in depth, experiences or texts to clarify their essences.
* There are several different forms of phenomenology: classical/realistic/transcendental; existential; and hermeneutic.
* Modifications of phenomenological approaches have been undertaken.

When to use: when the rich detail of the essence of people's experiences of a phenomenon is to be explored, described, communicated and possibly interpreted. Phenomena about which there are few in-depth data, e.g. domestic violence, high risk leisure activities, sexual ecstasy etc., are preferred topics.

Types of research question best suited: 'What has been the experience of … for you?'

Strengths: can document changes in feelings and experiences in depth and over time.

Weaknesses: a need to clarify which form of phenomenology is being used. Bracketing is difficult to do, and it is also very hard to judge when this process has been completed.

Classical phenomenology

One of the underlying issues prompting the genesis of classical phenomenology was a concern that the foundations of knowledge needed to be placed upon reality as it could be consciously interpreted. It was assumed that humans exist in the world as wakeful consciousnesses with little awareness of each other, separated by processes of socialisation and other social constructions. These constructed ways of being, it was thought, could be identified and suspended, allowing a refinement of consciousness to occur and enabling you to access the essential aspects of experiences in order to sol[...]

Edmund Hu[...] [phe]nomenology in his book *Ideas 1* (1913[...] [co]nsciousness' (1982: 33). The focus is o[...] [int]entionality (direction of experience tov[...] [t]he means by which an established wo[...] [...i]ng is brought into being. Intentionality [...] these established objects and ways of se[...] [t]he definition of an 'object' was that 'any s[...] [a]n object' (1981: 3); thus all phenomena are [...]jects. Husserl co[...]s by saying: 'To every object there corresponds an ideally closed system of truths that are true of it and, on the other hand, an ideal system of possible cognitive processes by virtue of which the object and the truths about it would be given to any cognitive subject' (1981: 3). Objectivity and subjectivity were clearly combined here and the anticipated outcome was that knowledge would be grounded and enhanced by this approach.

At the lowest level, how we see, hear, understand and intuitively experience everyday objects/phenomena such as sleeping, working, loving or hating defines meaning for us. Husserl saw meaning as being created by the mind through actions which have been directed toward these objects via a process of intentionality using concepts, ideas and images which form meaning for that individual. However, only objects which allow a process of critical reflection from the outside through phenomenological reduction or bracketing of the natural world were seen as useful for study, so that we can disconnect the world's 'taken for granted' reality, concentrate on the structures of our conscious experience, and gain a state of pure consciousness or ego. The disengaged consciousness can then be directed toward a specific focus, leading to a dual state of conscious awareness and reflective consciousness in which the essence of the phenomenon will become evident.

For example if my consciousness is directed toward someone such as a male person, then visually my experience will include size, shape, clothing, face shape, hairstyle. However, my visual experience of this person will also be coloured by my intentions in directing my consciousness toward this person and by whether he is viewed as a stranger, a lover, a child or a focus for research. These visual and emotional responses provide content and meaning or the sense of my experience.

This form of reality is referred back to consciousness and forward to meaning in a two-way process that seeks the ideal meaning. The 'ideal meaning' of an object remains, even though the physical object may be destroyed or may have died. The two 'realities' – the physical object and the ideal meaning – are both necessary (or at least need to have existed at one time) to comprehend meaning. In other words the actual spatial and temporal 'thing', together with the memories, feelings and multivisual pictures associated with that 'thing', comprise the whole.

Our natural day to day approach to intuiting experiences and creating meaning involves observing, describing and conceptualising or theorising them in the process of creating explanatory meanings which may be lightly linked to relevant concepts. If we formalise this approach and add phenomenological reflection to these natural processes, a phenomenological approach is achieved. Pure phenomenological reflection (bracketing) requires that one undertake 'to accept no beliefs involving Objective experience and, therefore, also undertake to make not the slightest use of any conclusion derived from Objective experience' (1981: 3). The putting aside of experiences of the particular phenomenon and the placing of brackets around the objective world should eventually enable a state of pure consciousness to emerge which will clarify our vision of the essence of the phenomenon and enable us to explore the structures and 'truths' which have constituted it.

So what aspects of the structure of conscious experiences should you be seeking in intuiting objects? According to Husserl (1981) phantasy, imagination, memory, emotion, action and their representations in language and culture are a useful starting point. Issues of perception, a capacity for self-reflection, intersubjectivity, temporal, cultural and linguistic awareness, and a capacity to identify intentionality, meaning and action in yourself and others, are also obviously essential here. The changing modes and your changing perceptions of a unified phenomenon add further complexity to this process as higher forms of consciousness are built. Husserlian phenomenology thus is an attempt to use a rigorous method to study experience both objectively and subjectively by going as close as possible to the experience of the things themselves.

The major outcome sought in phenomenology is the *description* of the structures of consciousness of everyday experiences as experienced at first hand. The grand theoretical frames from various academic disciplines are notably absent in interpretation and only description is highlighted.

Processes of phenomenological reduction

If you decide to undertake a classical phenomenology, then in attempting to bracket out your world views through phenomenological reduction, certain steps may be useful:

1 Identify the phenomenon or object.
2 Identify a recent experience of your own of this phenomenon in terms of how it appeared to you.
3 Take certain features of this experience, develop variations on aspects of this bracketed experience, and then delete these from the object.
4 Continue this process until you arrive at the essence or essential features of the object.

Say for example that the phenomenon you wanted to research was the experience of grieving. You may have had a recent experience of the loss of a personal item of value. This experience is separated out, examined and explored in terms of possible variations and is then discarded as potentially biasing in exploring the experiences others may have had of grieving – although ultimately some aspects of your experience may well be highlighted by respondents.

Michael Crotty (1996: 158–9, adapted) has clarified the process of bracketing more precisely by developing a step by step approach:

1 Develop a general question: for example, 'What is the experience of being HIV positive?'
2 Undertake a process of phenomenological reduction (bracketing):

(a) Ask more specific questions about your knowledge of and attitudes to what it is to be HIV+ ('What do I think of this?' 'What do I think this experience would be like?').
(b) Move back further, and remove all theoretical perspectives (the stigmatisation of men who are gay), symbols (such as the Grim Reaper) and constructs (safe sex practices) as well as your own preconceived ideas, experiences and feelings regarding the topic under research.
(c) Prepare to reconfront the phenomenon with a blank sheet, rather like taking the position of an alien from a distant planet.
(d) Focus on the phenomenon and become open and passive.
(e) Set reasoning aside.
(f) Listen carefully and allow yourself to be drawn in, in a sustained and receptive manner.

3 Document a detailed description of the experience based on answers to the question: 'What does the experience appear to be now?'
4 Examine this description, considering the question: 'Does it arise from my own experiences or from past knowledge or my reading?' All aspects which can be seen to have come from other sources must be abandoned.
5 Locate the experience's essence and identify and critique the essence's elements. Ask yourself the question: 'Would the phenomenon still stand without any of these?'
6 Negotiate the essence's elements with those observed/interviewed.

Data collection: intuiting and disclosure

Following the processes of phenomenological reduction, your intuiting (through close observation and listening) should enable the essence of the phenomenon to become more visible, allowing you to build up a picture over time in terms of emerging patterns, relationships and interconnections. Data which seek lengthy first-hand exposure of the complex layers of human experience can be collected by you from a range of sources via:

- Interviewing (of those who have first-hand experiences) but in a non-structured manner so that initial responses to open-ended questions lead you and your respondent in the direction of the respondent's experiences. You should return several times to seek clarification of issues raised by your respondent or to further explore potential aspects which are becoming illuminated.
- Observation (bathing in the experience as it occurs – observing the human experiences both of yourself and of others).
- Documentation including literature, poetry, biography, material culture etc. (immersion and reimmersion in the relevant texts under exploration, seeking the perspectives of others regarding these texts, meanwhile recording your own understandings and experiences).
- The identification and deconstruction of discourses.

Data analysis

You should use descriptions to uncover the essence of the phenomenon. Each text allows the uncovering of different layers of interpretation, which are constructed by you from within your social locations and cultural influences. These have to be identified in the analytical process. Meaning lies in the identification of the dominant themes in the encounter between you and your participant through a light form of thematic analysis where the data are kept largely intact. In-depth case studies are systematic, detailed and reflective and you will avoid comparing one case with another. The overall process will then involve:

- bracketing out your own experiences
- entering a dialogue with individual participants (or engaging with an existing text)
- reflecting on what you have gained through reading and rereading and through journalling your thoughts including any questions and responses
- identifying the major themes from the narratives/texts using processes of preliminary data analysis and/or thematic analysis.

Continue to question the data and any emerging assumptions so that new descriptions and new conceptualisations are then more likely to arise. Description of the experience's essence is gained through intuition and reflection and the thematic analysis should reveal different perspectives which can be written up through the use of metaphor or through conceptual linking. You must aim to reflect as closely as possible the essence of the experience. If you are certain that the description and interpretation correctly reflect experiences and that the reader will be able to recognise the experience's description as mirroring aspects of their own experience of the same phenomenon, then credibility is enhanced.

Example: phenomenological analysis

In an attempt to create specific steps for you in undertaking applied phenomenological analysis of the Husserlian variety for explication of interview transcripts, Stuart Devenish (2002: 5–6, adapted), utilised a combination of methods to undertake a form of thematic analysis as follows.

Stage 1: ideographic mode (the gathering of closely connected ideas, words or concepts)

1 From each transcript, identify categories of meaning from experiences by constructing a 'research key' of categories and subcategories related to the research question to highlight and isolate the themes and experiences occurring in the transcripts. This key will be expanded as more transcripts are perused.
2 Isolate 'natural meaning units' – phrases with a single meaning – and number these according to categories in the research key.
3 Select themes which are central to the experiences of participants, and write a phenomenological comment on each central theme.
4 Write a succinct subnarrative of the individual's experience of the phenomenon and relate it to the interpretive themes selected.

Stage 2: nomothetic mode (the search for abstract principles)

1 Collate succinct subnarratives and interpretive themes and use concept maps to place the interpretive themes into related 'fields' indicating interconnections around the phenomenon being researched.
2 Rank interpretive themes in order of importance (frequency × intensity) and group emerging metathemes and subthemes.
3 Identify explicative themes (those which appear to have a primary referential character) using bracketing of your own thoughts and biases, followed by creative writing through 'free variation' to multiply possibilities.
4 Creatively write using your own embodied experience of the phenomenon together with information from the literature to enhance phenomenological description of interpretive themes key to the phenomenon. Distil explicative themes into one final phenomenological description to form the conclusion of the research.

Three varieties of phenomenology

Various forms of phenomenology have developed over time. These approaches have been separated out to provide ideal types so that their differences are clearer for you to see, but overlapping is common. Three of the major streams are as follows.

Classical/realistic/transcendental phenomenology

This stream (Husserl), as clarified earlier in this chapter, describes:

- the structures of the world and how people act and react to them, in particular the structures of consciousness, intentionality and essences in an external world
- how objects are constituted in pure consciousness
- how these constitutions can be identified through processes of phenomenological reduction.

Existential phenomenology

This approach (Jean-Paul Sartre, Martin Heidegger, Maurice Merleau-Ponty, Clark Moustakas) questions Husserl's essences and their associated layer of consciousness which was seen to underpin experience, viewing these as not necessarily based in human experiences of everyday life, but some form of cerebral reconstruction. Sartre particularly emphasised reflection on the structure of consciousness using the issues of freedom and choice and the concept of the 'other', and Merleau-Ponty (1945) provided a focus on bodily selves, embodiment, the body experience and its reflection in the mind.

Existential phenomenology sees consciousness not as a separate entity but as being linked to human existence, particularly in relation to the active role of the body and to freedom of action and choices. In this manner, essences became part of human experience. People are inextricably immersed in their worlds (called by Heidegger *Dasein* or 'being-in-the-world'). Existentialism has a focus on the issues of in-the-world existence (which Sartre saw as preceding essence), in particular 'being' which provides an absolute beyond the essences which are being sought. 'Intentionality' links humans with their physical contexts. Within these contexts (*lifeworld,* mundane daily occurrences; *place,* temporal and spatial location; and *home,* a location and a state of mind in a particular situation), humans have the capacity to respond and react to the situations and to relationships with others that they confront, meet or are attached to in their worlds. In these worlds the notion of 'free choice' is seen as an individual responsibility not to be left to the group or society. The choices and responsibilities that are possible, the physical and intellectual experiences (actions, emotions etc.) that will eventuate and the interconnectedness of individuals in 'being-in-the-world' all provide a focus for 'being'. 'Nothingness' through death is viewed as the final outcome.

These writers also disagreed with Husserl's view that a process of phenomenological reduction was possible because of one's own interconnectedness in the world. They saw complete reduction as impossible because one must first experience oneself as existing in order to experience other aspects. As individuals we are inseparably part of the world. The fact and nature of our existence must affect our conceptualisations of any essences. Intentionality to these authors is revealable simply by involvement in the world, a focus on contextual relations and allowing things to show themselves rather than utilising processes of bracketing. The difference in approach here from the classical phenomenology of Husserl lies in the broad movement from the abstract to the real – the meanings for being must be uncovered first – in contrast with Husserl's movement in classical phenomenology from the real to the abstract.

Example: existential phenomenology

Joaquin Trujillo (2004) has used existential phenomenology to explore the human significance of crack cocaine abuse through conducting over 50 first-hand interviews with recovering and active cocaine users. To participate in the study respondents had to be able to communicate adequately and to have had experience of using crack cocaine. Trujillo found that for these user respondents there was a significant change in the structure of being. In terms of being, there had been a move away from interhuman significance and a transfer from being with others to being with crack. This had resulted in a focus on the self in the attempt to achieve a situation of being high but free of craving. The process of data analysis is not explicated but large chunks of interview texts are displayed to support the author's interpretation of this theme within the existential tradition.

Hermeneutic phenomenology

This form (Martin Heidegger, Hans-Georg Gadamer, Paul Ricoeur and Max van Manen) investigates the *interpretive* structures of experience of texts, whether public, private, in the form of art or in other material forms such as buildings. The interpretive focus in hermeneutics can occur either from the outside, from the perspective of the 'objective' researcher, or from the inside, with a focus on interaction between the interpreter and the text (Heidegger). The integration of part and whole in terms of overall interpretation is essential. Everyday transaction predominates and 'being' (existence) is the overarching hidden aspect which becomes evident via the activities of 'beings' (individuals). Bracketing does not occur but you will need to keep a reflective journal recording your own experiences, personal assumptions and views. It is also recognised that co-construction of the data between you and your respondent is occurring and that the outcome involves a continuous conversation.

Example: hermeneutic phenomenology

David Geelan and Paul Taylor (2001) have attempted a postmodern hermeneutic phenomenology of 'lived experience' (van Manen style) which emphasises the dialogic relationship of the researcher with the setting. Here the ways of being-in-the-world are allowed to speak for themselves but some linguistic interpretation is viewed as necessary. The authors use impressionistic fictive tales from a novel based in their data and an author voiced subjective observation of lived experience in middle school classrooms. These constructs are underpinned by the postmodern notion of *bricolage* (putting together all manner of bits and pieces of practices) to create pedagogically rich accounts.

The key criterion for trustworthiness in phenomenology overall lies in whether a reader, in 'adopting the same viewpoints articulated by the researcher, can also see what the researcher saw, whether or not he agrees with it' (Giorgi, 1975: 96). Your role as researcher is to provide transparency of process and to bring the reader as close as possible to the experiences and structures of the essences being displayed, and this will depend on creativity of re-presentation and display of information gained.

Modification of phenomenological approaches

Current modes of phenomenological analysis indicate that this approach is very flexible and that Husserl's classical orientation has in the main shifted towards either a hermeneutic or an existential approach, where some form of bracketing may or may not occur depending on whether the 'essences' are seen as harder to separate out from the human generated discourses that constitute them. Various forms of descriptive writings wherein the 'essences' can be identified by relevant persons are then seen as a sufficient outcome.

Peter Willis (2004) has however pointed to the problem whereby more traditional descriptions can dull essences, creating boredom in the reader. He suggested that in the description of 'lived experiences' a 'living text' would be more appropriate – one which uses metaphor or draws the reader in closer to the experience by utilising a range of literary approaches such as the autobiographical reflections and stories introduced by Moustakas (1961) in his descriptions of the loneliness which he experienced with his seriously ill daughter. Willis suggests fiction, poetry and graphic and visual arts are appropriate, following Moustakas's (1994) approach to phenomenology in which the focus is on subjective involvement and:

- immersion
- incubation
- illumination
- explication
- creative synthesis.

Creative synthesis using poetic forms of writing may result in intensifying attention but may also generate more critical reader appraisal. There is an element of risk here in that certain disciplines may find creative approaches problematic, despite the fact that literary portrayals have been common in some disciplines for many years and are now accepted practice within the postmodern tradition (Grbich, 2004).

Other methodological approaches such as grounded theory have been incorporated as analytical tools by Knight and Bradfield (2003) in their exploration of the experience of being diagnosed with a psychiatric disorder. Apart from the overarching focus provided by the study aim, research questions included:

1 What does the label mean for the individual being labelled?
2 How does the labelled individual understand that meaning?
3 How does the individual respond to that meaning in his/her world?
4 How does the individual's understanding of the label impact on his/her experience of self in relation to others?

Three people who fitted the criteria of the study were interviewed. Interview data were subjected to the three-stage coding process of Anselm Strauss (open, axial and selective coding) and models and theoretical propositions were constructed using the constant comparative process. The schema through these processes involved converting diagrams into narrative form to expose the tensions identified within and between the codes generated and abstract conceptual frameworks. The authoritative voice of the author presents the findings and discussion with interspersed quotes from the three participants. In terms of interpretation, the existential tradition dominated.

A study loosely situated within both the psychological and critical-ethnographic/action-research traditions explored the needs experienced by sufferers of late stage AIDS in KwaZulu–Natal (Rabbets and Edwards, 2001). The authors recruited 12 respondents from an AIDS care centre and interviewed them using non-directive interviewing techniques. The general approach to data analysis involved the collation of first-hand experiences where the essential research question was, 'What are your needs as a person with late stage AIDS?' This was followed up later by, 'Can you tell me more about your needs as a person with late stage AIDS?' From the detailed responses gained, reflective generative practice, which provides a focus on relevance and an emphasis on empowerment, was used to conceptualise the key issues and guide community interventions.

Summary

Phenomenological approaches involve you in intensive sampling of a small group and the detailed exploration of particular life experiences over time. Depending on the version of phenomenology undertaken, bracketing may or may not occur and the inclusion of other analytical approaches may be added on. Your final display varies from descriptive narrative to the more creative poetic/dramatic/literary displays of the postmodern tradition.

FURTHER READING

General introductory

Moran, D. (2000) *Introduction to Phenomenology*. London: Routledge. This book provides a history of phenomenology in the twentieth century including the versions of Husserl, Heidegger, Merleau-Ponty, Satre and Derrida. A very useful text for beginners.

Classical/realistic/transcendental phenomenology

Husserl, E. (1927) Phenomenology. An article written for the *Encyclopaedia Britannica*. Reprinted from *Journal of the British Society for Phenomenology* 2 (1971): 77–90; in *Husserl: Shorter Works*, pp. 21–35, revised translation by Richard Palmer. This article provides a clear summary of Husserl's ideas including epistemology, ontology, language theory and objectivity.

Smith, B. and Woodruff Smith, D. (2003) *The Cambridge Companion to Husserl*. Cambridge: Cambridge University Press. A series of essays which explicate Husserl's thought.

Existential phenomenology

Heidegger, M. (1962) *Being and Time*. San Francisco: Harper. The meaning of every-day life and the meaning of being is explored in this book. The translation is an accessible one.

Merleau-Ponty, M. (2004) *The World of Perception*, trans. Oliver Davis. London: Routledge. This is the translation and publication of seven radio lectures given by Merleau-Ponty in France in 1948. Suitable for both beginners and more advanced scholars, these lectures cover issues about the perceptual world.

http://www. mythosandlogos.com, accessed 26 April 2006. This website, *Mythos and Logos,* is dedicated to the exploration of existential phenomenology. It contains online essays and a comprehensive set of links.

Hermeneutic phenomenology

Moustakas, C. (1994) *Phenomenological Research Methods*. Newbury Park, CA: Sage. This book presents an historical overview of phenomenological research methods with an emphasis on hermeneutic, empirical and heuristic approaches as well as their philosophical underpinnings. Examples of research from a wide range of disciplines are also provided.

van Manen, M. (1990) *Researching Lived Experience: Human Science for an Action Sensitive Pedagogy*. Albany, NY: State University of New York Press. The focus here is everyday lived experience, the hermeneutic approach, reflection and thematic analysis, and writing up in narrative form.

7

Feminist Research

Feminism is a perspective with a set of principles (e.g. gender inequality, the value of women's experiences, social transformation) that inform research approaches. Feminists use a variety of approaches right across the qualitative research spectrum within which these principles are applied. One specific 'method' which has been developed and which incorporates and demonstrates feminist principles is memory work and this is discussed in detail later in this chapter.

Key points

- Feminist principles can be applied to all forms of qualitative approaches from ethnography to poststructuralism.
- Memory work is a feminist method which has been developed and widely used to illuminate women's life experiences and help relieve their oppression in society.
- The empowerment and emancipation of women participants through the research process continues to be contentious.

When to use: when undertaking overtly feminist research or research where the position of women in society is of primary importance.

Types of research question best suited: the exploration of gender inequalities and the lack of power of women in various situations.

Strengths: a focus on women's needs and a capacity to empower women.

Weaknesses: doesn't take into account the diversity within males and focuses only on them as a homogeneous group controlling the patriarchal structures which disempower women. Empowerment and emancipation tend to be presumed rather than demonstrated and evaluated.

Feminist principles

Although the content of the set of principles of feminist research has been hotly debated by feminists of various epistemological and political leanings, there is general agreement on the following aspects:

- That there is inequality in our society which has been constructed along gender lines and this has left women as a group unequal with and subordinated to men in terms of socio-economic status and decision making power. Structural and cultural expectations and practices continue to reinforce these inequalities.
- That current modes of knowledge disadvantage women by devaluing their ways of knowing and their forms of knowledge construction.
- That highlighting the experiences of women through research and allowing their voices to be heard may go some way to making these inequalities more widely recognised and may also encourage political action to redress oppressive practices.
- That transformation of society through the empowerment (the capacity to be able to assert personal power through having and making choices) and emancipation (freedom from the control of others) of women, particularly those participating in research, is seen as a desirable outcome.

The researcher and the researched

The relationship between the researcher (usually female, although some males have utilised feminist approaches) and the researched (women) seeks to conform to the following guidelines:

- The relationships between you and those you are researching should be non-exploitative.
- There should be exposure of your position, your personal biography in relation to the position you take on the topic, your emotions and values and how these impact on your view of reality and how this view of reality will be managed in the data gathering, analytical and interpretive phases.
- The voices of the researched should be heard in their own words, and ownership of narratives should be shared between you and these people in an egalitarian manner.

These guidelines have produced some interesting dilemmas. Ideally, your relationships should be as equal and as non-exploitative as possible; however, those who undertake research are usually educated students, academics, community or government researchers. Inevitably these people will maintain control over the topic, the design, the analysis and the final interpretation of data. Techniques used by researchers which may minimise differences between you and those you are researching have included divulging aspects of your self by clarifying who you are, what your interests in the topic are, and how you plan to conduct the research, including what you hope to do with the data contributed by participants. Friendships with participants have also been seen as a desirable outcome but the short term shallow relationships that usually develop during research can hardly be glorified with the term 'friendship'.

Issues of equality

Robyn Garrett (1999), in her research with senior secondary girls investigating the social construction of gender in sport and physical activity, went beyond the inter-action provided by the interview process to attend and observe sporting events, competitions, practices and rehearsals for dance performances. But despite this, she felt that the relationships developed were short lived and were terminated when she left the environment and went back to her university setting. In Garrett's view it is difficult, even when utilising egalitarian approaches in the research process, to avoid hierarchical power relations. Researchers are caught up in the challenge of having to produce research theses and articles and these processes have power imbalances built into them, especially when the outcomes will be judged via peer review by particular standards. In addition, the structural contexts in which women lead power impoverished lives (school, the workplace, the family unit etc.) are rarely changed just by the documentation of this powerlessness, although some consciousness raising may have occurred and these women's voices may have become more audible to a wider audience. Co-authoring of narratives is one way of giving women status in the research process but this can sometimes be compli-cated by the numbers involved and by issues of confidentiality and anonymity.

The empowerment of participants

The whole concept of emancipation and empowerment of participants raises several issues which you need to grapple with. What does this actually mean? And for whom? Who is actually emancipating whom and from what? And what would this look like in terms of outcomes? These terms together with 'consciousness raising' have overtones of a superior position inhabited by the researcher to which partici-pants might aspire. This places you as researcher in the space occupied by early Christian missionaries who with religious zeal set out to convert the 'natives' to a cul-ture and a set of beliefs which they perceived to be of a higher order than those of 'primitive' natives. The results of an investigation into the meaning of the word 'empowerment' for 15 women who believed they had experienced it (Shields, 1995) showed this experience to be multifaceted. Their experience centred on the develop-ment of an internal sense of 'self' (which had enabled them to take action) and on the development of interpersonal connectedness (a balance centred more on the self). These women had, however, achieved 'empowerment' in terms of their definition without the aid of researchers. This finding further questions the kinds of knowledge which are being produced, particularly when specific ontologies such as those embed-ded in feminism may not fit with the views of participants who have developed their own explanations of how things are and their own ways of self-empowering,

You will find that the oppression that women are seen to experience can be better addressed if the following are in place (Wadsworth, 2001: 4–5, adapted):

- The value driven nature of research is recognised and reflexivity is practised.
- Participants drive the research agenda.
- The focus is on improvement of participants' lives (rather than on researcher publication) as the major outcome.
- There is a diversity of participants including 'elites'.
- The language used is recognised and meaningful to participants.
- Data are contextualised and substantiated so readers can make their own judgements rather than you presenting a single 'truth' for their acceptance or rejection.
- There is some presentation of ways in which women may improve their situation.

In feminist participatory action research, empowerment of participants is seen as being gained through their participation in and reflection of the research process and through transformation of their perspectives via challenging new ideas provided by the researcher. However, participating in research has not always (or even often) led to life changes of the transformatory type – and is a greater understanding of one's oppression necessarily empowering? Power differentials still remain an issue, particularly where knowledge of the research process with regard to planning, interpretation, analysis and the writing up of the results and discussion is concerned. Do participants want to be involved in these time consuming processes anyway? Researchers trying to minimise the differences often take back these segments and present them to participants for their agreement or otherwise, thus recognising that researcher–researched relationships are basically unequal.

Feminist approaches to data interpretation

This can involve a direct imposition of frames such as the feminist intertextual deconstructivist approach within the poststructural tradition which was used by Leavy (2000) to undertake a content analysis of a range of media representations relating to the physical appearance and feminist orientations of Ally McBeal and Calista Flockhart. Leavy first outlined their positionality with regard to feminism and sought the contradictions within and between texts, which were viewed as reflecting the continuing impact of patriarchy and capitalism and the processes by which labels such as anorexia or feminism have come to be applied and commodified.

A less direct imposition can be seen in a feminist conversation analysis (Kitzinger, 2000) where participants' voices were utilised but the researcher refrained from imposing traditional feminist explanations. Rather than seeking the binary oppositions of gendered responses, two major principles were adopted: a focus on the voices and the viewing of female participants as active agents in refusing sexual interactions and in coming out; and an examination of how language use produces or resists the production of a gendered identity. There is an underlying assumption here that both males and females understand refusals in the same manner and experience similar issues when clarifying their sexual orientation.

An example of a reflective/reflexive approach can be seen in Magnusson (2000), where the researcher had become concerned regarding the complex interaction issues present between interviewer and interviewee in a project where she had carefully constructed non-hierarchical interviews by processes of oral and written feedback about results, by providing reflection on the interview experience, and by encouraging interviewees to develop questions (the interviews were longitudinal). Subsequently Magnusson decided to run a retrospective study with two external researchers reanalysing the original transcripts. Some of the original participants were recalled and independently to another researcher both they and the original researcher reflected back on the interview experiences, focusing on the issue of the location of power. Thematic analysis of the findings indicated that the original researcher's knowledge and ownership of the interview processes weighted power in her favour despite the equalising processes she had put in place.

Within the postmodern/poststructural tradition, disruption of traditional textual presentation forces a process of textual reflexivity onto the reader. Patti Lather and Chris Smithies (1995) attempt this in the presentation of their research on experiences of women living with HIV/AIDS. They use the metaphor of angels (ambiguous creatures, calm, cool, yet troubling tricksters) to stimulate reflection and multiple readings by the two targeted audiences: the women themselves and a wider public audience. The text is horizontally split on the page, allowing the interaction between two narratives to reflect issues back to the reader. The upper text portrays large continuous quotes – voices from the conversations among the female participants – while the lower text displays researcher voiced commentaries of the research process drawn from journal notes together with a discussion about the construction of this narrative. Short chapters or intertexts provide reflective commentary on the issues raised by the women interviewed in terms of the history of angels and the sociological and feminist commentaries related to AIDS. Any footnotes and further information such as statistics, research findings and useful resources are placed in sidebars – boxes alongside the other two texts. In this process of multiple layering 'the text turns back on itself, putting the authority of its own affirmations in doubt, an undercutting that causes a doubling of meanings that adds to a sense of multivalence and fluidities' (Lather, 1996: 543).

To show how feminist principles have been applied I have chosen the method of memory work. Although feminist principles can provide the underpinnings for any kind of qualitative approaches, there is only one actual 'method' which is uniquely feminist.

Memory work

The feminist narrative method of memory work was developed from the work of Frigga Haug and her collective in the late 1980s, so it is a fairly recent approach. It uses an emancipatory feminist focus within Marxism and social constructivism to help women rewrite memories of past oppression in order to liberate them. The underlying assumption is that women's oppression has occurred as part of their (unrealising) collusion with the wider (male) society to enter into societal roles and positions of lesser value than those occupied by men. As women go through life they are seen as experiencing important events and their memories and the reconstructions of these form a critical part of the construction of the self. This identity construction then feeds further into the interpretation of later events as they occur – reinforcing and justifying particular positioning. In memory work the group processes involve tracing back aspects of women's work and gender relations through memories in order to demonstrate how the women have taken an active part in oppressive female socialisation processes. The identification of processes of construction and reconstruction of memories in the presentation of self and clarification of meaning should result in considerable adaptation and change for the women, involved. Transformation of participating women, via increased awareness of their contribution to the exploitation experienced within patriarchal systems, is the outcome sought.

The role of the researcher

In pursuing notions of equality, you are required to become part of the group of participants under study. So although you have a facilitating role you are also examining and exposing your own life experiences and subjecting these to the gaze of the other participants (usually referred to as co-researchers) as well as to your own critically reflective analysis.

The method

There are three main stages:

1 The tracing of memories and the identification of processes of construction take place from each co-researcher's perspective.
2 The group then takes the collective memories and seeks to understand how each memory has come to be constructed in this particular way and how interaction within the wider society, including through the responses of other women, has reinforced interpretations. Common themes are then drawn out across the memories of the group. Finally new ways of interpretation are sought through the application of theoretical concepts.
3 Further application of theoretical constructs to the memories occurs, usually facilitated by you in the position of researcher.

The following sections describe these stages in more detail and using the basic processes developed by Crawford et al. (1992).

The tracing of memory and the re-presentation of it in written form

All participants identify a particular episode in their lives relevant to the topic of the research and write several pages about it. Sometimes it helps to write it initially in the first person to try to get inside the experience, but ultimately the third-person voice will represent the final product, i.e. 'Jane [pseudonym] went to ... and Jane felt this or did that ...' Describe the episode as vividly as memory permits to show the impact it had on you at the time. Bring in state of mind, mood, emotions, sound, smells, the environment etc. This helps to start distancing you from the action or event and allows the beginnings of another perspective to form. As much circumstantial and other detail as possible is encouraged, including anything that may seem trivial and inconsequential. Neither explanations nor interpretations are sought, just pure description.

Collective examination of memories to identify social meanings

This is a recursive process involving moving from the memories to cross-sectional analysis and back again. The participants in the group now discuss each memory in turn and question 'What did you mean by ... ?' and 'Did you experience that ...?' in order to clarify meaning. As the memories have focused on a particular topic and people's experiences of this, connections across the memories are sought and compared; but, more especially, lack of connections and differences are highlighted and these are not to be contextualised within that person's biography. Clarifications of ambiguities and any identified omissions are also sought; the silences and unsaid/unwritten aspects which might be expected to be there but are missing from the written memory are often very revealing of issues which have deep significance but have been too painful or too problematic to be written.

You then seek general societal explanations. The myths and clichés which have currency amongst media discourses and the general public, together with new concepts from such sources as Marxism, critical psychology and Michel Foucault as well as a range of feminist theorists, are discussed. At this point the memories may be rewritten to be more inclusive of missing aspects or they may not, depending on the group.

Reappraisal of memories

The general societal explanations identified in discussion in the second stage are then related and situated within academic literature and the group of women takes part in this process. These autobiographies should then have the capacity to illustrate how the formation of identity and the production of self within a particular social context have contributed to the reproduction of a particular societal order. The provision of a bridge between experience and theory will enable the development of new discursive frameworks. The disruption and destabilisation of past interpretations should break their continuity and provide the potential for transforming and liberating the women involved.

Studies using memory work

Researchers using memory work approaches have come from such diverse fields as tourism, health, psychology, sociology, women's studies, education, cultural studies and management and have included the topics of female sexualisation (Haug, 1987); women's negotiation of heterosexuality (Kippax et al., 1988); menstruation (Davies, 1990); emotion and gender (Crawford et al., 1992); older women's wellbeing (Mitchell, 1993); the experiences of women leaders (Boucher, 1997); links between bodies and the landscape (Davies, 2000); female sexuality (Farrer, 2000); customer service (Friend, 1997); leisure experiences (Friend et al., 2000); educational learning and assessment (Rummel and Friend, 2000; O'Conor, 1998); emotions and learning mathematics (Ingleton, 2000); pro-feminist subjectivities among men (Pease, 2000); women's speaking positions (Stephenson, 2001); and tourism experiences (Small, 2003).

The following example explicates both processes and dilemmas of this form of research.

Example: memory work, 'Bridesmaids revisited'

A study of the self-perceptions of the issues relating to the wellbeing of women who were older used memory work (Mitchell, 1993). The group of women who became participants lived in an outer suburban area and met regularly at a local social club; some had attended this club for up to 12 years. The researcher also met regularly with these women at the social club over a period of six months prior to the start of the study in order to get to know them, and when she felt they were comfortable with her she asked for volunteers for her project. Nine women between the ages of 50 and 80 years agreed to participate. Patricia Mitchell indicates that in her view five would be the ideal number for such a group. These women were apprehensive at the start and time was put aside both initially, and as the study progressed, to discuss any concerns.

Following feminist principles, feminist ethical issues were also addressed early by the researcher, including:

- Monitoring the emotional safety of participants. The researcher ensured that any distress caused by memories was managed in the group during the meeting, but she also followed up each meeting with an evening phone call to each member to discuss their feelings and to alleviate any concerns.
- Avoiding any deception by creating an atmosphere of honesty and transparency.
- Clarifying with participants all processes of the study and reassuring them that they would have control and ownership over all information to be revealed; promising confidentiality and anonymity as well as encouraging participant choice of pseudonyms; and affirming that the researcher would not delve into areas they individually or collectively considered private.
- Ensuring that the researcher's values were not imposed on or allowed to dominate group discussions.

- Taking back all researcher interpretations to the group for further discussion.
- Continuing to be in touch with the participants beyond the study.

In terms of the memory work process, this group met seven times over a three-month period with three follow-up meetings 12 months later for further review and confirmation of the researcher's interpretation of the data. This is a considerably shorter period than the three to four years that Haug, Kippax et al. and Crawford et al. used for their studies. In Mitchell's study most meetings were held in the social club with the final two meetings occurring in the home of one of the participants; the latter meetings were experienced as more informal and relaxed. Six women attended every session, with the others coming and going as family responsibilities intruded. All meetings took place over a light lunch and were taped using individual microphones. The researcher was open about her own life experiences but indicated that ultimately she had not been as transparent as she hoped the participants would be to her. The first session established a working model of the wellbeing of women who are older. Large sheets of paper were used to clarify the factors seen as most important; here a positive attitude and a need to counter the negative societal views of women who are older were identified. This model was further developed at subsequent meetings. At the first session the themes which were to be investigated in terms of memories were also nominated. These were:

1 the experience of illness
2 ambulances and emergencies
3 caring for others
4 menopause
5 weight
6 depression.

These themes were seen as potentially being relevant to all women. Prior to each session, memories of one of these topics from as far back as possible were written. However, as some women had difficulty writing in the third person they wrote the memories twice: the first time as they came to mind and the second time in the third person. Detail was encouraged and interpretation and biographical explanation were avoided. These written memories were brought to the group for discussion and analysis. Mitchell indicated that she found it difficult initially to convince the group that their views were paramount and that hers were not, and that it was their right to take her views and make what they could of them or to discard them in favour of their own – although the group soon developed strength in this area. The prior socialisation of the group meant that they sought leadership from her as an academic. In principle they were all 'in it together' (1993: 201) yet clearly the researcher had read the literature and knew what the issues in the wellbeing of women who are older were seen to be. The researcher had difficulty in not giving directions when the group decided on the above themes as they were quite different from those her literature review had highlighted. She also felt constrained by the need to conform to the goal of producing a thesis in a particular format. Ownership of memories was negotiated such that the written memories were to be the property of the women – to be returned to them at the final meeting. They also negotiated that the tapes and transcripts (only to be available to the researcher, to be displayed anonymously in the thesis and in subsequent articles) were to be destroyed at the completion of the study.

Analysis was necessarily collective, and meanings and understandings were interpreted by the group. Patterns and contradictions within the memories were sought, together with gaps, until a clear account emerged and the participants felt they had the complete picture. The written memories shared common themes which were categorised by the participants. Following analysis, the rewriting of the memories was not regarded as necessary by this group. The researcher took the transcripts and group discussions and undertook a deeper thematic analysis which enabled her to include casual remarks made during discussions, which often provided insights into the way these women were thinking. This analysis, and the more theoretical analysis also undertaken by the researcher, were taken back to the group for confirmation. In some memory work studies, participants will read extensively around the topic and engage in theoretical interpretation. However in this study, after discussion with the women, it was decided that they would not undertake theoretical and conceptual readings related to women's health; they clarified they had no interest in this, claiming that neither an understanding of their contribution to their own oppression nor the achievement of emancipation was important to them. This was despite the fact that when relevant issues emerged, the researcher would offer insights from her readings.

Memory work: methodological adaptations

Bronwyn Davies (2000) has provided a more autobiographical focus than the original method as described by Haug (1987), seeing the processes of writing and sharing and rewriting and reinterpreting as blurring the boundaries that normally separate researcher and researched. She has added a preliminary stage to the process which involves the group in choosing the topic to be explored and discussing it verbally in terms of individual stories and current societal/cultural interpretations. This process leads to uncovering the stories which are behind the more obvious accounts that may spring to mind and which may form the basis of the written memories.

Lorraine Friend (1997) has truncated the method by following the first two stages only. She asked women to write about a 'nasty retail clothing shopping experience', then went straight to individual and cross-textual comparison. The group discussions were taped and the researcher separately further analysed these, and as with Mitchell (1993) the interpretations were fed back to the participants to confirm accuracy. The separating out of the theoretical phase allows participants to share memories and identify socio-cultural explanations but may well limit any emancipation or transformation.

Criticisms of memory work

Criticisms of the memory work approach have included:

- Using friends or close acquaintances to form the group is not always ideal; some women may find it difficult or even impossible to discuss deep or buried emotional issues which may change others' perceptions of them in negative ways.
- Women who have no background in academic theory may become subjects and experience minimal emancipation or transformation.
- Women participants may prefer not to use academic theories to interpret their lives and this may relate to the education level of the group but will impact on emancipation and analysis of memories.
- The group may tend to indulge in primitive psychotherapeutics in the sharing of memories, which is not productive.
- The focus on Marxist frameworks emphasises a particular explanation of individual action as conformity rather than resistance, which may not sit well with group interpretations. Studies that have emphasised resistance and coping, despite the restrictions of a patriarchal culture, tend to have a more positive outcome for participants than those which emphasise women as victims.

Jenny Onyx and Jennie Small (2001) indicate other issues which have emerged from use of the method over time:

- The status of the individual's memories becomes somewhat problematic when they are challenged and reconstituted by the collective. To what extent can painful and personal memories be deconstructed, and what if this process is not an emancipatory one for the individual?
- What happens when the individual refuses to accept the collective's analysis or the whole collective rejects the researcher's theoretical frames as explanations too foreign to be of relevance to their lives?
- How are differences of opinion to be maintained and managed in the group process?
- Is it really possible to share ownership with a researcher who will also ultimately gain through publishing the work?
- In terms of analysis and final publication, what happens to the material from the first and second stages? Are these just discarded as not fitting the needs of academia and publishing? Where do they best fit?
- Whose voices are being silenced, particularly when issues of academic credibility are important?
- What happens to notions of emancipation and transformation when the groups are more interested in sharing than theorising their experiences?

Clearly the analytical processes in memory work will depend on the collective – their capacity for subjective, reflective discussion and their preparedness to take on the literature in terms of more abstract interpretations. But the issues surrounding both memory work and feminist research will continue to be hotly debated.

Summary

Feminist principles relating to empowerment and emancipation of women, who are seen as unequal to men in most societies, are well entrenched across research practice. Some of these principles, in particular the equalisation of power relations between researcher and researched, have become mainstream practice in qualitative research, although varying degrees of equality can be observed here. The contentious issues in feminist research continue to relate to who has the most power and control over the research design, data collection and analysis together with the issues of empowerment and emancipation of participants.

FURTHER READING

Anderson, E. (2000) *Feminist Epistemology* (Stanford Encyclopaedia of Philosophy). This book provides a focus on the central concept of feminist epistemology and the impact of gender. She further discusses feminist standpoint theory, feminist postmodernism, feminist empiricism, feminist criticisms of science and feminist science, the defining of the proper roles of social and political values in inquiry, evaluating ideals of objectivity and rationality, and reforming structures of epistemic authority. This is a book for those with a reasonable background in this topic.

Ardovini-Brooker, J. (2002) Feminist epistemology: the foundation of feminist research and its distinction from traditional research. *Advancing Women in Leadership*, http://www. advancingwomen.com/awl/spring2002/ARDOV%7ECG. HTM, accessed 19 April 2006. The article attempts to answer the question 'What makes feminist research distinctive from traditional research within the social sciences?' The intertwining nature of feminist epistemology, methodology (theory and analysis of how research should proceed), and methods (techniques for gathering data) utilised by feminist researchers is discussed and these issues are contrasted with traditional approaches.

Haug, Frigga (1999) *Female Sexualization,* trans. Erica Carter. London: Verso. This collective work explores the sexualisation of women's bodies, charting the complex interplay of social, political and cultural forces which produce a normative 'femininity'. In particular an examination of the role of hair, legs, the slave girl stereotype and women's gymnastics all lead to a broader examination of the relationship between power and sexuality, the social and the psychological.

Johnson, A. (2005) *The Gender Knot: Unraveling Our Patriarchal Legacy,* rev. edn. Philadelphia: Temple University Press. This text provides compelling analyses of patriarchy and the powerful ideology that supports it and inhibits change. Accessible but doesn't oversimplify the complex issues involved.

Millen, D. (1997) Some methodological and epistemological issues raised by doing feminist research on non-feminist women. *Sociological Research Online* 2(3), http://www.socresonline.org.uk/2/3/3.html, accessed 26 April 2006. This article addresses the two key concepts of empowerment of women and the equality of the research relationship. The author suggests that whilst there is a need to conduct gender-sensitive work, a too orthodox definition of feminist research may inhibit rather than facilitate research. A better strategy might be to define feminist research in terms of values which it might uphold rather than the techniques it might use.

Tong, R. (1998) *Feminist Thought.* Boulder, CO: Westview. Tong, R. and Tuana, N. (eds) (1995) *Feminism and Philosophy.* Boulder, CO: Westview. These two books provide a very accessible introduction to the varieties of feminisms currently evident, their underpinning philosophies, and the relationships of these to broader philosophical ideas.

Part Three

Analysis of Documentation

Analysis of documents within the qualitative domain is all about *shaping*. It focuses on how social, cultural and political events and individual and group understandings shape what is said and written, and how these influences can be tracked through natural conversations and stories, collected through observation or identified in the perusal of existing documents. You will find that analytical approaches such as content analysis, conversation analysis, narrative analysis and discourse analysis overlap and sometimes duplicate each other, but each has a particular orientation – a distinctive flavour which identifies it as a discrete entity. For example, content analysis involves taking large documents and coding and categorising their contents, while conversation analysis focuses on conversation sets, narrative analysis focuses on stories told by participants, and discourse analysis can cover conversations and stories as well as including analyses of media and other documentation of a written or visual nature in the tracking of power bases from which the discourses have evolved.

8

Content Analysis of Texts: Written/Visual Documentation

In this chapter you will be introduced to various forms of content analysis including: the enumerative version with its focus on word frequencies and key words in context; the combined version where enumerative tools combine with a generic thematic approach; and thematic versions where coding frames are developed from the data, from existing theory, or from previous literature and imposed on the data set.

Key points

Content analysis requires up-front decisions regarding:

- the size and aspects of the data set to be analysed
- sampling approaches
- predesigned protocols
- inter-rater reliability
- whether codes will be generated or imposed on the data
- analytic techniques (enumerative, combined or thematic).

The analytical tools which are commonly used in enumerative content analysis are:

- word frequency
- rank ordering of words
- key word in context.

When to use: when you have large sets of existing written or visual documentation which require analysis.

Types of research question best suited: what is the percentage of occurrence of … (words, events, types of approaches etc.)? What is the dominant word use? How have particular concepts been used in context, and why? And for what purpose?

Strengths: the different approaches – enumerative, combined and thematic – provide different information regarding what is in the documents: enumerative provides a numerical overview; combined provides a numerical overview and a thematic slant; and thematic adds depth of explanation as to why and how words have been used in particular ways and what the major discourses are.

Weaknesses: enumerative data alone provide only a superficial overview, and thematic alone lacks the detailed numerical information to situate and structure the data.

Content analysis: purpose

Content analysis is a systematic coding and categorising approach which you can use to unobtrusively explore large amounts of textual information in order to ascertain the trends and patterns of words used, their frequency, their relationships and the structures and discourses of communication. You can use this approach to analyse media and policy documents, visual images and actions, medical and other personal records, speeches and transcripts. The researcher's creation of coding frames highlights certain aspects of the text, providing the reader with one particular view, but other views are possible and different researchers may achieve varying results because of different protocols developed and imposed. Enumerative approaches have tended to dominate here but in many cases these have been combined with thematic forms of analysis.

Content analysis: process

Six questions need to be addressed in every content analysis:

1   Do you have sufficient documents to make this form of analysis useful? And which aspects of these documents are to be analysed? All of the documents? Part of the documents? And pertaining to what topics?
2   What sampling approach will be undertaken? In the case of large numbers of documents you will need to judge whether random, stratified, cluster or non-probability approaches to sampling will be of benefit or whether this may mean that certain key documents get left out of the data set.
3   What level of analysis will be undertaken and what particular concepts or situations will be coded for? You may need to develop a prior protocol rather like a matrix which can then be imposed on subsequent documents in order to gain enumerative data. And how will you incorporate any thematically analysed data: as a basis for the generation of codes? As a basis for cross-checking? To identify discourses? Or to provide depth information and case studies?
4   How will the protocol and/or your codes be generated? Will you seek these from the database via preliminary data and thematic analysis or will you impose a predecided (*a priori*) coding frame derived from the literature and your own experiences of this field? And if the latter, what inclusion or exclusion criteria will you use to develop predecided codes?

5 What relationships between concepts, codes and their contexts will be taken into account? And how will this be managed? Will you look at context? Or stay with a broad numerical overview?

6 How reliable is the approach or protocol that you have decided on? Can a high level of inter-coder reliability be sustained? Can validity be achieved through cross-referencing to other documents or through triangulation and the inclusion of qualitative data?

Having addressed all these prior issues, how does this process translate into practice?

Example: enumerative content analysis of advertisements

Daniel Chandler and Merris Griffiths (2000) attempted a content analysis of the features of 117 toy advertisements broadcast on British television. Firstly they drew up a series of investigatable predictions derived from their review of the literature. These were:

- More *shots* are likely to be used within each advertisement aimed at boys and consequently the average duration of each shot will be shorter.
- More *dissolves* (the fading out of one frame and the dissolving in of another) are likely to be used in advertisements aimed at girls.
- More male than female *voiceovers* are likely to be used overall, even in advertisements for girls.

This focus on camerawork was to add a new dimension to a literature which had concentrated largely on editing and voiceovers. Toy advertisements which occurred between 7 a.m. and 9.30 a.m. on Saturdays were recorded for six weeks from the beginning of November on the HTV Wales channel. The first coding task was the identification of the target audiences for each advertisement. This was done by classification of the presence or absence of boys or girls in the advertisement, with those targeted at girls generally having mainly girls on screen, those for boys tending to have mainly boys on screen, and those targeted at both sexes having both boys and girls fairly equally included. The outcomes were compared with a previous study on parental classification of the target audience of toy advertisements. Inter-coder reliability was undertaken using five males and five female coders who were parents. Each was interviewed alone in their home and shown a 35 minute edited video containing the sample of 117 different advertisements. These coders were asked to decide whether each advertisement was aimed primarily at boys, primarily at girls, or at a mixed audience and to clarify their judgements. The coders for 115 of the 117 advertisements in the sample were in total agreement, resulting in an inter-coder reliability level of 98.3%.

The second coding task was the classification of various formal features of each advertisement:

- *editing and other post-production features* such as transitions (e.g. cuts and dissolves), duration of shots, and voiceovers
- *camerawork features* such as shot sizes, angle of shots, and camera and lens movement.

This coding was done by the authors independently and rechecked and readjusted by them at a later stage. Of the 117 advertisements, 43 were classified as being targeted at boys, 43 at girls and 31 at a mixed audience, but the boys' advertisements occurred 132 times while the girls' advertisements were screened only 94 times. With regard to editing, boys' advertisements had 684 cuts (a clean break dividing one shot from another) compared with 384 for girls and 422 for mixed advertisements. Dissolves occurred nine times for the boys' advertisements and 77 for the girls', with three for the mixed advertisements. In terms of camerawork features, in particular shot duration, the average duration of each shot in boys' advertisements was shorter (1.23 seconds as opposed to 1.73 seconds for girls); thus there were more shots per advertisement and they were faster paced. With regard to voiceovers, boys' advertisements had only male voiceovers while those of girls had three with male, 27 with female and 13 with no voiceovers. Differences also appeared with the shot sizes, with the boys having a greater percentage of long shots (full body) and a smaller percentage of closeups than the girls; and in terms of shot angles the boys had more low (lower than eye level) shots while girls had more pedestal (up and down) shots. These results were then theorised in terms of gender inequalities and the production and maintenance of gender stereotypes.

Tools for content analysis

As the repetition of words in content analysis is assumed to indicate their level of importance in the document, enumerative information is favoured in terms of gathering and assessing data. These enumerative quantitative processes are centred on seeking dictionary-based 'key words in context', 'key words out of context' and 'word frequency' indexes as well as 'space measurement' (of the columns in newspapers) and 'time counts' (of pauses and amounts of time given to particular topics in radio and television presentations). Computer programs with these tools provide a quick way of breaking into particular data.

Computer programs

In order to utilise computer tools, first your text needs to be able to be read by machine in either electronic or scanned format. One tool you might contemplate is word frequency in order to identify how often particular words are turning up in your documents. It is sensible to exclude such words as 'a', 'the', 'of', 'and', 'in', 'like' and 'which' as well as any other joining words which are being widely used in your document set. Having identified the frequency of key words you might like to select several of these to identify their contextual use (key word in context or concordance). The advantage of the dictionary approach is that other related words (synonyms) will also be picked up, e.g. if you identify 'economy' then related words like 'employment', 'unemployment' and 'inflation' will also be searched for. Equally 'family' would pick up 'mother', 'father', 'sibling', 'son', 'daughter', 'parent', 'grandparent' etc. Lemmatisation is another tool where the base form of the word and its variations are gathered, for example 'go' picks up 'goes', 'gone' and 'going'. In addition, you might want to check on the co-occurrence of particular words such as 'security' and 'terrorism'. Or you might decide to start out with a list of words that you want to check on to find out how often they occur in proximity to each other.

To facilitate your enumerative content analysis there are a large number of computer programs available for your consideration. I have found TEXTPACK a solid workhorse in the past. TEXTPACK (for PCs running on Windows) uses the dictionary word approach – whereby it can tag defined words for word frequencies (which can be sorted alphabetically or by frequencies). Key words in context (single words, word roots or multiple word combinations) can be shown with 8–10 words on either side to clarify the context; cross-references, concordances and vocabulary comparison of two texts are also possible. The cost varies from 50 to 100 euros for non-profit users. See http://www.gesis.org/en/software/textpack/index.htm (accessed 26 April 2006) for more information. Detailed links to most of the available software for quantitative content analysis, audio, image and video analysis and management, and the generation of statistical information can be perused and accessed at http://bama.ua.edu/~wevans/content/csoftware/software_menu.html (accessed 28 April 2006).

Open-ended questions can be managed using Verbastat (a very expensive program designed for government agencies) or Statpac (http://www.statpac.com, accessed 26 April 2006) which has an automatic coding module and is more accessible to individual researchers.

Let's look at the capabilities of these enumerative strategies in greater detail.

Word frequency: rank ordering

The rank ordering of the frequency of words in the election speeches of key politicians from various political parties will clarify how often these people refer to such issues as health, education or national security and how the frequency of use of these terms may change from party to party and election to election. If you go to http://tactweb.humanities.mcmaster.ca/tactweb/doc/twgbsec5.htm#KWIC, TACTWeb 1.0 experimental software (accessed 26 April 2006), you will find a simple illustrative program in which you can undertake a search for different words on a couple of databases. Taking the play by William Shakespeare *A Midsummer Night's Dream*, you can seek to identify the frequencies of particular words. The example below shows the results for words beginning with the word root 'ba'. From this you can see that in this play 'back' is the most frequently occurring word of the 'ba' root.

Database: *A Midsummer Night's Dream*
Query: ba.*

bacchanals (1)
bachelor (1)
back (10)
badge (1)
bait (1)
balance (1)
ballad (1)
band (1)
bank (2)
bankrupt (1)
barber's (1)
bare-faced (1)
bark (1)
barky (1)
barm (1)
barren (2)
base (1)
bashfulness (1)
bated (1)
battle (1)
batty (1)
bay'd (1)

Key words in context (KWIC)

Equally, identifying a particular word – in this case I have chosen 'love' – and printing out some words on either side of it whenever it appears will provide greater detail about the contexts in which 'love' has appeared. Only a small selection of the 99 occurrences of 'love' in this play appear in the example shown.

Database: *A Midsummer Night's Dream*
Query: love

love (99)
I.1/577.1 thee with my sword, I And won thy <u>love,</u> doing thee injuries; I
I.1/577.1 feigning voice verses of feigning <u>love,</u> I And stolen the
I.1/577.2 The sealing-day betwixt my <u>love</u> and me, I For everlasting
I.1/578.1 You have her father's <u>love</u>, Demetrius; I Let me have
I.1/578.1 Lysander! true, he hath my <u>love,</u> I And what is mine my
I.1/578.1 my love, I And what is mine my <u>love</u> shall render him. I
I.1/578.1 as he, I As well possess'd; my <u>love</u> is more than his; I
I.1/578.1 I'll avouch it to his head, I Made <u>love</u> to Nedar's daughter,
I.1/578.1 Come, my Hippolyta: what cheer, my <u>love</u>? I Demetrius and Egeus,
I.1/578.1 I I [LYSANDER] How now, my <u>love</u>! why is your cheek so
I.1/578.2 or history, I The course of true <u>love</u> never did run smooth;
I.1/578.2 [HERMIA] O hell! to choose <u>love</u> by another's eyes. I
I.1/578.2 is a customary cross, I As due to <u>love</u> as thoughts and dreams
I.1/578.2 I I [LYSANDER] Keep promise, <u>love</u>. Look, here comes
I.1/579.1 I give him curses, yet he gives me <u>love</u>. I I [HELENA]
I.1/579.1 I I [HELENA] The more I <u>love</u>, the more he hateth me.
I.1/579.1 me: I O, then, what graces in my <u>love</u> do dwell, I That he hath
I.1/579.2 and vile, folding no quantity, I <u>Love</u> can transpose to form
I.1/579.2 transpose to form and dignity: I <u>Love</u> looks not with the eyes,
I.1/579.2 unheedy haste: I And therefore is <u>Love</u> said to be a child, I
I.1/579.2 themselves forswear, I So the boy <u>Love</u> is perjured every where:
I.2/579.2 kills himself most gallant for <u>love</u>. I I [BOTTOM]
I.2/580.1 It is the lady that Pyramus must <u>love</u>. I I [FLUTE]

You could then undertake further classification of the use of the word 'love'. For example the following four groupings, which can be imposed on or generated from your data, provide a starter:

- 'in love'
- personal loves – my love, his love, thy love
- to make love
- 'love' as a force in its own right.

Variable display of key word in context

If you seek greater depth in contextual information you might like to display several lines surrounding your chosen word rather than just a few words. Simply type in your word and specify the lines to appear. In the example shown, three lines on either side of the word 'love' have been requested. Again, only a small sample of the possible total of 99 is displayed.

Database: *A Midsummer Night's Dream*
Query: love

love (99)

[Exit PHILOSTRATE]

Hippolyta, I woo'd thee with my sword,
And won thy <u>love</u>, doing thee injuries;
But I will wed thee in another key,
With pomp, with triumph and with revelling.

I.1/577.1

Thou, thou, Lysander, thou hast given her rhymes,
And interchanged love-tokens with my child:
Thou hast by moonlight at her window sung,
With feigning voice verses of feigning <u>love</u>,
And stolen the impression of her fantasy
With bracelets of thy hair, rings, gawds, conceits,
Knacks, trifles, nosegays, sweetmeats, messengers

I.1/577.1

My soul consents not to give sovereignty.
[THESEUS]   Take time to pause; and, by the next new moon –
The sealing-day betwixt my <u>love</u> and me,
For everlasting bond of fellowship –
Upon that day either prepare to die
For disobedience to your father's will,

I.1/577.2

[DEMETRIUS]   Relent, sweet Hermia: and, Lysander, yield
          Thy crazed title to my certain right.

[LYSANDER] You have her father's <u>love</u>, Demetrius;
          Let me have Hermia's: do you marry him.

[EGEUS]   Scornful Lysander! true, he hath my love,

I.1/578.1

(Continued)

[LYSANDER]   You have her father's love, Demetrius;
             Let me have Hermia's: do you marry him.

[EGEUS]   Scornful Lysander! true, he hath my <u>love</u>,
          And what is mine my love shall render him.
          And she is mine, and all my right of her
          I do estate unto Demetrius.

I.1/578.1

Graphical representation

In addition, distribution patterns of the occurrence of the word 'love' over different segments of the play can be graphed as shown in the example.

Database: *A Midsummer Night's Dream*
Query: love

	#	Graph
0–10%	17	*****************
10–20%	8	********
20–30%	11	***********
30–40%	10	**********
40–50%	5	*****
50–60%	25	*************************
60–70%	9	*********
70–80%	5	*****
80–90%	5	*****
90–100%	4	****

Total: 99. Total in database: 16,065.

[About TACTweb] (Ver. 1.0 (Beta A))

Text: William Shakespeare: *A Midsummer Night's Dream* from The Online Book Initiative (OBI).

As you can see, in this play the word 'love' is most used in the earlier part (the first 60%) and in particular the middle section (around halfway at 50–60%), tapering off in the last 40%.

Inter-coder reliability

This is an important aspect of ensuring the reliability of your findings, and it is suggested that you get another coder to look at your data. Seeking the percentage of agreement is usually done through the use of Cohen's kappa (Cohen, 1960), which can be calculated using the following formula:

$$\kappa = \frac{Pr(a) - Pr(e)}{1 - Pr(e)}$$

where $Pr(a)$ is the relative observed agreement among two raters and $Pr(e)$ is the probability that agreement is due to chance. If the two raters are in complete agreement, kappa = 1. A kappa statistic of 0.00 would indicate poor agreement, while 0.21–0.40 would be considered fair and 0.81–1.00 would be considered high in agreement.

It is assumed that the units coded are discrete (independent of each other) and that the categories of the nominal scale (names) are mutually exclusive and don't overlap.

Example: combined enumerative and thematic content analysis

This approach involves the use of both enumerative and narrative descriptive data, bringing together the categorisation and typologising of written text, images, responses to open-ended questions and systematic observations in context. Preliminary data analysis and thematic analysis are useful tools here, together with any of the enumerative approaches already outlined. This combination of quantitative and qualitative methods allows for a more reflective approach to the analysis of documents and enables contextualisation and the development of theoretical interpretations which can link to the structural organisations producing the events.

David Altheide (1987) undertook an ethnographic content analysis of television programmes on the news coverage of the Iranian hostage crisis (4 November 1979 to 24 January 1981) which involved 52 Americans who were held for 444 days. The research examined 925 news reports. The major research focus was the role of formats in the television news coverage of an international crisis. Formats were defined here as organisational devices – the rules and procedures for presenting information as news such as visual imagery, narrative form and aural information. Other foci included accessibility (of events for journalists); visual quality of the events; encapsulation and thematic capacity for summarising the event and linking it meaningfully to others; as well as the relevance of such events to a mass audience.

All 925 newscasts were viewed and preliminary data analysis was undertaken. Random and stratified sampling were rejected on the basis that these would distort the coverage to be assessed because of the interlinking of newscasts where each day builds or borrows from the news of the previous day. The analytic procedure involved viewing several reports, and identifying through preliminary data and thematic analysis the major themes of: hostages; families; the Shah of Iran; Iran (government operation); Iran (internal problems); Iran (external problems); the USA (government); international responses; and Iranian students in the US. This thematic analysis identified depth of information and revealed clusters and groupings which were linked to the origins of reports and to the visuals, and which would have been missed in a solely enumerative analysis.

The original protocol was designed to collect numeric and descriptive data on: network; presenter; length of report; origin of report; news sources; names and statuses of individuals presented/interviewed; their dress, appearance and facility with English; what was filmed; and the correspondence between film, speech and overall emphasis. Utilising a constant comparative process, Altheide was able to break open the text and to discover its complexity. For example, by transcribing a news broadcast down the left-hand column of a page, with identification of the speaker in the centre column and descriptions of the accompanying visuals in the right-hand column, greater insight as to the messages being constructed could be obtained through the juxtapositions that comparisons between the left and right columns naturally offered. The visuals were then further broken down into three categories:

- What was shown?
- Who was shown?
- What were they doing?

Altheide found that the families of hostages were featured in 12% of the sample but were clustered around certain rituals, such that they appeared in 37% of all reports around the hostages' first Christmas, falling to 25% around the second Christmas. In contrast, Iranians in street demonstrations in Iran appeared in 87 film reports (9.7%), and Iranians in the US, who were also involved in local demonstrations, appeared in 31 reports.

The advantages of this reflexive combined approach are that both enumerative and narrative descriptive tools can provide different perspectives in the analysis of the text and can serve to illuminate critical questions and issues beyond what is presented. They can also clarify the potential impact of these constructions on mass audiences while providing more behind the scenes information on the actual nature and operation of the media.

Example: thematic content analysis, codes
generated from the data

Motivations for the creation of hyperlinks (Vaughan et al., 2005) on business websites in the United States and Canada were investigated. The database was gathered by using Google to identify the links to www.abc.com and also by using Yahoo through the command 'linkdomain'. For each link sampled, the linking page (the page that initiated the link) was retrieved and the content of the page as well as the context of the link were examined to record the following: country, type of website, and qualitative information – the motivations for linking. A classification scheme was developed through an induction process based on grounded theory, and the category of 'motivations for linking' was developed by a three-stage process: one researcher examined a group of linking pages and identified and defined eight preliminary categories; the other authors classified a group of linking pages using the preliminary categories and added more categories as needed. Ten categories were finally negotiated by the three researchers and used to classify the 808 links identified. It was concluded that the final motivations for linking included, in order of numerical strength: online directories; lists of companies; news articles; acknowledging sponsors; links to business partners; links to customers; lists of products; links to job advertisements; and list of clients.

Advantages and disadvantages of content analysis

The advantages of content analysis are:

- It can simplify very large documents into enumerative information.
- It can combine both qualitative and quantitative approaches to look at both numbers and the relationships between these and the context.
- It can identify intentions, attitudes and emotions as well as reveal lines of propaganda, inequality and power.
- It can analyse interactions from a distance (enumerative), providing a sense of 'objectivity'.

The disadvantages are:

- It can be criticised for being too positivist in orientation, particularly when only enumerative approaches are used.
- It can end up focusing only on word counts, leaving no possibility of more detailed interpretations.
- It can decontextualise information.
- It can often be atheoretical, with minimal interpretation, on the assumption that numbers say it all.

Summary

Content analysis uses a variety of approaches from enumerative to thematic as well as various combinations of these. The computer-based tools of word frequencies, key word in context and other graphical representations of occurrences within documents are a useful way of turning a large set of written or visual documentation into something manageable and meaningful. These processes are extremely valuable in their own right but the addition of some thematic codes derived from mining down much deeper into the documentation can provide other levels of interpretation and theorising and a more complete picture of what is happening.

FURTHER READING

Budge, I. (2001) *Mapping Policy Preferences. Estimates for Parties, Electors and Governments 1945–1998*. Oxford: Oxford University Press. An interesting example of the application of content analysis methods in political science, dealing with political parties and their impact on electoral systems.

Krippendorf, K. (2004) *Content Analysis: An Introduction to Its Methodology*, 2nd edn. Thousand Oaks, CA: Sage. Currently one of the most detailed and useful books available; the first edition was published in 1980.

Mayring, P. (2000) Qualitative content analysis. *Forum Qualitative Social Research* 1 (2) June, http://www.qualitative-research.net/fqs-texte/2-00/2-00mayring-e.htm, accessed 26 April 2006. Provides a discussion about qualitative content analysis including: history, basic ideas; procedures; inductive category development; deductive category application; computer programs; and examples of projects.

McKeone, D. (1995) *Measuring Your Media Profile*. Aldershot: Gower. A general introduction to media analysis and PR evaluation for the communications industry.

Roberts, C. (1997) *Text Analysis for the Social Sciences: Methods for Drawing Statistical Inferences from Texts and Transcripts*. Mahwah, NJ: Erlbaum. An edited volume that examines recent developments in content analysis. It provides helpful insights on the types of data matrices that can be created from texts and how these matrices can be analysed.

Weber, R. (1990) *Basic Content Analysis*, 2nd edn. Newbury Park, CA: Sage. Recommended introductory reading for content analytical approaches.

9

Narrative Analysis

Narrative analysis focuses on stories told by participants. The story aspect is seen as a complete entity in itself with a beginning, a middle and an end. There is an underlying presumption that much of our communication is through stories and that these are revealing of our experiences, interpretations and priorities. Eliciting narratives of personal experience is seen as a more natural form of communication than face to face interviews, although it is possible that the question and answer format of this approach may elicit often lengthy responses in the form of a story. In this chapter we explore the structure and sequence of personal events portrayed by the speaker, their content and context, how things are portrayed and by whom, how people make sense of events, how these relate to the original event, how in the analytical process one story compares with other accounts, and how story construction conveys meaning to the receiver and to the reader.

Key points

- There are two main versions of narrative analysis:
  - socio-linguistic
  - socio-cultural.
- Socio-linguistic analysis focuses on 'plots' or the structure of narratives and how they convey meaning.
- Socio-cultural analysis looks at the broader interpretive frameworks that people use to make sense of particular incidents in individuals' lives.
- Although these two approaches tend to be used separately, their combined use provides a powerful analytic tool.

When to use: when you are collecting stories from participants.

Types of research question best suited: those that explore either the structure of narratives or the specific experiences of particular events, e.g. marriage breakdown; finding out information which is life changing; undergoing social/medical procedures; or participating in particular programmes.

Strengths: gives insight into how individuals structure communication for effect and how they construct meaning from their life experiences.

Weaknesses: when only one approach (socio-linguistic/socio-cultural) is used, the perspective is limited.

Historical definitions and changes

How can we define a narrative? It is evident that the term can cover a wide variety of textual possibilities from fairy tales, myths and legends, paintings, movies, books and journalistic articles to personal autobiography, but not, however, instructions regarding how to do things. The key defining feature appears to be that the stories are narrations of events which unfold sequentially over time. The definition of what constitutes a narrative and how it should be treated has shifted and polarised over the past half century. Drawing on a detailed review of this topic (Franzoni, 1998: 519) it is evident that a structuralist approach dominated the middle of the twentieth century. This approach was strongly influenced by Russian formalists who emphasised the difference between the *story* (the actual action or event which occurs) and the *plot* (the orderly arrangement wherein events are presented to the reader.) This distinction was further emphasised by French structuralists who introduced different terminology but with a similar meaning: *histoire* (story) versus *Discours* (the actual textual narration). In English speaking countries the events of the story and their textual presentation have continued to be separated through the 'plot' work of Labov (1972; 1997) which emphasises structure through clauses. At the other extreme there is the approach of the Personal Narratives Group (1989) which focuses on content and contextual interpretation derived from the stories.

Two major orientations are currently evident for you to consider: a structuralist socio-linguistic approach and a socio-cultural approach. Following the historical division into plot and story this dichotomy now dominates analysis in the field. There has been a recent re-emphasis on stories in the shift toward postmodern ways of thinking which has led to a focus on the subjectivity of the author as the person either writing (autobiography) or transmitting the narrative. We now ask questions like: who is this person? What is their background and socialisation? Why are they doing this? For what purpose? And who benefits?

Narrative genres

These encompass a broad range of presentation and re-presentation and are usually tailored for particular audiences. Three of the more widely accepted types of texts – lyrical, dramatic and essayist – have largely been constructed by the narrator, who is not the actor, in the form of re-presentation. The fourth – narrative – is where the actor who has had the actual experience has control of its telling. Because they are told for a purpose it is possible to classify narrative stories into particular types. Northrop Frye (1957) identified four conventional narrative forms or generic plots: *tragedy*, *comedy*, *romance* and *satire/irony*. Despite being separate in purpose these depend on contrast or the incorporation of other genres. For example, tragedy and comedy form a contrast, as do romance and irony, but comedy can blend into either satire or romance. Equally, romance may become comic or tragic, while tragedy can also be romantic or ironic.

Apart from these broad genres of narrative, which are more applicable to literary conventions, it is possible for you to identify particular narrative styles in the telling of personal stories. Stevens and Doerr (1997: 523–38) found three types of narrative in the subjective responses of women to being informed that they were HIV positive:

- *epiphany*: a revelation which suddenly clarified for them the meaning of their lives, often leading to dramatic changes such as geographical relocation, the reseeking of contact with family members, or leaving a job and pursuing more meaningful ways of living
- *confirmation*: of something suspected, leading to more matter of fact or more resigned responses based in recognising their own contribution to the diagnosis through drug habits, prostitution, own sexual preferences or practices, or those of partners
- *calamity*: a sudden and unexpected event causing considerable distress, extreme fear, shock, terror and panic as well as feelings of anguish, occasionally involving consideration of suicide.

In her work on women's experiences of relationship breakdown and divorce, Catherine Reismann (2003) has identified other narrative styles including: *habitual* narrative, when events are repeated again and again with no peak in action, often seen in patterns of grieving; *hypothetical* narrative, that is the presentation of events that did not happen; and *topic centred* narrative, namely snapshots of events which have occurred and are linked into current discussions as exemplars. Further styles were evident in the narratives of managers and workers in different organisations which were attempting to improve organisational performance through management of human resources (Beech, 2000). The *heroic director* involved a story of transformation through aggressive individual action taken by a heroic leader which was successful in managing a conflict situation to the benefit of all, but especially enhancing the honour and glory of the manager. The *romantic ward manager* involved a story of an assertive type of manager who pushes ahead team individuals and the group despite setbacks, who is positive and pragmatic and maintains direction toward an improved future for all. The *tragic skilled worker* occurred where individual action by workers is viewed as personally costly and not worth taking; an example of an individual who attempted this but became alienated from the organisation is presented, and from this example the future is not seen as positive and passivity is viewed as the safest path. Finally, the *ironic response to human resource management* involved a story of passive resistance of workers to what is viewed as pointless top-down organisationally directed change which will not benefit them.

Your purpose in identifying different styles of narratives is to generalise them to other settings. The habitual and hypothetical styles can clearly be applied to a number of story types in a range of settings, as can the epiphanous, calamitous and confirmatory narratives of Stevens and Doerr; while those of Beech are more confined and are probably most relevant to organisational settings where change is being attempted.

The socio-linguistic approach

This approach came to the fore with the research of William Labov and Joshua Waletzky (1967) who were interested in looking at the speech narratives of Afro-American people. These researchers became fascinated by the structure of these narratives, in particular the match between the reported chronological verbal sequencing of personal events and their actual order of occurrence, as well as how their construction conveyed meaning to the receiver. Labov assumed that sequential ordering of narrative clauses would form the basis of the narrative. Todorov (1990) added into this the element of transformation; he suggested that narratives usually involve some form of disruption and, in order to demonstrate change in equilibrium, narratives move backwards and forwards between changed events, usually ending with the achievement of a final state of equilibrium.

According to Labov (1972: 360–1) the most basic narrative comprises at least two clauses which are sequentially ordered. For example:

1 I usually shop at X.
2 Last week the girl at the checkout overcharged me.
3 I complained and gained a refund.

Clause 1 is a free clause because it can be moved to any position without changing the meaning of the story. Clauses 2 and 3 are narrative clauses which need (in this case) to stay in this order for the story to make sense.

Process

From their research on Afro-American narratives, Labov and Waletzky concluded that a well developed narrative displays a six-part macrostructure of ordered recurring patterns comprising six elements. These elements are as follows (adapted from Labov and Waletzky, 1967; Labov, 1972: 370; 1997):

1 *Abstract*: an initial clause that reports or summarises the entire sequence of events of the narrative.
2 *Orientation clauses*: the time, place and events of the narrative.
3 *Complicating action clauses*: these form the main body of the story and provide the next sequential event to respond to the question 'And what happened then?'
4 *Evaluation*: interpretation of the significance of events and meanings and also the importance of the narrator's situation, socialisation, experience and views.

5   *Result or resolution*: the final outcome of the narrative.
6   *Coda* (often missing): ties narrator and audience back to the present.

The underlying assumptions here are that it is possible to break down all narratives into units of meaning and to map them in such a way that their common properties will be revealed.

An example is as follows:

1   She gave birth after a long labour (abstract).
2   She went into labour on Thursday (orientation).
3   On Friday they said she would have to have a Caesarean (complicating action).
4   I think they should have let her have a normal birth, but these gynaecologists won't work weekends (evaluation).
5   And she had a lovely baby girl (result).
6   They're all fine now (coda).

A more detailed analysis can be provided by identifying the classes of narrative clauses and examining each in terms of their range and impact (Labov, 1997):

- The *range* of a narrative clause is the sum of the number of preceding clauses it is occurring simultaneously with (left subscript in the notation) and the number of clauses it is followed by and linked to (right subscript).
- A (temporarily) *bound* clause is an independent clause with a range of 0.
- A *free* clause is defined semantically as non-sequential and refers to a condition which remains unchanging throughout the narrative: it cannot be a sequential clause.
- A *restricted* clause is sequential with a range greater than 0.

Example: socio-linguistic analysis

The following is an example of this form of analysis.

Interview with Harold Shambaugh			
Range	Elements	Type of clause	Transcript
$_0a_2$	OR	restricted	Oh I w's settin' at a table drinkin'
$_1b_0$	CA	restricted	And – this Norwegian sailor come over
$_0c_0$	CA	bound	an' kep' givin' me a bunch o' junk
			about I was sittin' with his woman.

(Continued)

d	OR	free	An' everybody sittin' at the table with me were my shipmates.
$_0e_0$	CA	bound	So I jus' turn aroun'
$_0f_0$	CA	bound	an' shoved, 'im,
$_0g_0$	CA	bound	an' told 'im, I said, 'Go away,'
$_0h_0$	EV	bound	[and I said,] 'I don't even wanna fool with ya.'
			An' nex' thing I know
$_0i_2$	CA	restricted	I'm layin' on the floor, blood all over me,
$_1j_0$	EV	restricted	An' a guy told me, says, 'Don't move your head.'
$_0k_0$	CA	bound	[And he said,] 'Your throat's cut.'

The Layout is as follows:

- In the first column, the lines are all given letters in sequence from (a) to (k), except for the fourth and tenth lines which are not independent (not sequential) clauses. The subscripts for line (a), shown in $_0a_2$, indicate that (a) is not simultaneous with any preceding events, but does overlap with the two following (and with the free clause (d)). But (a) is not simultaneous with (e), since at that point Shambaugh has moved beyond just sitting and drinking at the table.
- In the second column, the orientation (OR) clauses (a) and (d) are picked out, as are the evaluation (EV) clauses (h) and (j). There is no abstract or coda, and the other sequential clauses are all complicating action (CA).
- In the third column, each sequential clause is identified as free, bound or restricted.
- In the fourth column, the narrative is transcribed.

Labov has constructed the causal sequence of events of this narrative as follows:

1 Shambaugh is sitting with his mates at a table drinking (orientation).
2 A Norwegian sailor comes over to complain to Shambaugh about his sitting with the Norwegian sailor's woman (complicating action).
3 Shambaugh rejects the complaint (complicating action plus evaluation).
4 Shambaugh turns his back on the sailor (complicating action).
5 The sailor cuts Shambaugh's throat (complicating action and result).
6 Shambaugh is warned not to move by another person (evaluation).

Source: adapted from Labov (1997: 28/7/70), reprinted with permission and available online at http://www.ling.upenn.edu/~wlabov/sfs.html, accessed 24 April 2006.

Criticisms of the socio-linguistic approach

- The focus is the text and the sequence of events. What is missing are: the inter-action between the actor and the audience; the power relations; the shifts in meaning; the outcomes in terms of impact on the listener; and the development of shared understandings. The plot – its performance via clauses and the structure of its construction – is alone what is analysed.
- The assumption that language represents reality does not take into account the arguments that language is power laden, embedded in culture and socialisation patterns, and actually constitutes and constructs reality.
- Narratives are complex constructions of meaning linking personal lives, community and culture and should be preserved intact, not fractured.
- The context is completely omitted and the impact of the issues of race, class, gender and hierarchy are not considered.
- Narratives may not follow a chronological sequence in a linear way through time; they may be linked by themes which are not necessarily sequential.

The socio-cultural approach

Lives and stories are narrated as meaningful, coherent entities. However, the socio-cultural approach goes beyond language structures to the broader interpretive frameworks that people use to make sense of everyday happenings/episodes, usually involving past–present–future linking. These personal narratives tend to be fairly-concise and relate to specific incidents which have been observed or experienced. The segmentation of data into themes and other forms of fragmentation such as coding is avoided in this process as the stories which are told are complete entities in themselves and resist such processes. The assumptions underpinning this approach are that stories not only reflect culture, ideology and socialisation, but also provide insights into the political and historical climates impacting on the storytellers' lives. As when stones are dropped into water, the ripples reach out in ever increasing cicles.

Process

- Identify the boundaries of the narrative segments in the interview transcript. These may be entire life stories or specific life episodes recorded in interactive talk or interviews.
- Explore the content and context of the story. How do people make sense of events? What emotions and feelings are displayed?
- Compare different people's stories (if examining similar events).

- Link stories to relevant political structures and cultural locations.
- Interpret stories, being aware of your own positions and reactions and how these shape the final text.

Example: socio-cultural analysis

In one response to the question 'How did your mother respond to you becoming a father at home?', the following was given (Grbich, 1987):

> Well mum thought I was being taken for a ride by an older woman when she first found out I was going to be a father. Her first reaction was horror that I wasn't still a virgin, which shows where her thinking lay. She's now good, she's come round a lot. She gets on very well with Dan [his partner's child by another relationship], and she gets on well with Jen [partner]. Once she got over the problem of Jen being a terrible woman – a single mother who wanted someone to hang her bloody hat with – they got on very well, so that's been a substantial change.

Identification of boundaries

Using Labov's framework, this narrative appears in structure to be bounded by an orientation clause, complicating action, a result and a coda to bring it back to the present. This approach allows us to see that it is a fairly well developed narrative, with a beginning, a middle and a resolution.

Interpretation of content: political and social context

The context of gaining the narrative was that it emerged from within the bounds of research interviews of men who stay at home to rear young children while their partners take on the breadwinner role. This is a narrative response identified in the first of several interviews. These interviews recurred at intervals over a period of five years and were backed up by further interviews with the partner and the househusband's parents. In this narrative we have John, a male in his late 20s, who 18 months previously left his job as a manager of a small credit union to become a househusband to look after two children: his stepson Dan who is two years old, and his own child Emily who is three months old. Jen, his partner, who is in her early 30s, is a social worker. They share a house with a priest, another couple and a baby. John's mother lives in a rural town in a fairly remote area, and the emotions reported here indicate that she initially had a negative response both to the relationship and to the role change involved.

Other interview data confirm that the mother's views stem from a strongly conservative Catholic upbringing. Her husband died when John was 20 and she is close to her son, who is her third and youngest child, despite the fact that they live about 3000 kilometres apart. Her expectations for her son were very high as he was the only child to attend university even though he only attended for five weeks. It appears that her initial reaction reflected the socialised expectations of many western cultures: that the male should be older and that the female should not be the breadwinner, particularly in a situation where there was a young baby at home still being breastfed. Her indicated concern that John wasn't still a virgin at 26 is also a reflection of earlier moral standards no longer seen as relevant to metro males in western societies who are well past their teens.

Further indications are that this initial response from John's mother also stems from geographical distance. And it was interesting to note that prior to the birth of their shared child the couple had travelled to spend time with her, and this face to face contact had obviously allowed other factors to impinge on her view of the situation. Having met both Jen and Dan she realised that they were likeable people and that Jen was not just out to capture her son for her own selfish wellbeing. A young child and a future new baby to whom she would be grandmother were undoubtedly also an influence here, but in addition Jen's very practical, no-nonsense, down-to-earth nature would also have provided reassurance that despite being a 'city person', Jen was in fact very close in character to many country women and therefore probably the right person for her son.

Contrasting stories

John's frustration and anger at his mother's response that Jen was just 'taking him for a ride' and looking for 'someone to hang her bloody hat with' is revealed in the language he uses and suggests he feels strongly about the relationship being seen in a truer light. The strength of his response also indicates that his mother's views are important to him. These emotions probably prompted the long trip with a pregnant wife and a one-year-old child to demonstrate to his mother that she was wrong. He later stated that he was 'very fond of her … she doesn't understand what we are doing … but we get on well. We're good mates, we love each other very much.' The stories presented – his mother's and implicitly his own views, which are quite different from hers – provide the contrast in the account and match Todorov's aspect of transformation: the disruption of equilibrium through change and the movement over time to another form of equilibrium.

Positioning of the actor and the researcher

But what about the position of the actor and the interviewer? The actor had strong ideological views about the importance of relationships and the need to avoid allowing workforce requirements to dominate and to undermine the time and energy levels available to develop these relationships. Commitment to community, social action and personal growth were also important. This was summarised later in this interview when he said: 'When you work in the fast lane, you live in the fast lane … we found that we just were not enjoying our life, it was too empty, too much going on.' Choosing to live in a group household, with people who were equally committed to such views, reinforced and supported this situation. The researcher was also largely committed to these values: she was undertaking her doctoral thesis on the topic of househusbands because she believed that this form of role change was important to allow the development of greater equality in the home division of labour; and also because, in being the breadwinner herself while her partner was the househusband at home to their three young children, she was interested to see how other couples were coping, given that there was little research on this topic at that time and none of it had been undertaken longitudinally. Her own position, which had been clarified to each participating family, undoubtedly placed her inside this group and facilitated acceptance, but also may have resulted in a belief that there was shared ideology and therefore too much elaboration was not required (the 'insider' dilemma).

The narrative and in fact the whole interview needs to be seen as a dramatic performance. The use of the word 'bloody', often used as an expletive by men in this culture, emphasises the fact that despite his mother's views and the traditionally 'feminine' role he is inhabiting, John is definitely a male. The statement that he 'wasn't a virgin' emphasises that he is sexually experienced, with the implication that he also knows what he is doing regarding his choice of partner and role change. The language used to portray his partner from the perspective of his mother – 'taken for a ride by an older woman', 'a single mother who wanted someone to hang her bloody hat with' – serve to position the mother at a different end of the spectrum from himself and his partner and make the resolution involving 'substantial change' more impressive. Using other information from the interview, the narrator can be seen as positioning himself as a heroic and powerful knight in shining armour, galloping forth to the ends of the earth with partner and child in hand to right wrongs and mitigate the impact of his mother's negative opinions on his immediate family unit.

In choosing to display and to analyse this narrative, the researcher is highlighting her own views that although parents may not initially respond positively to their sons' choice to take on what has previously been seen as the 'female' nurturing role, it is very likely that eventually such parents may abandon negative views, particularly if these are challenged. These views then change and become subsumed into a desire to accept, to justify and to protect their offspring from the responses of others by taking an accepting position. Another researcher might have chosen to omit the father's voice or to report it minimally while highlighting the voices of the partner and mother for consideration.

The reader: other interpretations

Each narrative is subject to many readings and interpretations. A feminist reading might focus on a generational clash between two women and their capacity to resolve this, viewing the role of the male as diminished except as one perspective on the situation. A reading based on power relations would look at male, female and intergenerational relations between son and mother; while an emphasis on the concept of socialisation might view this male as deviant or suggest that the socialisation toward traditional gender roles has not been enduring either for himself or for his partner. But even without the utilisation of theoretical concepts, the reader brings to the open narrative a considerable amount of background knowledge which they will use to add their own interpretations which may be quite different from those presented by the researcher/writer. This allows the text to be further produced in the reading process in an ongoing and transformative process (Eco, 1979).

Longer narratives

Longer or more complex narratives may be reduced to their elements by grouping lines which relate to a single topic and then linking these to form scenes, each of which represents a geographic, temporal or reported voice shift in the narrative. An illustration of this from the above short example would then look something like the following.

Scene formation

Question
How did your mother respond to you becoming a father at home?

Scene 1
Well mum thought I was being taken for a ride by an older woman
when she first found out I was going to be a father.
Her first reaction was horror that I wasn't a virgin, which shows where her thinking lay.

Scene 2
She's now good, she's come round a lot.
She gets on very well with Dan [his partner's child by another relationship],
and she gets on well with Jen [partner].
Once she got over the problem of Jen being a terrible woman –
a single mother who wanted someone to hang her bloody hat with – they got on very well,
so that's been a substantial change.

This form of division helps to distinguish the sections which serve to build the narrative and to clarify their sequencing.

Summary

So which approach is preferable, socio-linguistic or socio-cultural? You need to choose here. The literature has polarised the two orientations and it is clear they operate on different principles and produce very different readings. However, it may be possible for you to use both together in the one study, but for different purposes. Although Labov's segregation has been criticised, it provides one way of gaining insight into the structure of a narrative, while the socio-cultural approach allows the contextual constructions and interpretations of the actor and the researcher to emerge.

FURTHER READING

Boje, D. (2000) *Narrative Methods for Organisation and Communication Research.* Thousand Oaks, CA: Sage. In this book, Boje sets out eight analysis options for dealing with storytelling and recognising the complex natures of stories. The notion of post-structuralism can be seen in the introduction of 'anti-narrative' methods, where fragmented and collective storytelling can be interpreted.

Herman, L. and Vervaeck, B. (2005) *Handbook of Narrative Analysis.* Lincoln, NB: University of Nebraska Press. These authors look at the ideas and approaches of various theorists and their practices with regard to narrative analysis.

Labov, W. and Waletzky, J. (1967) Narrative analysis: oral versions of personal experience. In J. Helm (ed.), *Essays on the Verbal and Visual Arts.* Seattle, WA: University of Washington Press, pp. 12–44. A classic work focusing on the importance of evaluative statements in first-person narratives, http://www.clarku.edu/~mbamberg/LabovWaletzky. htm, accessed 26 April 2006.

Milroy, L. and Gordon, M. (2002) *Sociolinguistics: Method and Interpretation.* Oxford: Blackwell. This book covers models and methods, locating and selecting subjects, data collection, language variation in the social world, issues in analysis and interpretation, social relations and social practices, phonology and style switching, and code shifting.

Reissman, C. (2003) *Narrative Analysis.* Thousand Oaks, CA: Sage. Socio-cultural principles and techniques are accessibly presented with central examples from feminist research and further examples from medical sociology.

Wardhaugh, R. (2002) *An Introduction to Sociolinguistics,* 4th edn. Oxford: Blackwell. This is useful as a comprehensive advanced undergraduate text focusing on four major areas: languages and communities, inherent variety, words at work, and understanding and intervening.

10

Conversation Analysis

The central goal of conversation analysis is the exploration, through the use of the spoken word, of the procedures which speakers use to communicate in a variety of socially mediated situations. Your analysis needs to focus on the forms of exchange in naturally occurring conversation sets and how any accompanying visuals and non-verbal interaction add to this.

Key points

- Transcriptions of naturally occurring conversations form the substance of the data in conversation analysis.
- Identification and discussion of the 'devices' used by participants in the communication process provide the major focus.
- Structures and social systems are reflected in interactive behaviours.
- Analytical approaches include:
  - seeking the mundane in everyday conversations
  - reading the language of environmental settings
  - understanding chatroom conversation.

When to use: when you have access to naturally occurring conversations which can be transcribed.

Types of research question best suited: how do people interact through the medium of conversations within particular environments?

Strengths: clarifies the dynamics of interaction by looking at the minutiae of turn taking.

Weaknesses: when we only have access to transcriptions of spoken dialogue, the revealing facial expressions and non-verbal communication are missing.

Conversation and social interaction

Conversation analysis (CA) is a research tradition that grew out of ethnomethodology – a theoretical position developed by Harold Garfinkel (Lynch and Sharrock, 2004). Ethnomethodology is a study of the ways in which people make sense of what other people do in the processes of social interaction. Such study should illuminate not only the micro level of interaction but also the broader social systems which are in place and which constrain or enable our behaviour. As much of our interaction is carried out through conversations with others, the study of ordinary conversations as they occur has become an important area of research. In particular, ordinary conversations shed light on the rules of social behaviour and indicate what is acceptable and what happens when these rules are broken or bent. In studying conversations every aspect becomes significant, from the smallest pause to the loudest yell and all that goes in between. The dynamics of interaction are also relevant. What happens when a person of higher status talks to a person of lower status? How do conversations between women and between men differ from those when the genders are mixed? How do we manage both our own and others' emotions and impressions? For example, death can be discussed on a continuum from the light hearted parrot sketch of 'Monty Python' – 'He is no more, he is an ex-parrot' – to the unctuous 'He is in a better place' of the funeral director.

The underlying assumptions here are that the conduct of society is socially organised and that much of this organisation is reflected, reinforced and shifted into new dimensions by both verbal and non-verbal interaction. The objective of CA is that you describe the procedures by which conversationalists produce their own behaviour and understand and deal with the behaviour of others. A basic assumption throughout is that these activities – producing conduct and understanding and dealing with it – are accomplished as the accountable products of common sets of procedures. Thus the central goal of CA is the description and explication of the procedures that ordinary speakers use and rely on in participating in intelligible, socially organised interaction. The focus on a conversation (defined as at least two turns, i.e. two people interacting verbally) provides you with a fairly precise way of analysing the organisation of verbal interaction. The socio-cultural content and context of conversation or interactive talk in the construction of meaning making can be explored through a detailed inspection of tape recordings and their transcriptions. Analysis focuses on conversation sets, visuals, non-verbal interaction and environmental structures that impact on everyday behaviour as well as individual (conversations) with behavioural boundaries.

Most practitioners of CA tend to refrain, in their research reports, from extensive theoretical and methodological discussion but this varies from discipline to discipline. As researcher you will tend to use your habitual expectations, derived from established social scientific practice, as a frame of reference. A CA report will not generally have an extensive *a priori* discussion of the literature, details about research situations and the subjects and participants who have provided the data, descriptions of sampling techniques and coding procedures, or testing and statistics. Instead, the reader is confronted with a detailed discussion of transcriptions of recordings of (mostly verbal) interaction in terms of the 'devices' used by participants.

Speech acts

In the process of conversation, several recognised patterns of interaction or devices have been documented. In the analytical process, the presence or absence of these is sought in order to provide insight into what is happening in particular texts:

- *Assertions* are statements which state, describe, predict, announce or specu-late. For example, 'It is cold today'; 'I wonder what the weather will be like tomorrow'; 'I think it will be fine'; 'There are long flakes of snow catching on the leaves and sliding to the ground.'
- *Declarations* are a stronger form of assertion: 'I pronounce you man and wife'; 'You're hired/fired/redundant'; 'I sentence you to 10 years' imprisonment.'
- *Directives* attempt to produce some form of action/response in another per-son, through requests, commands, questions, suggestions and orders. For example, 'Do this'; 'Tell me what happened'; 'Would you like to come with me?'; 'Why did you do that?'
- *Commissives* involve the elicitation of guarantees and vows of the order of: 'Promise not to tell anyone else.'
- *Expressive statements* enable the speaker's feelings to be shared through apologies, thanks, greetings, acknowledgements and compliments. For exam-ple, 'I'm really sorry about that'; 'I think that definitely suits you'; 'Thank you so much for your help.'

Sequential features

Turn taking interaction in the display of interactional meaning can be more specif-ically indicated by the investigation of timed gaps and overlap between or among speakers. It is assumed that one speaker will dominate at a time although various people may speak at different times and no set order can be predicted. There are occasionally gaps and overlaps in turn transition and most conversations will tend to occur in pairs called *adjacency pairs* which are expected paired interactions of matching responses, such as: 'Congratulations!' and 'Thank you very much'; 'Promise not to tell anyone' and 'I promise'; 'I wish to complain about ...' and 'I'm very sorry about ...'; 'How are you?' and 'I am well, thank you'; 'Are you respon-sible for this?' and 'No I had nothing to do with that.' They may also be question and answer pairs, such as 'Can I come round to visit you this evening?' and 'Yes/no.' Some question/answer pairs are more complex and contain conditional interactions, for example:

> 'Shall we go for a walk this evening?'
> 'Do you think it will rain?'
> 'No.'
> 'Then I'd love to.'

Silences in conversation can be interpreted in one of several ways: as natural gaps between speakers, as significant pauses because of the content and one person's response to this, or as a lapse in the continuity of the conversation. Another aspect worthy of note is alignment which provides an indication that mutual understanding has occurred. This can be seen in echo/reinforcing statements, e.g. 'I had a terrible time …' and 'That must have been terrible for you'; in exclamatory reinforcers such as 'Really!' and 'Uh huh'; or when one person completes the sentences of the other, e.g. 'I wonder if I might have a …' '… cup of coffee?' It is when the conversation does not take an expected turn or responses don't match that interaction becomes more complex and, from the conversation analyst's point of view, more interesting.

Researcher options

The term 'conversation' can be used very broadly and often involves (as well as language) visuals, non-verbal interaction, the environmental structures that impact on everyday behaviour, and the individual pushing of behaviour boundaries.

You can:

- examine situated activities with audio/video equipment, seeking order and mundaneity in the constructed interaction of everyday happenings
- attempt to make sense of information/visuals which are very different from those of the usual conversational interactions, such as reading the language of a coffee bar which converses with patrons both in terms of signs and through the layout of tables and counter
- put yourself in unusual situations where routine sense making may not work, for example following the conversations recorded in chatrooms.

A model of CA's research practices

1 Select conversations to be analysed, e.g. consultations between health professionals and clients; the casual conversations which occur between and among people who meet in public places; gatherings of family and friends; talkback radio etc. Only ordinary conversation as it is naturally occurring should be included, not interviews or staged scripts. Record the material to be analysed.
2 Transcribe recordings.
3 Select episodes to be analysed, such as in a consult: the opening conversation, or 'discussions' about the understandings of the client regarding their particular problem. An episode will generally consist of one or more sequences, in which an interactant initiates an action and (the) other(s) react(s) to it.
4 Try to make sense of the episode, using informal understandings of what utterances 'mean'. Your analytic interests will tend to 'predispose' you to certain hearings and these may need to be checked with the participants and their sense making must be taken into account. Interpretation is directed at a typification of what the utterances that make up the sequence can be held to be 'doing' and how these 'doings' interconnect with other instances.

5   Interpret the material in a comparative manner and, if desired, use any of the concepts/theories/explanations which are meaningful in your own discipline. (This sequence is adapted from ten Have, 2006.)

A useful way in which you can gain an overview of a total conversation would be to identify the kind of conversation that has occurred: is it an amicable or a heated discussion, or an outright argument about personal or political issues? Is it an equal exchange? Or is one person leading? What happens when one person moves to a dominant questioning or declarative mode, and how does this structure or impact on the conversation? Are any misunderstandings evident? If there is any tension, how is it created? Maintained? Reflected in the structure of the conversation? What is your response as a reader to this conversation?

On a more structural and contextual level: how do speakers manage sequences and turns? What patterns are evident? What adjacency pairs can be identified?

Notation for conversation analysis

Notation is important in that it gives life to the conversation and allows it to be read in the manner in which it was spoken. Clarification is provided as to where the pauses have occurred, where the voices have risen, fallen, added emphasis or become very quiet, and where overlapping speech has occurred. It indicates where breath and laughter have been audible and what other non-verbal sounds may have impacted on the interaction. Table 10.1 contains the major notational signs based on the Jefferson system (Jefferson, 1984a; 1984b) currently in use.

Conversational interactions

The following is an example of a brief interaction using the notation from Table 10.1.

1   *Jan*:   ↑Ste:ve:
2   *Steve*: ↑Ye:h?
3   *Jan*:   What you ↑do:ing.? Come ↓here.
4   (1.0)
5   *Steve*: I'm ↓bu:sy. You come he:re.
6   *Jan*:   ↑O:h d'I ha:ve ↓to?
7   *Steve*: =I'm do:ing something.=
8   *Jan*:   =°Oh:.°

This interaction can be analysed as follows. At the start, you can see that Jan emphasises the 'e' in Steve's name and that his response of 'Yeh' is drawn out and rises in a questioning tone. Her directive to him to come to her results in a long

TABLE 10.1 *Notation for conversation analysis*

(.)	Just noticeable pause
(0.3), (2.6)	Pauses in seconds
↑word, ↓word	Rise or fall in pitch/intonation
wor-	A sudden pause in speech
=word or word =	No pause between two speakers, or shows that their words are running together
word,	Underlined sounds are loud or emphasised
WORD	Capitals indicate very loud speech
°word°	Words between signs are quietly spoken
word: wo:rd	A colon indicates stress on and an extension of the sound it follows
word,	A comma indicates intonation
word?	A question mark indicates a rising inflection
( )	Unidentifiable speech
< >	Talk between these signs is slower/compressed
[[	Successive brackets on two lines with utterances from different speakers indicate the start of overlapping speech
]]	A right bracket bridging two lines indicates that overlapping or simultaneous utterances at this point have stopped
//	One speaker overlapping with another speaker
*	Indicates end of overlap
.	Indicates falling intonation
> <	Words between these signs are spoken fast
(( ))	Descriptions of events, e.g. ((cough)) or ((smile))
.hh, hh / .hhh hhh	In-breath or out-breath (sometimes more than two h are used)
wo(h)rd	(h) indicates laughter within the word

pause where no interaction appears to occur. Steve issues a counter-directive to her to come to him. Jan raises her voice to question the need for this and to emphasise that she doesn't really want to come to where he is. Steve provides an excuse for his inability to come to her, and Jan gives up at that point with a quiet overlapping 'Oh' of resignation/acceptance. Adjacency pairs can be seen in the relatively expected response patterns of the couple, after which it is unclear whether the conversation will continue. If the researcher wanted to go further into an analysis of gender relations it is clear from this short extract that power lies with Steve and his 'busyness' and that tension is provided by Jan attempting to get him to meet her demands while he successfully resists.

Another example of unscripted interaction is that between a mother (Lyn) and her daughter (Zoe) in a situation where Lyn is sitting at a table (possibly studying) in front of a video camera when her daughter comes into the room. This can be viewed as video clip 2 at http://www-staff.lboro.ac.uk/~ssca1/analysis2.htm (accessed 26 April 2006). Part of this interaction, following the initial greeting, is as follows:

17		(6.0)
18	↓Zoe	th' camera's on.
19	Lyn	>yes<
20		(1.8)
21	Zoe	w'(h) are you ta(h)lking to it while you
22		wORK?
23	Lyn	no:,
24		(.5)
25	Lyn	[heh heh °heh heh°=
26	Zoe	[hh what ye' DOINg then
27	Lyn	=hahh hahh hahh
28		(1.0)
29	Zoe	what's the ↑point:h
30		(1.5)
31	Zoe	↑oh ↑god (.) look what ↑I'm wearing

(Antaki, 2002, http://www-staff.lboro.ac.uk/~ssca1/analysis1.htm, reproduced with permission)

Analysis requires reference to both the video and the script. Lyn is sitting at a table looking down, apparently thinking for some considerable period of time before Zoe comes in and notices that the camera is recording. Lyn's response to this is a very compressed 'Yes' and her disinclination to clarify why the video is going can be seen in the pause of over one and a half seconds. Zoe again attempts to find out what Lyn is doing with the camera but again no explanation is forthcoming, and Zoe's queries regarding the purpose of having the camera recording are met initially with laughter followed by no response. Zoe then notices that her voice, appearance and actions are also being recorded and becomes distracted, drawing attention to her appearance (she appears to feel her clothes are unsuitable for an appearance on camera).

One central part of the interaction is Lyn's reluctance to respond to Zoe and to clarify why she is apparently recording herself sitting at a table in front of a camera. More detailed conceptual analysis could examine mother–daughter interaction in terms of questions, responses, resistance, and the shifting power dynamics.

Examples: conversation analysis

There are many possibilities for CA, and three different examples are provided for you.

The mundaneity of everyday conversations

The first analytical possibility involves examining situated activities with audio/video equipment in order to reveal order and mundaneity in everyday happenings. Devorah Kalekin-Fishman (2000) examines the construction of mundane culture in Israel through the reported chance/not-chance interactions of individuals unknown or known to each other in public places, including the following. Two men, waiting in a line at the bank, end up discussing a recent TV programme. Two women friends meet in a crowded restaurant and briefly explain to each other why they arc there; one was attending a birthday party and the other couldn't be bothered cooking that night. A husband and wife who are students, lunching at a table in the university café, discuss the imminent delivery of a friend's baby and the most convenient day the birth might occur from their perspective in terms of their having to make a duty visit to the newborn. Two female shoppers queueing at the supermarket share information on the tedium of after-work shopping, the numbers of children in their families and the lack of help they get at home with cooking. Two mothers talk on a train about the naughtiness of one of their young sons. Two women, waiting in a queue at the travel agency to book flight tickets, discuss the fact that one of them is booking a ticket for her husband whom she has not yet informed of the trip. Two male students in the university cafeteria discuss the war-torn situation in Lebanon and their differing perceptions of the role of Arab people in the unrest. Female neighbours at the entrance of an apartment building discuss the weight loss of a female acquaintance known to both. A female soldier on leave and a female acquaintance meet at a crowded fair where the acquaintance castigates the soldier for her untidy uniform and quizzes her on her position in the army; she changes tack on realising the soldier has quite high status in the army. A husband and wife, at home with a member of their extended family present, argue and the wife challenges her husband over forgetting her birthday. Finally, two friends in mourning at the house of the deceased share information on the actual details of how the death occurred and the implications of this death for the living who remain.

Going beyond into visual/non-verbal 'conversations'

Public places such as cafés create their own forms of conversation with the public through signs and symbols indicating that coffee and various forms of food can be purchased and imbibed and eaten on these premises. They also use written information such as 'enter here' or 'close the door' or 'please order before you sit down' as directives to patrons indicating how the establishment runs. But other forms of 'conversation' can be seen in the arrangement of tables with which clients will interact. Pathways between the tables encourage patrons to move in a particular direction and the types of tables also provide interactive possibilities. For example, if there are only two-person tables available a larger group entering will tend to put tables together to form one to fit their numbers, or will seek out another café. If

143

only long tables are available then some singles will use the opportunity to mix with others but other singles will seat themselves in such a way as to minimise interaction – perhaps by leaving a gap between themselves and the next person – and this separation will be reinforced by gaze avoiding or by the reading of a book or the positioning of a newspaper to screen the individual from others and to make it difficult for others to read the day's headlines. Other non-verbal forms of conversation can be seen on the tables themselves when individuals 'take' or reserve a table by leaving glasses or a coat or some other possession to show they have just gone to order or to visit the restroom and will be back soon. In contrast, empty glasses and plates and the absence of possessions indicate the table is vacant and waiting to be cleaned and taken. Cultural settings such as cafés invite and reinforce certain interactions and the extent and type of social order which has been established can only be ascertained by pushing the boundaries of indicated expectations. Examples include sitting down and reading but refusing to order; shifting tables to quite different areas of the inside or the outside of the café without seeking permission; going and sitting opposite a single patron at a two-person table without seeking their permission or checking whether the seat is already taken; or talking loudly to oneself.

New forms of conversation: chatrooms

In chatrooms, the assumptions that turn taking and agency pairs will dominate interaction in a linear progression are thrown by the intertwining nature of the 'conversations' where one statement/question may not be responded to until several players later. Responses in between will be read by all the interactants and will tend to dilute later responses or act as intersection points for a number of conversation streams. In 15 minutes of chatroom talk, Parrish (2006) identified 20 starting statements within which there were 25 instances of branching away from linear progression. In this situation a participant may be involved in multiple conversations, simultaneously jumping from one response stream to another or just inserting a general response into a stream which does not directly interact with any of the previous players. Parish found that in chatrooms adjacency pairs are almost never adjacent and may occur with anything up to 17 statements in between. The slowness of typing responses creates issues here, particularly if the site is an active one.

Summary

The assumption of a structured society with rules of interaction and behaviour which can be read and analysed to reflect social conventions in the perusal of conversations still holds in terms of face to face interaction. However, it is questionable as to how realistic these assumptions are with regard to the newer forms of internet online communication where conversations occur along the lines of chaotic interactions and bifurcations (branching).

FURTHER READING

Antaki, C. (2002) An introductory tutorial in conversation analysis, http://www-staff.lboro.ac.uk/~ssca1/sitemenu.htm, 25 April 2005. This site provides several examples (one of which has been used in this chapter) of conversation analysis in tutorial format. It also provides links to other teaching and learning resources.

Arminen, I. (2005) *Institutional Interaction: Studies of Talk at Work.* Aldershot: Ashgate. This book provides a fairly advanced discussion of conversation analysis and looks at talk and interaction in institutional settings, in particular the classroom, counselling settings, the courtroom and the doctor's surgery.

Ethno/CA News, http://www.paultenhave.nl/EMCA.htm, or the older more detailed version at http://www2.fmg.uva.nl/emca/index.htm, accessed 25 April 2006, is a site that provides information and accessible examples and links on both ethnomethodology and conversation analysis.

Hutchby, I. and Wooffitt, R. (1998) *Conversation Analysis: Principles, Practices and Applications.* Cambridge: Polity. This is a very accessible introduction to the field including its theory and methods with practical examples from social science, and includes human–computer interaction, political communication and speech therapy.

Nevile, M. (2004) *Beyond the Black Box: Talk-in-Interaction in the Airline Cockpit.* Aldershot: Ashgate. This book looks at the organisation of talk in a complex technological work setting. He examines how airline pilots use language and gestures linked to the equipment they are using to build action and to share meanings. Includes 24 pictures and 23 video stills.

Seedhouse, P. (2004) *The Interactional Architecture of the Language Classroom: A Conversation Analysis Perspective.* Oxford: Blackwell. This book comprises a compilation of work from Seedhouse's doctoral thesis together with various journal articles, to explore classroom discourse as institutional interaction. He describes the interactional architecture of the language classroom across cultures and the teaching of different languages in different institutions.

Ten Have, P. Methodological issues in conversation analysis, http://www2.fmg.uva.nl/emca/mica.htm, accessed 23 April 2006. Within the framework of ethnomethodology, ten Have provides a seven-step approach to undertaking conversation analysis and illustrates some of the current debates within this field – in particular the tension between a phenomenological approach and quantification.

Wooffitt, R. (2005) *Conversation Analysis and Discourse Analysis: A Comparative and Critical Introduction.* London: Sage. If you are finding difficulties in clarifying the similarities and differences between conversation and discourse analysis, this book provides a clear exposition of the fields of conversation analysis, discourse analysis, critical discourse analysis and discursive psychology.

11

Discourse Analysis

Discourse analysis can include analysis of media and all other documentation of a written or visual nature. One version, the Foucauldian approach, uses the historical and political tracking of documentation over time and tends to utilise the conceptual preconceptions of power as a basis for interpretation.

Key points

- Discourse analysis spans a broad field from formal linguistic approaches through Foucauldian analyses to cultural and communication studies approaches, and has been used in many disciplines including: linguistics, psychology, education, artificial intelligence, sociology, health, management and administration, and communication.
- Foucauldian discourse analysis identifies statements and tracks their changes and challenges historically in the mapping of the creation of power-laden discourses.
- Various hybrid approaches to discourse analysis, combining with other forms of analysis and interpretation, continue to be developed.

When to use: when the identification and tracking of powerful discourses is useful.

Types of research question best suited: how did this way of thinking/behaving/writing/talking eventuate? What other ways of knowing have been marginalised?

Strengths: capacity to track historically the origins of and challenges to mainstream ideas and to illuminate marginalised ideas.

Weaknesses: incapacity to do much beyond record the dominance of powerful discourses unless feminist/action research is undertaken to attempt to reinstate other ideas.

Michel Foucault and discourse

The term 'discourse analysis' came into vogue in the 1960s as interest started to emerge in the representations of reality through language. The notion of discourse has been used extensively by Foucault who was concerned about the technologies of power utilised in the creating and sustaining of mainstream cultural knowledge.

He defined discourses as: 'practices that systematically form the objects of which they speak ... Discourses are not about objects; they do not identify objects, they constitute them and in the practice of doing so conceal their own invention' (1972: 49). Foucault was particularly interested to document the ways in which power had been developed and exercised through the control of knowledge and how, in creating and maintaining particular discourses, powerful interests had obscured the voices, protests or challenges put up by others with an interest in this piece of knowledge. Foucault exposed the manner in which the state had created the powerful discourses of 'madness' and 'sexuality' and how through sovereign (the monarchy) and disciplinary (the agents of the monarch, government etc.) power these ideas had filtered down to the (largely unresisting) population and had become the basis of their understandings and explanations (written and inscribed on their bodies). In this situation, he demonstrated that language would not necessarily be reflecting reality and the location of 'truth' could become very controversial. In tracing the discourses, hidden or buried truths are not sought; the search itself is an active process of detection and creation.

In more detail, Foucault uses the metaphor of the body and the circulatory system to describe the mechanism through which a discourse is dispersed throughout society. The heart (the person/people with an interest in developing and controlling this discourse) pumps these ideas and discourses via the arterial, venous and capillary systems (ways of feeding the discourse to the wider populace through various media) and these views are then internalised by the population and fed back into the system, enabling reinforcement. The binary opposites of structuralism, in particular 'good' and 'evil', serve to persuade the population that truth is singular and these 'truths' are 'normalised' through the processes of 'surveillance' and 'monitoring' which together with notions of 'confession' are reinforced by legal structures. The discursive practices within disciplines and specialisms further serve as a micro form of control, allowing meaning and myth to become the product of power relations. Foucault is also interested in how these discourses link and interweave across other domains of cultural knowledge. He has led us to a form of historical analysis where the terminology of 'discontinuity, rupture, threshold, limit, series and transformation' (1972: 9) abound.

In order to break open (rupture) these discourses it is necessary to track the historical processes by which they have been constructed: 'history is that which transforms documents into monuments. In that area where, in the past, history deciphered the traces left by men, it now deploys a mass of elements that have to be grouped, made relevant, placed in relation to one another to form totalities' (1972: 7). He utilises Nietzsche's historiographical approach – genealogy – to access the voices which have not been recorded, in order to expose the hidden power plays, the memories and knowledge which have been covered over in the maintenance of powerful interests by dominant institutions. 'Genealogy ... seeks to reestablish the various forms of subjection: not the anticipatory power of meaning, but the hazardous play of dominations' (1984b: 83). 'The search is directed to "that which was already there", the image of a primordial truth fully adequate to its nature, and it necessitates the removal of every mask to ultimately disclose an original identity' (1984a: 78).

The process of tracking these images somewhat resembles that of an archaeological dig, involving turning over and exposing the traces which have been left, many largely erased 'like a face drawn in sand at the edge of the sea' (1970: 387). By unearthing and following these traces, it is possible to identify gaps, interruptions, discontinuities, missing pieces, erased voices or obliterated events and to clarify how the material remains became grouped into meaningful entities. In the archaeological dig of discourse analysis the artifacts found comprise a set of statements which can transform and change over time with new knowledge and new challenges. Notions of discontinuity and dispersion underpin this process. Unity is unlikely to be a feature of any discourse, so your task is to discover the rules which define the discourse, not to interpret it, but to identify the limits to unity and the forms of disunity which hold groups of discursive statements in a particular pattern.

According to Foucault (1972) the basic element of discourse analysis is the *statement* which is made up of signs (objects). Signs are the building blocks of statements. A set of signs becomes a statement if they have an internal relationship and there is also a relationship between the objects and the statement. The resulting statement is then viewed as existing in a wider domain, overlapping with and abutting to a complex web of other statements. Thus a statement is more than just a sentence and depends on the conditions of emergence, where it is located and the practices which allow it to have claims to 'truth' – although truth and meaning are of minimal interest here. Relations between statements and groups of statements (made by other authors) are important, and socioeconomic and political events need to be described so that the interplay of statements can be documented and a potential discourse identified. Definitionally speaking, a statement then becomes 'a function that cuts across a domain of structures and possible unities, and which reveals them with concrete content, in time and space' (1972: 15).

A statement then needs to comprise the following aspects:

- to be associated with an identifiable person who is making the statement
- to be part of an arena where other statements can be found, e.g. a domain such as law, medicine, economics or politics, which will have had an impact on delimiting, excluding, appropriating or controlling the discourse
- to be meaningfully related (relevant) to the issues around which the discourse has developed.

Discursive regularities (objects, forms, concepts, statements and themes relating to a particular issue) are the aspects which constitute a discourse and govern discursive formations.

In order to record the emergence of the object of a discourse you need to first map the surfaces where the object has emerged. In identifying the location of an object such as 'sexuality', the mapping of perceptions and their interplay would involve investigation of the family, social groups, work, religion, medicine, art, literature and pornography. Then the clarification of the rules of cultural institutions such as education, medicine and law in dealing with sexuality/ies will need explanation as will the identification of who has been responsible for these rules. In tracing the paths of sexuality as they are named, redefined, challenged and erased, it is important to identify disunity, dispersion and discontinuity. For example, different kinds of sexuality need to be 'divided, contrasted, related, regrouped, classified, derived from one another as objects of psychiatric discourse' (1972: Chapter 3: 2).

The conceptual organisation of the discourse is made up of:

- forms of succession (particular arguments)
- forms of coexistence (relations among all statements – accepted or excluded)
- procedures of intervention (the rewriting and ordering of information into systems of ideas, usually by powerful individuals or groups).

In more detail, you should be very critical of statements and groups of statements which appear to have become grouped and bounded within a particular discipline and should seek their use elsewhere. Foucault takes the example of 'madness' and indicates that such a word will be used differently when it appears in psychiatry from when it appears in the legal system, in police action and in the media. Following this, the transformation, replacement and type of connection of groups of statements and their concepts need defining. Then the final regrouping of statements, their interconnection, their consolidation in particular fields, the persistence of particular themes and their systems of dispersion within which regularities may be evident, can be undertaken.

Guidelines for discourse analysis

The following broad guidelines have been drawn from Foucault's writings:

1 Track the historical development of the discourse over time and identify the players and the social, economic and political climate which fostered its development.
2 Identify constituents in terms of objects, statements, themes, arguments, traces of challenges, traces of ideas which changed directions. Seek disunity and discontinuity and the limits to the discourse. Monitor dispersion in other fields.
3 Locate challenges and see what happened to these: where did they come from? Why? And if they were rejected, how were they dispensed? And by whom? For what purpose?

Discourse analysis guidelines in use

The following nursery rhyme provides a brief illustrative example of how a Foucauldian discourse analysis might be attempted:

> Jack and Jill went up the hill
> to fetch a pail of water;
> Jack fell down and broke his crown,
> and Jill came tumbling after.

> Up Jack got and home did trot,
> as fast as he could caper;
> He went to bed to mend his head,
> with vinegar and brown paper.

This is a short narrative about a male and female of indeterminate age climbing a hill to fetch water. Both fall down and Jack receives an injury to his head necessitating treatment. The key active descriptors are: 'going up', 'falling down' and 'mending'.

Track the historical discourse over time and identify the social, economic and political players.

This is not easy as there have been a number of explanations of this nursery rhyme:

- *Mythology*: in old Norse legends (Harley, 1855) the Moon God Mani (male) took from the earth two children: Hjiki (pronounced Juki, which has a close resemblance to Jack), a word which also means to assemble and increase in amount; and Bil (also close to Jill), which means to break down or dissolve. Mani put these two on the moon. The children were each holding the end of a pole on which was being carried a bucket, and from that time forth could be seen from the earth as markings on the moon. Their shapes were said to mark the vanishing of moon spots one after another as the moon wanes, but they also represent the waxing of the moon which affects rainfall patterns (water) as the phases of the moon change.
- *Gender*: the imagery of the masculine moon and the feminine sun as well as the use of Jack and Jill as generic masculine and feminine terms in England, plus the link to water, can be seen reflected in Act III Scene II of *A Midsummer Night's Dream*:

> And the country proverb known,
> That every man should take his own,
> In your waking shall be shown.
> Jack shall have Jill;
> Nought shall go ill;
> The man shall have his mere [boundary/pond/mare] again,
> And all shall be well.

- *Economics/politics*: in the 1640s Charles I of England attempted to reduce the liquid measure of a jack (two jiggers or two mouthfuls) which also impacted on the measure of a gill (two jacks is a gill (Jill)) in order to increase tax revenue to balance some fairly severe fiscal mismanagement. The jack/jackpot was a particularly relevant measure for the sale of ale. After a reign of heavy taxation and civil war, Charles was beheaded for treason in 1649 while his wife Henrietta Maria was in exile in France.

  Another interpretation involved the French King Louis XVI (Jack), who was married to Queen Marie Antoinette (Jill) and who also initiated a system of heavy taxation and reforms to deal with a financial crisis. The bourgeoisie of France resisted the reforms which impacted on them and the angry populace razed the Bastille and imprisoned the royal family in the Tuileries. Louis was beheaded in 1793 and nine months later his wife was also beheaded.

A more detailed analysis would track these stories much more precisely and their long term impact on policy and practice in a range of areas.

Themes, arguments and ideas, disunity and discontinuity

The major theme of aggregating and building up and then losing what has been gained permeates all the stories, from the waxing and waning of the moon to the unfair aggregation of the wealth of the population by a powerful monarch followed by loss of position, power and life as the population rise up and take control through civil war. The masculine–feminine dichotomy is evident in the different stories but is not viewed as significant: some earlier versions stemming from the Norse legend suggest that there were two male children involved and that one became feminised over time – perhaps harking back to the sun–moon dichotomy, or just a convenient change to provide balance and contrast and to incorporate the role of the Queen.

Challenges

As the discourse moved over time and country it shifted from moon mythology to a political and moral tale about the overreaching and exploitation of the populace by greedy monarchs and the fate that awaits such behaviour. The power and might of the general population in triumphing over the monarchy is a strong challenge to the God-given power the monarchy had experienced. This challenge now appears to dominate the discourse. Again, the impact of this and dispersion into other fields would need further exploration.

Examples: discourse analysis

The forms of analysis which are currently being undertaken appear only loosely to follow the indications to be found in Foucault's work (although calling upon it) and often lack any historical context or any real tracking of changes and challenges. Many appear to comprise a fairly limited collection of documents which have been subject only to thematic analysis and coding and any other approach which looks as though it might be useful in clarifying the data.

Deborah Lupton and Simon Chapman (1995) investigated four years of press clippings in national and regional newspapers to identify the discourses regarding diet, cholesterol control and heart disease. Historical tracking was limited to a review of the literature. Twelve focus groups were held with 49 members of the public to understand how they were making sense of the conflicting information which was appearing in the news media. The public expressed considerable cynicism regarding health promotion information on the above topics. Cynicism was fuelled by conflicting reportage, the discourses of pleasurable indulgence, and the 'work' required to control one's health. Resistance to 'official views' led to the generation of the compromise 'everything in moderation' which was regarded as the safest pathway in the light of both conflicting advice and the unknown factors of 'luck' and 'fate'. The outcomes of this study highlighted individuals' capacity to adapt and transform events received through the medium of language. The concept of risk and risky behaviour underpinned the findings and power was found to be located in two competing areas – medicine and individual life experience.

In contrast Julie Hepworth (1999) used a more directly linked Foucauldian approach and took a much larger written sample of all published medical articles relating to *anorexia nervosa* since the emergence of the term in 1874 to identify relevant discourses. She also conducted interviews with current health professionals. The cultural and historical underpinnings of the diagnosis were situated in the view that the illness appears as a result of the failure of middle class women to move without fuss into their preordained domestic roles (Hepworth and Griffin, 1990). In the rapid orientation of the documentation toward psychological aetiology and over time, five discourses were exposed: *femininity*, i.e. women as emotional, deviant, irrational and perverse psychological, mental and reproductive entities; *medical*, the search for scientific organic causes; *clinical*, the prescriptive treatments and the (moral) quality of relationships; *discovery*, the link between medicine and psychiatry; and *hysteria*, the link between femininity and the psycho-medical framework. The power of medicine in the maintenance of the enduring discourse of femininity (irrational female behaviour) was revealed. The conclusion was that the coherent set of linguistic practices evident since the late nineteenth century has been very strong.

The shift and overlap of analytic processes can be seen in the use of a combination of discourse and content analysis by Clive Seale (2002) of media portrayals of the emotions of women with cancer. English language newspaper articles with the words 'cancer' or 'leukaemia' which had been published worldwide during the first week of October 1999 (2419) were downloaded from LEXIS-NEXIS. A subsample of 358 articles pertaining to adults with cancer was chosen from this. Of these, 69% were females largely with breast cancer. Iterative thematic analysis and coding were undertaken and the analysed texts were stored and managed in the qualitative computer program NVivo. The semantic segments were then checked for concordance. Identification and classification of 'good' and 'bad' feelings indicated that 'fear/anxiety' was used most often to portray women's emotions (19) compared with men (6), while 'feeling supported' was the major aspect characterised as important for women (19 compared with 12 men). The main metaphor which emerged was that of the 'journey', with 'going through' this being the dominant image. Women were displayed as 'courageous' (20) in undertaking this journey while men were more likely to be highlighted as 'altruistic' (thinking of others first). Through analysis of media language, Seale has identified a strong psychological discourse with an emphasis on heroic resistance to the experience of cancer.

Limitations of Foucauldian analysis

Feminists have criticised Foucault for not addressing the social position of women as being different from powerless groups in general, noting that this has impacted on the historical production of gender relations and range of associated discourses. The absence of praxis – actually doing something about any imbalances of power which have been uncovered – is another criticism but Foucault has made it clear that he was only seeking to expose the complexity and discontinuity of the discourses which dominate western culture.

Summary

Although Michel Foucault did not provide a specific guide to the process for undertaking his form of discourse analysis, guidelines can be derived from his writings and applied to the identification of discourses and to a clarification of which discursive practices have held particular discourses in place in a particular discipline or in society. However, like all forms of qualitative research, discourse analysis has had its share of creative adaptation by researchers, resulting in the dilution of method and the addition of content, narrative, conversation, feminist, critical, grounded theory and other analytical entities in the formation of hybrid approaches.

FURTHER READING

Andrejevic, M. (2004) *Reality TV: The Work of Being Watched*. Lanham, MD: Rowman and Littlefield. This is a detailed explanation of reality TV: its history, its seductive interactivity with audiences, and the notions of the use of surveillance to enhance this form of entertainment as an economic entity.

Bayley, P. (ed.) (2004) *Cross-Cultural Perspectives in Parliamentary Discourse*. Amsterdam: Benjamins. This collection of nine papers focuses on parliamentary talk in western democracies. European (British, Swedish, German, Italian, Spanish) and United States and Mexican settings are examined from a cross-cultural perspective. The analysis combines techniques of functional linguistics and critical discourse analysis.

Cordella, M. (2004) *The Dynamic Consultation: A Discourse Analytical Study of Doctor–Patient Communication.* Amsterdam: Benjamins. The focus here is the dynamic interaction and forms of talk used by both doctors and patients during consultations in an outpatient clinic in Chile. Issues of power in the form of social status, knowledge and personal beliefs are identified.

Levine, P. and Scollon, R. (eds) (2004) *Discourse and Technology: Multimodal Discourse Analysis.* Washington, DC: Georgetown University Press. This book looks at the complexities of multimodal discourse including cell phones, video recorders, visuals, internet chatrooms, online journals, speech, gesture and the landscape of text making. Education, social and workplace service encounters are explored through the additional influence of space and layout in the environments.

Speer, S. (2005) *Gender Talk: Feminism, Discourse and Conversation Analysis.* London: Routledge. This text links feminism, gender and discourse with ethnomethodology, conversation analysis and discursive psychology. Both discourse and conversation analyses are described in detail and applied to the feminist concepts of language difference, power, masculinity and femininity.

Thiesmeyer, L. (ed.) (2003) *Discourse and Silencing: Representation and the Language of Displacement.* Amsterdam: Benjamins. The filtering of knowledge in discursive language communication is the focus here. Examples are provided from courtroom trials, domestic violence, censorship, marital discussions, news media and penal institutions in eastern and central Europe, Canada, the United States, New Zealand and Japan. The political silencing of anti-Semitic, Polish and Aboriginal (Canadian) voices as well as those from performance art is also discussed in detail.

12

Visual Interpretation

This process of understanding and interpreting the world uses visual images rather than words and these images are seen as reflections of reality in particular contexts. This chapter will look at four forms of visual analysis: ethnographic visual analysis, historical analysis through iconography and iconology, and structural and poststructural analyses of visual images.

Key points

- Visual images, either alone or in conjunction with other data, provide a rich source of research information.
- Depending on your research question, any of the following analytic approaches may be useful: ethnographic content analysis, historical (iconography and iconology) analysis, or semiotic structural or poststructural analysis.

Visual data

Visual records can be one of three kinds. The first kind comprises those which are currently in existence such as:

- film
- newspaper images
- artwork (paintings, posters, cartoons)
- computer images
- architecture and all forms of design
- video
- photos
- aspects of material culture such as clothing, graffiti etc.

Analyses of these records are complicated by their location and the devices of presentation and re-presentation contrived for consumption by particular audiences. Many are embedded in non-visual contexts such as words and link to a multiplicity of other texts and cultural and structural settings. Our earliest visual research records were undertaken by anthropologists and comprise black and white photography and moving films. A structuralist approach involving classification and the development of taxonomies formed the dominant analyses of these.

The second and third kinds of visual records are those which have been collected either by you as researcher or by the participants in your study, separately or together with you in a collaborative approach. The capacity to capture conversations, interactions and events as they occur in natural environments is enormous, although the presence of fixed cameras may well disturb routines if they are intrusively located or left in place by you for only short periods of time. Participants are usually involved in using non-fixed video cameras for the collection of personal narratives (auto photography) where there is an inbuilt notion of power transfer or empowerment. Sometimes filming is directed into data collection of specific events and situations which have been predefined or suggested by you and sometimes these are at the discretion of the participant. Collaborative approaches can lean more toward you collecting data with direction from your participants as to what should be highlighted. Photo elicitation – the provision of photos, captured by you or your participants for further interview discussion – is another approach. The collection of verbal or written responses and participant authored drawings and paintings can also provide an adjunct to visual data, allowing one to complement or comment on the other.

Who should interpret visual images collected by you or by your participants? It is suggested that the participants can provide considerable insight here regardless of who has collected the data. Conversation analysis, content and context, spatial movements and interaction can be used to provide specific analyses here, although thematic analysis and deconstructive approaches are more common. The positioning of you and your audience also needs to be taken into account as visual images have the capacity to create the audience (readers) as consumers of particular images.

You can analyse visual records through a range of approaches. The following represent four of these:

1 ethnographic content analysis
2 historical analysis: iconology and iconography
3 structural analysis
4 poststructural analysis.

Ethnographic content analysis

Ethnographic content analysis seeks to identify the signifiers/signs within visual images and to understand their accepted meanings within the culture in which they are located.

When to use: when you have access to visual images.

Types of research question best suited: what is going on in this visual image? What aspects of the cultural context or social organisation are reflected in these images?

Strengths: enables visual images to be 'read' within cultural or historical contexts.

Weaknesses: the origin and the purpose of the construction or collection of the images may be unclear.

The following steps will enable you to undertake an ethnographic content analysis:

Content and context

- What is the image of?
- What is the context of its production?
- Who was involved in the production? And for what purpose?
- How do the outcomes convey meaning?

Links

- Each image will be linked to or embedded in a variety of other signs through intertextuality. What are these other signs?
- How do other signs impact on and affect the image?
- How does this image reflect or depart from dominant cultural values?

Interpretation

- What is the most obvious reading of the image?
- What alternative readings can be made?

Example: mental illness in movies

Content, context and links

An ethnographic content analysis of representations of psychiatric disability in 50 years of Hollywood films was undertaken by Levers (2001). Twenty-one films were assessed in a cross-case cultural context analysis to identify the following aspects:

- *structured narratives* (content and context) which included credit information, description of main theme/setting and plot, stereotypical portrayals and context
- *presence of previously identified stereotypes* (links), including dangerous people, objects of violence, atmosphere, pitiable and pathetic, asexual or sexually deviant, incapable, comic figures, their own worst or only enemy, and 'super crips' or burdens
- *frequency of icons* (links) associated with the traditional historical portrayal of madness in art, especially through images of lighted window/door, seated, caged, restrained, held/guided by warders, carrying a staff (long stick), eyes cast down, music icons, and holding hands.

Interpretations

Interpretations were cross-checked with a psychiatric rehabilitation professional, a sociologist, a psychologist and a filmmaker. The iconography of 'insanity' or 'madness' – terminology which changed to 'mental illness' after changes in the production code in 1968 – allowed mental illness to be used as a major theme in films. The change resulted in more positive portrayals and more serious explorations of relevant issues, although the use of iconography (icons with recognised meanings) and stereotypes also increased. The icons most noted overall in the 21 films were: hospital white, bandages, wheelchairs, glazed stare, and locked doors/keys. The stereotypes identified were: dangerous people, passive objects of violence, atmosphere, pitiable and pathetic, asexual or sexually deviant, incapable, comic figure, own worst or only enemy, 'super crip' or burden, artistic/creative genius and pathology.

Example: war bonds

FIGURE 12.1 World War II war bonds, 1944–5: 'Put all *your* might into the Mighty 7th War Loan' (reprinted with permission of the Hartman Center, 24 October 2005, http://scriptorium.lib.duke.edu/dynaweb/adaccess/war/warbonds1944-1945/@Generic__BookTextView/4027;nh=1?DwebQuery=7th+war+loan+in+%3Cc01%3E#X, accessed 26 April 2006)

Content and context

The image in Figure 12.1 relates to the 7th War Loan and was published in the New Yorker in 1945 by F. & M. Schaefer Brewing Company. The image comprises six men striving to raise a flagpole with the flag of the United States unfurling upon the top of it. The foreground appears to be covered in broken wood in shapes reminiscent of the bones of the dead. A helmet also lies in the foreground. From behind a cloud the sun's rays illuminate an elevated gilded statue of a soldier holding a gun. The statue is of a 'minuteman', a member of the American Militia who fought against the British as they tried to quell the American revolution of the eighteenth century. Minutemen had a special duty to protect their towns of origin. The purpose of this poster is clearly to remind the public that the people who have given their lives for freedom should not be forgotten and that the public should continue to support the war effort, in particular those who are struggling to win and maintain democracy.

Links

- Clouds have the capacity to hide and to reveal.
- Graven images suggest immortality, glory, youth captured, perfection sustained, adulation of those remaining.
- Sun illuminates, warms, glorifies, gives life.
- Wood/bone remains suggest death, altruism, sacrifice for the greater good.
- The flag and pole link to national pride, identification and power.
- Water links to cleanliness, peace, tranquility.
- Six men pulling together: strength in numbers and teamwork.

Interpretation: obvious reading

The clouds move back to reveal the statue of the soldier caught by the sun's rays. His elevated image above and beyond the struggle symbolises hope and provides intimations of glory, perfection and immortality – caught in time and providing an ongoing memory. This contrasts with the struggle of those still alive and still fighting to lift the flagpole, reflecting the battle to win, to conquer and to retain the values that the flag represents. The forward looking face of the statue focuses on a distant future, one of peace and security, also emphasised by the expanse of water flowing tranquilly in the background.

Interpretation: alternative reading

War is destructive; it leads to death and decay. Peace through physical fighting is costly in terms of lives lost and is difficult to gain and maintain. Those who have given their lives will soon be forgotten and will be remembered only by generic images reflected on special occasions.

Iconology and iconography

Iconology tends to refer to the interpretation of art and religious images, while iconography refers to the meanings of these symbols. In practice the two have become closely interwoven.

When to use: when you have access to images from art or religion.

Types of research question best suited: what are the meanings of the signs in a painting?

Strengths: enables the identification of the meanings of the icons/signs being used.

Weaknesses: interpretations may change over time, so the original meaning is lost.

Erwin Panofsky (1974) proposed three levels of analysis for these kinds of images:

- *primary*: description of factual and expressional representations
- *secondary*: iconographical analysis, examining representation at a more abstract level
- *tertiary*: iconological interpretation, seeking the deepest meaning reflecting the underlying principles or period.

Example: the Mona Lisa

Primary level

Leonardo da Vinci's *Mona Lisa* is an oil painting measuring 31×21 inches, painted on a panel, using the *sfumato* (blended smoke) method in which translucent layers of paint are applied in such a way that the transitions between colour changes on the clothing are hard to detect (Figure 12.2). The chiaroscuro technique of light and shade for skin contrast is also used. The portrait is of a Florentine woman dressed in the fashion of the sixteenth century, hands folded, with a face which appears to be made up of two not quite matching halves and a half smile (lips almost closed) portrayed against a mountainous, watery landscape.

Secondary level

Here symbols are linked with accepted meanings or themes. The painting represents beauty and the enigmatic power of women; the complex smile can be both alluring and mocking at the same time. The complexity of the composition seen through the male/female face is another (somewhat contentious) theme. Other signs lie in numbers and measures, particularly the geometry of the figure (comprising 12 circles and the pyramid-like placement of the figure in the landscape) which provides a possible link to ancient cultures and to astronomy. Other signs lead to a form of numerology and to myths. For example, using a simple Latin code of values for particular letters, 'Mona Lisa' and 'La Gioconda' and 'Leonardo' all come to the same number value 84, suggesting some connection. Going into mythology, the title *Mona Lisa* has been seen as a rebus (a code) for *sol* + *anima* or sun and moon or male and female, again giving support to the argument regarding the male–female dimensions of the face.

Tertiary level

Here the focus is on the links between nature, mythology, astronomy, mathematics- and the power and beauty of women (or males and females) in their dual creation of human life and the environment. The primary link between nature and beauty characterises the major value of the Renaissance period.

FIGURE 12.2 *Mona Lisa* (http://commons.wikimedia.org/w/index.php?title=Image: Mona_Lisa_frameless.jpg&p, accessed 10 May 2006. The two-dimensional work of art depicted in this image is in the public domain worldwide due to the date of death of its author, or due to its date of publication. Thus, this reproduction of the work is also in the public domain)

Example: Guernica

Primary level

A more detailed analysis of a single painting can be undertaken using Pablo Picasso's *Guernica* (Figure 12.3). At the primary level the painting falls within the synthetic cubist tradition with its grey, brown, white and black colours and its incorporation of geometrical experimental constructions of collage forming layers which can be seen through to create and impart other, less obvious, meanings. The purpose is to represent images as the mind rather than the eye sees them. The painting, measuring 350×750 cm, was undertaken for the Spanish Pavilion at the Paris World Fair of 1937 for the Spanish Republican government. It represents a massacre of civilians at Guernica, the capital city of an independent republic in the Basque country of northern Spain. The massacre occurred as the outcome of German military practice and was permitted by Franco in exchange for military aid for the Spanish Civil War. The Germans bombed the town and surrounding area for three hours on 26 April 1937. Two thousand five hundred people were killed or wounded and the town burned for three days. The painting uses two- and three-dimensional imagery to depict dead and wounded people and animals – some dismembered, others mutilated. The agony and horror experienced by the victims is evident on their faces. A woman wails, head thrown back, holding an inert baby; another woman with outstretched arms and head thrown back weeps, body split. A bull's head looks impassively over the scene while a horse's head is open mouthed in horror and pain. In the centre is a representation of Hitler impaled by a spear.

A fallen warrior lies in crucifixion position holding a broken sword. A hand holds a flower in the foreground. Another hand holds out an oil lamp to the exploding electric lamp which occupies a central position on the top of the painting. Rays of light penetrate the dark and lines intersect at points creating apparent explosions. There appear to be layers within the painting; a Lucifer is present as well as a second bull's head goring the horse, and a human skull penetrated by a spear can be deciphered beneath the wounded horse. The horse has been stabbed by a spear which has a diamond tip – the symbol of a harlequin. A harlequin, mouth open, looks down on the scene, and four other hidden harlequins can be seen when the painting is inverted.

FIGURE 12.3 *Guernica*, Pablo Picasso, 1937 (reprinted with permission of the Museo Nacional Centro de Arte Reina Sofía, Madrid, Spain)

Secondary level

At the secondary level and according to Picasso, any analysis of the painting lies solely within the meanings that the observer takes from the symbols. Some suggestions include: the bull may represent fighting in general but more likely represents Franco; and the gored (sexual imagery) and speared horse represents the Spanish Republic. The weeping women symbolise suffering and loss, while Lucifer is often the bringer of light and evil – the light of the bomb explosions. The crucified warrior with the broken spear is Christ, or the incapacity of good to reign over or to combat this situation. The surviving flower represents hope and peace. Harlequins are often seen as having power to combat death.

Tertiary level

At the tertiary level, the major reading is a negative representation of the horrors of war through the portrayal of a barbaric act, the death of hope and goodness, the self-serving duplicity of political leaders, and the resulting pain and suffering of innocent people and animals.

Example: longitudinal iconology

An example of longitudinal iconology (Fritz Saxl, 1957) involved historical documentation and interpretation of the image of a figure holding two snakes. Its emergence was traced to the third millennium BC, where the figure was thought to symbolise the power of a divine being, and it was followed to its disappearance during the twelfth century Christian era.

Another example of this form of analysis can be seen in the tracing of early tarot images of the tower from the fifteenth and sixteenth centuries (O'Neill, 2006). These are linked to religious art, the apocalyptic tradition of the fall of earthly kingdoms, and the joint symbols of death, the devil and towers from the fourteenth century.

Structural analysis

The signs and patterns of visual symbols are viewed as being directly related to concepts within particular cultures which have meanings that can be read. The signifier (image) is connected to the signified (meaning).

When to use: when you wish to identify the commonly accepted meanings of signs.

Types of research question best suited: what do these signs represent? What are the meanings of these images for participants?

Strengths: enables visual images to be 'read' within cultural contexts.

Weaknesses: the static nature of sign and signifier doesn't allow for rapid changes in meaning.

There are different kinds of symbols:

- *iconic*: a realistic representation or strong resemblance between image and object, e.g. a picture of a horse
- *symbolic*: a learned symbol such as a crown, representing royalty and the power of the monarchy
- *indexical*: a symbol that links to natural events via a physical connection, e.g. steam relates to hot water, and a red sky at night relates to good weather the following day.

Clearly all of these signs or symbols can operate on more than one level and the boundaries may overlap. For example, a crown is iconic, indexical (sign of a particular kind of administrative organisation) and symbolic (power) at the same time. In addition, signs are often not just single entities, they can be made up of other signs. The openness and widespread availability of visual images mean that those viewing images may well come up with a range of analyses, but the underlying assumption is that these will have common codes (systems to which signs refer and into which they can be organised) identified through similarities and oppositions and categorised.

Example: the 1984 Apple Macintosh advertisement

This commercial advertisement (Moriarty, 1995), which can be seen at http://www.uiowa.edu/~commstud/adclass/1984_mac_ad.html (accessed 26 April 2006), provides a useful basis for a semiotic structural analysis (Figure 12.4). The 45 second advertisement was shown to a Superbowl audience in 1984 regarding the advent of the Apple personal computer.

The advertisement featured a line of marchers or walkers in identical grey prison style clothing moving along a circular enclosed tunnel while a Big Brother figure's face on a screen continuously speaks in the background in an idealistic sloganeering style. There is a flash of white as a woman in a white singlet and red shorts carrying a sledgehammer runs into view followed by guards with face shields. The Big Brother image is then seen speaking to a hall of seated passive unmoving and expressionless workers dressed in grey. The woman, lit from behind, comes into this hall and runs to the screen swirling the hammer and sending it into the screen as Big Brother says, 'We shall prevail'. An explosion occurs, flooding the scene with white light. Then a voiceover explains that Apple will introduce Macintosh on 24 January 1984 and that 1984 will not be like *1984*. There are clear links to the original Orwellian text, to Fritz Lang's film *Metropolis*, to the film *Blade Runner*, and negatively to the conformity of the IBM culture.

In an analysis of this advertisement undertaken in 1991 (Moriarty, 1995), 200 undergraduate students were asked to observe it and complete a short survey. The survey comprised open-ended questions designed to identify the symbols evident, to

FIGURE 12.4   The *1984* Apple Macintosh advertisement (reprinted with permission, Apple Mac)

capture meanings and to understand the messages students were receiving. Content analysis of the responses was undertaken to cluster the meanings identified and to categorise them. All responses were grouped in terms of being *iconic*, *indexical* and *symbolic*. A question on the dominant images revealed that 92% mentioned a woman, a hammer and a TV screen. The woman was seen as a bright (white in colour) athletic runner (iconic), a change agent, a representative of the future, a saviour and a metaphor for freedom (symbolic). The sledgehammer was viewed iconically as a tool and symbolically as a destructive force and creator of new possibilities. The TV screen was iconically linked to various other screen technologies and symbolically linked to the power of the media, control and censorship. The researcher concluded that overall, iconic images impacted more than symbolic or indexical images and that people and objects had greater impact on viewers' impressions than did dynamic or audio elements.

Poststructural analysis: deconstruction

When to use: when you have access to visual images and their deconstruction/unravelling will enhance the clarification of your research questions.

Types of research question best suited: what is the meaning of the sign components of this visual image?

Strengths: enables in-depth analysis of visual images as they are deconstructed within cultural and historical contexts.

Weaknesses: multiple readings and multiple conclusions mean there are no finite answers, everything is transitional.

Taking the guidelines for deconstructing written texts presented in Chapter 13, the process of deconstructing visual images involves a sceptical reading together with an identification of the arguments which will need to be positioned against each other to clarify ideas, metaphors, contradictions, generalisations and binary opposites. Images present and images missing also need identification. Alternative readings and multiple interpretations are essential in the recognition of the transitional and open-ended nature of images.

Process

In seeking threads to rupture the text:

- Allow the arguments to challenge each other.
- Identify any contradictions and generalisations.
- Disentangle the complexities of all dichotomies.
- Seek alternative readings and links with other texts.
- Seek marginalised voices.
- Avoid finite interpretations.
- Seek alternative readings.

Example: Three Sphinxes of Bikini Atoll

Within the poststructuralist tradition, layers and complexity should be sought. In Salvador Dali's painting, the notion of the Sphinx in the title first needs to be

FIGURE 12.5 Three Sphinxes of Bikini Atoll, Salvador Dali, 1947 (reproduction rights: approved mandatory credit, copyright Salvador Dali, licensed by VISCOPY Australia, 2006)

explored (Figure 12.5). In Greek mythology the Sphinx was a creature with a lion's body, the wings of an eagle and the head and breast of a human female. This animal–female–bird combination emphasises strength, flight and fertility and was viewed as both a guardian (protector) and a destroyer. In the plays of Sophocles around 400 BCE, the Sphinx was to be found on a high rock near a road into Thebes where he posed a riddle to passers-by: 'What is that which has one voice and yet becomes four footed and two footed and three footed?' (Apollodorus, 1921: 1.349). Those who failed to solve the riddle were killed. Only Oedipus was able to answer correctly that man crawled on four legs in infancy, walked on two and resorted to a stick in older age. The Sphinx committed suicide on the rocks below when its riddle was correctly answered.

In terms of the atomic bomb test explosions around Bikini Atoll from 1946, the two human Sphinx heads portrayed face away from the viewer (hidden power, hard to decipher) and – in contrast to the image of the tree, which may represent life and knowledge (transparent, but fragile) – reflect the dual capacity of the Sphinx for destruction (man) and regeneration (earth and tree). Can the creative power of man which, as knowledge has increased, has produced so much destruction, also use this creative power to save the earth? Or is the whole painting an ironic postmodern play by an intelligent artist who likes to combine the bizarre for visual effect but with no particular message except that created by the reader?

In avoiding finite interpretation, many questions arise. Why is the front head severed and bloody but set upon the earth? Why is the tree one entity but comprised of two, and what does the situation of the distant head on the mountains mean? Is man really creative and intelligent or just destructive (lemmings following each other to self-destruction)? Do the mountains reflect the rocks upon which the Sphinx suicided when Oedipus answered the riddle correctly? What is the connection between the similar shapes of the mushroom cloud hair and the leaves of the tree: is it man's individuality that is dangerous compared with the power of nature? Why are the human heads solid while the tree can be seen through to a vegetated vista, and the front head looks toward a fading reflection of itself in the distance placed in a whitened landscape (denuded by atomic fallout?) with a bright white sky? The colours of the earth and foliage – green and gold brown – are more evident than the black sky and the shadows cast. This reading would appear to indicate that man's destructive capacity may well terminate his/her own existence, but another reading would point to the continuing capacity of man to survive despite blindness, lack of vision and the inability to emulate nature.

Example: family photograph

A poststructural analysis of a family photo of a young woman from an earlier generation was undertaken by Karen Crinall (1999). She collected family stories about this person, who is pictured as a lively young woman, dressed as if for a formal social occasion and smiling – face made up, lipstick and earrings on. The author attempted to understand the constructed narratives regarding this person and how these had changed over time. Firstly the location of this photo (on grandmother's walnut-veneered buffet) is contextualised. The photo is of her grandmother's child – the author's aunt. The narratives regarding the person in the photo shifted over time from identification as 'a lady I knew once' to 'your aunty', and eventually the silenced stories started to emerge. Intimations of 'talent ' and 'struggles' and 'victimisation' within a family context of violence and despair lead to the young woman's final escape to homelessness and death by accidental means. Crinall links this photo with other photos of homeless women which she has previously analysed in order to see further into the smiling face portrayed.

Summary

You can analyse visual images using different approaches but your choice will depend on your desired outcome. You might choose ethnographic content analysis, where cultural meanings are important; or iconological and iconographical approaches, where historical icons are present; the structural approach, where the commonly accepted interpretations of signs are sought; or the poststructural approach, where deconstruction through a sceptical reading is seen as useful.

FURTHER READING

Banks, M. (2001) *Visual Methods in Social Research*. London: Sage. Banks combines both practical and technical approaches and uses a wide range of examples from research conducted on Egyptian television soap opera, to the sale of ethnographic photographs in London auction houses, to pornographic images on the web. New technologies are also included, with image digitisation and computer-based multimedia extensively covered. There are sections on using film and photographic archives and useful practical advice on publishing and presenting the results of visual research.

Knowles, C. and Sweetman, P. (eds) (2004) *Picturing the Social Landscape*. London: Routledge. Contributors explore the following ideas: self and identity; visualising domestic space; the urban landscape; and social change. Methods covered include photo and video diaries, juxtaposing official and unofficial views, using images as triggers in interview work, working with children through photographs, and combining visual methods with interviews and text-based research.

Pink, S. (2001) *Doing Visual Ethnography: Images, Media and Representation in Research*. London: Sage. Using visual ethnographic approaches, the author draws on research and paradigms from anthropology, sociology, cultural studies, photographic studies and media studies to describe visual methods in particular photographic and video images in qualitative research.

Preziosi, D. (1998) *The Art of Art History: A Critical Anthology*. Oxford: Oxford University Press. This book provides an introduction to the links between semiotics and iconography. Included in the selected readings are Panofsky's essay on Poussin's *Et in Arcadia Ego* and Louis Marin's essay on the same painting.

Rose, G. (2001) *Visual Methodologies: An Introduction to the Interpretation of Visual Materials*. London: Sage. The author provides a comprehensive overview and history of this field and examines the approaches of: semiology, psychoanalysis, discourse analysis and content analysis.

Van Leeuwen, T. and Jewitt, C. (eds) (2002) *Handbook of Visual Analysis*. Thousand Oaks, CA: Sage. This book explains methods for visual analysis, content analysis, historical analysis, structural analysis, iconography, psychoanalysis, social semiotic analysis, film analysis and ethnomethodology. Each approach is applied and detailed analyses of a variety of data, including newspaper images, family photos, drawings and art works, are provided.

13

Semiotic Structural and Poststructural Analyses

These forms of analysis involve determining how the meanings of signs and symbols are constructed and how they can be read. The meanings of signs are not assumed to be inherent but are taken to come from relationships with other things. Structural approaches involve identifying the commonly accepted layers of meaning within texts, while poststructuralism calls on Jacques Derrida's processes of deconstruction to illuminate the many possibilities of meaning.

Key points

- Semiotics is the study of signs, sign systems and their meanings.
- Structuralism assumes that signs have a limited range of meanings which can be identified.
- Poststructuralism assumes that superficial and static meanings provide only one layer and that deconstruction can reveal many more options as meaning slips away into multiple possibilities.

Chapter 12 gives examples of these approaches applied to visual analysis.

Structuralism

When to use: when it is important to identify the language forms, structures and processes of meaning transmission.

Types of research question best suited: what are the commonly accepted meanings of signs within a particular culture?

Strengths: the approach helps to clarify broad cultural values.

Weaknesses: this form of precision signifier–signified may not sufficiently represent the complexity of meaning (leading to poststructuralism).

Structuralism to poststructuralism

You may find a brief exploration of structuralism and poststructuralism helpful here. Poststructuralism is a very complex field, theoretically speaking, and it is worthwhile trying to understand it and to be prepared to read some of the French theorists mentioned here if you decide to attempt it.

The ideas that can be termed 'structuralist' seek to describe the world in terms of systems of centralised logic and formal structures that can be accessed through processes of scientific reason. Individual objects are viewed as being part of a greater whole, for example a particular building is seen less as an individual entity and more as a representative of an architectural style based at a particular point in time in a specific culture and reflecting identifiable values. Similarly, people are seen as objects/products with the self and the unconscious being classified and constructed by their webs of cultural networks, perceptions and values. This allows people to be seen largely as mechanical organisms produced by systems, with defined needs, predictable behaviours and actions. Thus the underlying *forms*, *structures* and *processes* of construction and transmission of meaning, rather than the *content*, become the main focus.

Language, signs and meaning

Under structuralism, language was seen as a key process in the creation and communication of meaning. It was viewed as a self-referential system: all perceptions and understandings were seen as being framed by words. Meaning lay within the text, a coherent and unified structure derived from pattern and order, and analysis simply involved uncovering these patterns and ascertaining their meaning through the particular order in which they have been constructed.

Much of this view derived from the early twentieth century work of a Swiss linguist Ferdinand de Saussure (1857–1913) who, in viewing language as a system of signs and codes, sought out the deep structures, the rules and conventions which enable a language to operate at a particular point in time. He saw individual words as arbitrary signs with meaning only in relation to other signs in the cultural system. Within each rule-based language system (*langue*) the linguistic sign is the spoken or written word (the signifier) which attributes meaning to objects, concepts and ideas (the signified – the mental picture produced by the signifier) in the construction of reality. For example, the word 'rain' produces a mental image of rain falling. We recognise the meaning of the word 'rain' not from the word in itself but from its difference to other similar sounding words such as 'ran' and 'lain' which produce different mental pictures. In comprehending meaning we also utilise the difference between rain and similar concepts such as 'hail, 'sleet' and 'snow' as well as opposing concepts such as 'drought'. Meaning is seen as being structured through binary opposites.

There developed widespread acceptance of the assumption that, through signifiers and signifieds, reality is socially constructed and that any utterance (*parole*) is meaningful only in relation to other words within the larger cultural system in which all of these have been constructed. Binary oppositions were sought to clarify meaning and were seen to provide a localising (within specific cultures) focus, and the interrelationships among signs were viewed as crucial in the analysis of language. Some signs were seen as embodying broader cultural meanings and were termed 'myths': for example, a Ferrari sports car is a mythic signifier of wealth and a particular lifestyle.

Texts

The focus on signs, signifiers and codes (the frameworks in which signs make sense), and on order and meaning through repetitions of patterned relationships, enabled texts and cultures to be 'read' using structural forms of analysis. Here construction of meaning, representation of reality and the privileging of binary opposites is integral. Everything then became 'text' and the ways of presenting 'reality' within 'cultures' was meticulously documented.

However, the view of the usefulness of some signs in determining universal cultural values became questioned. Returning to the example of the Ferarri sports car, this mythic signifier would have minimal use and quite different value and meaning for the pygmies of the Congo forests in comparison to the value and meaning it might hold for the elite of Milan. This focus on the universality and centrality of structures and signs even across cultures also tended to diminish the role of history in constructing and influencing current values and behaviours.

Process

1 Seek the way effects are created through metaphors, repetition and binary opposites.
2 Identify meanings of signs in context and in the culture.

Example: Jack and Jill

The first two verses of the nursery rhyme 'Jack and Jill' can be used to simply illustrate the process from first a structural and then (later) a poststructural perspective.

Jack and Jill went up the hill
to fetch a pail of water;
Jack fell down and broke his crown,
and Jill came tumbling after.

Up Jack got and home did trot,
as fast as he could caper;
He went to bed to mend his head,
with vinegar and brown paper.

Structural analysis

Here the signifiers are presumed to have meanings which are easily recognisable within the cultural language. In the first stanza we can then assume that Jack is a male person and Jill a female person. The fact that Jack is referred to first may indicate that males are of greater importance in the culture. Going up a hill to fetch a pail (older name for a bucket and probably made of metal) of water suggests also that water is valued in this story and that getting it involves effort (climbing a hill), or that as water collects in low lying areas it was necessary to get to higher ground in order to descend to a water collection point. Water as the basic constituent of life on the planet is clearly a resource worth travelling for. Jack's fall and the breaking of his 'crown' (either his head or a crown, suggesting he may be a member of the royal family) indicate his ultimate lack of success in achieving the goal of gaining water, resulting in a painful outcome – either a broken skull or a fall from grace. Equally unsuccessful in their quest, Jill tumbles and falls after him. Their fortunes appear to be linked.

In the second stanza only Jack is mentioned, reinforcing the lesser importance of Jill whose fate we now know nothing about. Jack is sufficiently intact as to be able to get himself home at a fair speed (trot) and to put himself to bed and to treat his head with a mixture of vinegar and brown paper. This combination produces a substance known as dimethyl sulfoxide or DMSO (currently under trial for its medical uses). This substance is a byproduct of the wood industry and its elements are present in paper. A dilute form of this substance has been used in the past as a topical analgesic, as it was viewed as having the capacity to reduce pain and inflammation almost immediately through its ability to enter the body quickly. The overall rhyme of the poem falls into a walking/trotting rhythm supporting the narrative.

Criticisms of structuralism

You can see that in developing arguments regarding the limitations of structuralism, many authors were providing the foundations of what would later be termed poststructuralism.

Is there meaning beyond the text?

Jacques Derrida challenged the notion from Saussure that meaning was to be found in the difference between particular words and other concepts in the language system by emphasising both the simultaneous referral and deferral of meaning. He supported this view in his statement 'There is nothing outside of the text [*Il n'y a pas de hors-texte*]' (1976: 158). This meant that textual signifiers did not relate to any clear centred 'reality' or 'signified' outside the text, they simply slid away toward multiple possibilities.

Roland Barthes also asserted that structural analysis could not seek meaning beyond the text itself: '"What takes place" in a narrative is from the referential (reality) point of view literally nothing; "what happens" is language alone, the adventure of language, the unceasing celebration of its coming' (1977: 124). In his essay 'Death of the author', Barthes suggested that the author did not have total control of textual meaning and had no greater insight into the text than the reader. This emphasised the notion of free play of meanings and the impossibility of originality under structuralism where the text becomes a product of the system and any possibility of uniqueness is lost. 'We know now that a text is not a line of words releasing a single "theological" meaning (the "message" of the Author-God) but a multidimensional space in which a variety of writings, none of them original, blend and clash. The text is a tissue of quotations drawn from the innumerable centres of culture' (1977: 146).

Jean Baudrillard (1993) also emphasised the death of the possibility of originality in the recycling of images by referring to Andy Warhol's repeated identical paintings of Marilyn Monroe's face, and Jacques Derrida shared Friedrich Nietzsche's critique of the level to which 'truth' had descended under structuralism:

> What, then, is truth? A mobile army of metaphors, metonyms, and anthropomorphisms – in short, a sum of human relations which have been enhanced, transposed, and embellished poetically and rhetorically, and which after long use seem firm, canonical, and obligatory to a people: truths are illusions about which one has forgotten that this is what they are; metaphors which are worn out and without sensuous power; coins which have lost their pictures and now matter only as metal, no longer as coins. (Neitzsche, 1911/1954: 46–7, quoted by Spivak in the preface to Derrida, 1976: xxii)

The problems of binary opposites

Derrida (1976) pointed out that in poststructural analysis using deconstruction of texts, binary opposites (each of which always contains traces of the opposing entity) collapse, challenging Saussure's ordered systems of meaning (for example the opposites '*male*' and '*female*' have both linguistic and biological traces). Luce Irigaray (1985) also strongly critiqued the limited social frames which binary opposites imposed, in particular the binary opposites of penis/vagina. She noted that this privileging of the male organ has led to a phallocentric orientation for all sexuality. Her concern lies with female sexuality and gender which are seen to have been rendered invisible except through the male 'gaze', or dissolved into reproductive activities. 'There is only one sex, the masculine, that elaborates itself in and through the production of the "Other"' (1985: 18).

With the collapse of binary opposites, Deleuze and Guattari introduced the concept 'rhizomatic' to explain the infinite nature of meaning:

> the rhizome connects any point to any other point, and its traits are not necessarily linked to traits of the same nature; it brings into play very different regimes of signs, and even nonsign states ... It is comprised not of units but of dimensions, or rather directions in motion. It has neither beginning nor end, but always a middle (milieu) from which it grows and which it overspills. (1987: 21)

This notion of the rhizome, capable of constant adaptation, shifted the field of semiotics light years away from previous linear structuralist orientations.

Transition between structuralism and poststructuralism

Many of the above critics came from the structuralist tradition and have been responsible not only for initiating the move into poststructuralism but also for the continuity and linking of this newer approach with that of structuralism. As time passed, the overall focus shifted from the structures which generate meaning, to documenting how the generative capacity provided by the framing and content of the texts themselves was displaced by the possibility of an endless deferral of meaning amongst a range of signifiers.

Poststructuralism

When to use: when a deconstruction of the text/texts is desirable.

Types of research question best suited: what are the deeper meanings of and links to this text?

Strengths: the capacity to go beyond superficial meanings.

Weaknesses: too much pulling apart of the text can lead to meaninglessness.

Deconstruction

One of the major aspects of poststructuralism, the notion of deconstruction of the text through the critique of its structural integrity, was introduced by Jacques Derrida (1976). The word 'deconstruction' itself has been subject to different forms of interpretation, but the meanings as Derrida understood them are clarified in a 'Letter to a Japanese friend' where he explains the orientation of this term by utilising several dictionary definitions: 'Deconstruction: action of deconstructing. ... Disarranging the construction of words in a sentence. Of deconstruction, common way of saying construction ... To disassemble the parts of a whole ... To deconstruct verse, rendering it, by the suppression of meter, similar to prose' (1985: 1–5).

Thus the deconstruction of text appears to be a positive and a negative process of change, although it has been argued by some that it is more a destructive process (Habermas, 1987: 161). However, 'Rather than destroying, it was also necessary to understand how an "ensemble" was constituted and to reconstruct it to this end' (Derrida, 1985: 1–5). Deconstruction is less a method or stage by stage approach and more a natural unravelling which the text invites by presenting this opportunity within its own structure. The word 'deconstruction' like all words is not a unity in itself but is also subject to deconstruction. Its value is relative to the other words, sentences and concepts against which it appears in context and to which it is linked.

Most systems constructed during the era of structuralism were seen as centred and self-referential and all meaning emanated and referred back to this centre.

According to Derrida in poststructuralism 'the center is, paradoxically, within the structure and outside it', allowing 'the free play of its elements inside the total form' (1978: 278–9). Derrida talks of the hidden areas inside systems, which can be accessed by various approaches. He uses the analogy of his own veins: their internal action can be viewed by various pieces of medical imaging equipment, but if cut they reveal their action outside the body – an action which will display the workings of the circulatory system (the pumping of blood), but can lead to loss of the original form or death (Derrida online, http://www.hydra.umn.edu/derrida/content.html, accessed 1 May 2006).

Centred systems are usually created and maintained on the basis of binary oppositions, for example 'God' and the 'Devil', 'Good' and 'Evil', where one reflects a positive value and the other a negative value in society. These central concepts provide meaning and the sense of something existing beyond the system – something indefinable – the 'constant of a presence … consciousness or conscience, God, man, and so forth' (1976: xxi). For Derrida, hierarchical oppositions cannot be absolutes as each contains a trace of the opposite term. Derrida uses the binary opposition of 'presence' and 'absence' to clarify this. He saw presence and absence as being unable to be easily separated. Presence is only meaningful in the context of the notion of absence and because in each present there is a trace – a sign left by the absent thing. The concept of *différance* (1972/1982) has two aspects – difference (to differ, linked to identity) and deferment (time and the constant deferral of meaning) – which serve to break down the power of such oppositions. Every sign is a signifier and every signifier is linked to other signifiers in a never-ending process.

The overall purpose of deconstruction is to erase the boundaries of these binary oppositions in order to illuminate the similarities and interdependencies between each oppositional pair. This is done by demonstrating that each member of the pair is not a complete opposite and to show how the marginalisation of one member has in fact centred it. This exposure of societal values causes rigid boundaries to blur and collapse and the oppositions to become meaningless.

Thus both deconstruction (boundary removal) and construction – putting into free play the relationships among signs and allowing new possibilities of meaning to emerge – have occurred. Rather than new binary oppositions being developed, conclusions become infinite with the constant referral/deferral of multiple interpretations of meaning. Sometimes a 'hinge' (*la brisure* – an internal device such as double meaning, trace, statement) can break open the text and put *différance* into play (1976: 65). Many meanings thread together to make up the discourses within any one text. With deconstruction, one thread leads to another and to another and slowly the text unravels. Roland Barthes has said that 'In the multiplicity of writing, everything is to be *disentangled,* nothing *deciphered;* the structure can then be followed, "run" (like the thread of a stocking)' (1977: 147).

Each sign carries traces of references to many other signs in an interconnected (rhizomatic) network of possibilities. Language and meaning depend on difference (from other signs) and deferral of meanings. Interpretations are thus intertextual, differing among the author, the text, and the viewer, as well as constantly shifting and subject to revision. The viewer is empowered and both viewer and creator are part of the 'jubilant multiplicity of self-references' (Derrida, 1984: 174). Closure or finite meanings are impossible.

Process in deconstruction: some indications

Derrida is quite clear that there is danger in formalising a method of deconstruction:

> I would say that deconstruction loses nothing from admitting that it is impossible ... For a deconstructive operation *possibility* would rather be a danger, the danger of becoming an available set of rule-governed procedures, methods, accessible practices. Deconstruction is inventive or it is nothing at all; it does not settle for methodological procedures, it opens up a passageway, it marches ahead and marks a trail; its writing is not only performative, it produces rules – other conventions ... Its *process* involves an affirmation, this latter being linked to the coming [*venir*] in event, advent, invention. (1992: 312–13)

Although the disentangling or unravelling process appears fairly simple as a visual construct, when you are faced with a complex text the actual process of locating a key thread could be fairly daunting. Rosenau (1992: 120–1, adapted) has collated a number of principles from various sources and these have been expanded in an attempt to provide you with some suggestions for guiding the procedure.

1   Take the position of accepting nothing and rejecting nothing in a critical and skeptical reading, the overall outcome of which should be the production of an understanding of the text's structure, its content and its omissions.
2   In the seeking of threads to rupture the text:

   (a)   allow the arguments of the text to challenge each other
   (b)   identify any contradictions and inconsistencies (ideas, metaphors etc.)
   (c)   locate any generalisations and use these to undermine any principles used
   (d)   place argument against argument
   (e)   seek out and disentangle the complexities of all dichotomies, binary oppositions and hierarchies
   (f)   try reading against the grain of the document to discover alternative readings
   (g)   seek out links with other texts.

3   Examine the margins and identify marginalised voices and concealed information.
4   In writing up:

   (a)   write so as to allow as many interpretations as feasible
   (b)   avoid making any absolute statements

(c)   stay close to the language of the text

(d)   cultivate ambiguity and ambivalence

(e)   remember that this is a transitional not a finite text that you are creating – it should resist closure.

Example: Jack and Jill

The first two verses of the nursery rhyme 'Jack and Jill' (see earlier this chapter) can also be used to simply illustrate a poststructural analysis.

Arguments and challenges

Both going up a hill to fetch a pail of water.
Jack falling down and breaking his crown.
Jill tumbling after him.
Jack trotting home fast.
Going to bed to mend his head.

Oppositional elements, hierarchies, contradictions

Jack	Jill
up	down
pail of water	empty pail
head	crown
out of bed	in bed
broken	mended
out of home	in home
vinegar	water

Ideas, metaphors, generalisations

crown	head
water	life (for life maintenance or as a medium for new life – sperm)
tumbling	(sexual metaphor)
up the hill	moving up in status

Simple reading

It is possible to climb high, but such a climb may lead to a fall with personal/political damage as the outcome.

Alternative readings

Nordic mythology, political/economic (see Chapter 11 on discourse analysis for detailed alternative readings of the rhyme). In addition the breaking apart of the text through the identification of oppositional elements allows for a straight sexual reading where the monarch has dallied (with a female) whom he may or may not have made pregnant (breaking the royal line 'head') and is obliged to retreat and lay low (from his wife? or from the public gaze) until things are calmer. This encounter can of course be read as political/economic dalliance with ideas or another country or a particular project: in all cases some damage appears to have occurred requiring caution and the outcomes are unclear. A positive reading against the grain could see Jack and Jill, as male and female representatives of the population, seeking new and powerful knowledge which they gain, but in doing so they need to break with traditional ways of thinking in order to encompass these new ideas. A reading against the grain of patriarchy would point to the weaker, more easily damaged male of the species in contrast with the more resilient female. Another reading might assume that Jack and Jill were both male or both female and the narrative was a warning tale about public displays of homosexuality or lesbianism.

Marginalised voices
Jack, Jill, partners/family of these two, the general public and so on.

Transitional conclusion
The poem can be read as relating to either gaining or losing by individuals, pairs or heads of state and these gains/losses may be further linked to mythological, sexual, political, economic and social readings. One potential outcome indicated is that when losses are suffered it may be possible to retrieve or mend some of the damage if you retreat and lie low, but the reverse may also be true because lying low may become a lifetime occupation.

Research examples of deconstruction

Researchers who have attempted deconstruction have employed various approaches to display or re-present data for the reader, such as: placing texts against each other in order to trouble them; interrupting texts in an attempt to prevent them closing and avoiding finite interpretations; and creating another structure to allow a freer play of language.

Placing texts adjacent to each other
David Boje (2000) has attempted this: it can be viewed at http://web.nmsu. edu/~dboje/pmdecon9705.htm (accessed 1 May 2006) and the first couple of paragraphs and accompanying visual images can be viewed in Chapter 16. Boje has placed an article from *Popular Mechanics* on the left side of a two-column page against researcher collated reports of community action and celebration. This juxtaposition allows the joyousness of community life to be put into hard relief against the aggression of police in the maintenance of order in urban culture, thus dislodging threads for unravelling.

Avoidance of closure
This can be seen in an article by Karen Fox (1996) and involves placing several different sets of data in three columns. This study looked at the impact of

childhood sexual abuse on the perpetrator and his now adult victim. The first column has the voice of the perpetrator discussing his feelings, in the centre is the voice of the author (reflecting on the interview and on herself as a victim of childhood sexual abuse by a priest), and in the third column is the voice of the victim of the relationship under interview. The juxtaposition of these three voices provides the reader with a complexity of interacting threads to pursue.

Creation of a new structure

Alan Aycock (1993) has attempted a new structure to facilitate a preliminary deconstruction of the term 'play' with particular reference to the Fort-da game as described by Sigmund Freud and played by his young grandson. This game involved throwing a wooden spool attached to a piece of string and retrieving it to the accompaniment of 'ooo' and 'ah' sounds. Derrida (1987: 257–409) had previously used this game as a trope (metaphor) for Freud's writings – how he sends away and retrieves his arguments. He also uses it as a trope for love, love letters, work, and a commentary on the ideas of other philosophers. Aycock applies Derrida's approach of Fort-da to five different forms of chess which he has observed – casual play, tournament play, correspondence play, computer play, and skittles – in all cases focusing on data gathered relating to play talk, structures of play and player self-awareness. This process appears to weaken the centrality of 'play', identifies the traces of absence and picks up on difference and deferral of meaning.

Criticisms of poststructuralism

- Poststructuralism has been criticised regarding the complexities that it provides. In particular its tendency toward nihilism – the deconstruction of the deconstructed text – can very quickly lead to meaninglessness.
- The lack of finite conclusions through the constant deferral of meaning also presents difficulties in terms of evaluation and policy decisions.
- The decentring of the author doesn't take into account the fact that the author still composes the structure of the text, has selected the 'voices' and manipulated the direction of interpretation. Although deconstruction should clarify this, it is a lengthy and painstaking process.
- The difference between deconstruction and good critique is unclear.
- Is deconstruction any more than an older authorial desire to appropriate a text (however momentarily)?
- How will the contradictions between culture and science be explained without recourse to the language claims of structuralism?

Summary

Semiotic approaches to textual analysis fall into two broad categories: structuralism, where there is an assumption that signs have clearly recognised meanings and that binary opposites will serve to clarify these meanings; and poststructuralism, where, meaning is seen as more complex, deferring endlessly to many possibilities which are only limited by the imagination of the writer and the reader. In structuralism your analytic process is straightforward, involving analysing the construction of language and documenting the accepted meanings of words in order to make sense of them. In contrast a poststructural analysis involves you in a sceptical reading to identify arguments, challenges and metaphors, as well as unravelling binary opposites, seeking alternative interpretations and presenting your conclusions in such a way as to avoid closure.

FURTHER READING

Belsey, C. (2002) *Poststructuralism: A Very Short Introduction.* A simple but concise introduction to poststructuralism from Ferdinand de Saussure to today.

Chandler, D. (2002) *Semiotics: The Basics.* London: Routledge. This book provides an easy-to-read jargon-free introduction to the study of semiotics from Saussure and Freud to Lacan, Eco and Derrida, It covers structuralism, sign systems, and poststructural deconstruction. Plenty of examples are provided. Daniel Chandler's online 'Semiotics for beginners' covers similar ground, http://www.aber.ac.uk/media/Documents/S4B/semiotic.html, accessed 1 May 2006.

Johansen, J. and Larsen, S. (2002) *Signs in Use: An Introduction to Semiotics.* London: Routledge. An accessible introduction to the study of semiotics which presents semiotics as a theory and a set of analytical tools: code, sign, discourse, action, text and culture. The book is illustrated with numerous examples, from traffic systems to urban parks.

Royle, N. (2000) *Deconstruction: A User's Guide.* London: Palgrave. This book shows practical applications of deconstruction at work, illustrating what it is not and linking it to feminism, poetry, psychoanalysis, love and drugs.

Sarup, M. (1993) *An Introductory Guide to Post-Structuralism and Postmodernism.* Athens, GA: University of Georgia Press. This is a comprehensive but fairly basic introductory text – a good place to start for those with no previous knowledge in these areas.

Part Four

Writing Up Data

There are several decisions to be taken once you have assembled your data into groupings from which you can then begin to think about writing up. The first is to see if it is possible to develop a more abstract explanation regarding the results you have gathered. The depth to which you undertake this will depend on whether the method you have pursued has a particular philosophical bent that you would like to follow or from which you can develop and build on existing underpinnings. You may of course decide to minimise your theorising and to display your data in creative ways so that the reader can decide where your findings fit with their knowledge and experiences; or you may decide on a position midway between these two and combine theorising with interesting displays, but in such a way that the reader is clear about what you have found and where it all fits (in your view). If you have collected some quantitative data to provide a broader overview, you will need to decide if, when and how you will combine them with your qualitative data. The three chapters in this part attempt to help you with these decisions by discussing theorising, the use of mixed quantitative and qualitative data, and the variety of data display options which are available.

14

Theorising from Data

This chapter will help you undertake the process of developing a more abstract theoretical explanation of data collected through the range of approaches that have been covered in this text so far. This process can be initiated early and should have strong links to the research question, to the approaches to data collection that you have chosen as being best for this question, and to the forms of data analysis that have been undertaken. Sometimes this is an almost seamless process where, at one extreme, previously identified theories are applied (theory testing or theory directed), while at the other, light theoretical interpretations of a conceptual nature may occur. In between these two extremes, emergent explanations closely linked to a range of theoretical positions (theory generation) currently tend to dominate the field.

Key points

- Your choices regarding theorising range over:
  - adopting your chosen theoretical underpinnings from the beginning
  - closely following the theoretical underpinnings of your method
  - linking your emerging findings to any relevant theories
  - minimising theorising (postmodernism).
- Theory testing and theory generation are the two major theorising procedures.
- Theories can fall into one of three levels: micro, middle range or grand.

Theorising

The process of theorising involves you in taking the results which you have collated and looking at them again through the lens or frame of one or several theoretical or conceptual positions in order to make further sense of them and to lift the analytical discussion to a more abstract level. The whole notion of theorising from qualitative data can be looked at from one of four options. The first relates to your *pre-chosen theoretical positions* which will drive your research and against which you will place your findings (theory direction). The second relates to *methodological underpinnings* which may constitute the orientation and processes of data collection: for example, the grounded theory approach has elements of symbolic interactionist theory which may lead you toward this or some related form of interactive theorising; phenomenology has a variety of philosophical theoretical possibilities which may be called upon; and feminist approaches are usually directed by and the results discussed primarily within feminist principles. The third option, *researcher choice,* allows you to call upon the huge variety of conceptual models and theoretical ideas that exist across all available disciplines in order to provide a more abstract explanation of your findings. The fourth option, *theory minimisation,* lies in the postmodern tradition where minimal interpretation but maximal display of data occurs so the reader can get close to the participants' experiences and make their own decisions based on their own life experiences.

Theory testing versus theory generation

One other complicating factor is whether you have adopted a *theory testing* or *theory directed* type of approach – where the relevant theories have been stated early, the implications for the study have been drawn out, and the data have been collected to meet these implications and in effect to 'test' the theory. However, you can also use this initial theory to move to the second option, that of *theory generation,* where you draw a range of 'theories' from the literature and from available theoretical ideas of relevance. Some of these will fall by the wayside as their explanatory power cannot be sustained in view of your research findings, while you may combine others with what is emerging from the data to form the basis for new theoretical explanations and models of practice.

Theory

But what is theory? Theory is abstract knowledge which has been developed as an account regarding a group of facts or phenomena. It is derived from the exploration of phenomena, the identification of concepts and the interrelationships between concepts surrounding phenomena, from which an explanatory framework can be developed.

There are different levels of theory: micro, middle range and grand. At the *micro* level, theoretical framing is mostly provided by the *concept*. Concepts are simple units of abstract thought which identify the common aspects of phenomena: examples would be 'power', 'socialisation' and 'locus of control'. Various concepts are combined with *variables and propositions* to form the next level up: theories of the *middle range*. These are explanations with a particular discipline focus, such as nursing or architecture. Finally, *grand theories* combine concepts, propositions and *statements* to provide an abstract overview which should be able to be applied in a range of disciplines.

Example

At the *micro* level we have concepts which refer to limited aspects of social organisation, e.g. 'Women carry the burden of care in our society'.

Lifting this example to the *middle range,* concepts (gender roles, burden etc.) are joined by variables (sex, class) and propositions (made up of concepts plus variables), e.g. 'Women of low socio-economic class, as the least powerful members, will carry the burden of care in some societies.'

Taking the example further to the level of *grand theory,* this would involve an abstract explanation of the uniformities of social behaviour, organisation and change and would comprise definitions, concepts, variables, statements and theoretical constructs. For example, a Marxist analysis would become: 'In capitalist societies, women's powerless lower class position will ensure they always have lower status work. Strong socialisation into nurturing roles means they will continue to be unwaged domestic slaves.'

Thumbnail sketches of examples of how other researchers have dealt with theory, chosen from within the particular approaches previously outlined in earlier chapters, are provided for you below.

Classical ethnographic approaches

The in-depth exploration of a culture, however this has been defined – whether it be the operation of tribal groups or the culture of a classroom or a department – can be undertaken in either a theory directing or a theory generating manner.

Theory directing

Some of the older ethnographies closer to the original anthropological tradition fall into the theory directing mode. For example Margaret Mead in her work in Samoa set out to apply the concept of 'adolescence' to the group under study. This can be seen in her initial application for funding to do the research, which she titled: 'A study in heredity and environment based on an investigation of the phenomenon of adolescence among primitive and civilized people'. Later in 'Life as a Samoan girl' she states: I had been sent to the South Seas to study ... the life of Samoan girls. 'I was to find out what sort of life girls lived in Samoa, whether they, like American girls, had years of tears and troubles before they were quite grown up' (1931: 94). She did discover that in fact the concept of adolescence had little value in Samoan culture:

> So, the sum total of it all is – Adolescence is a period of sudden development, of stress, only in relation to sex – and where the community recognizes this and does not attempt to curb it, there is no conflict at all between the adolescent and the community, except such as arises from the conflict of personalities within a household (and this is immediately remedied as I have shown by the change to another relationship group) and the occasional delinquent – of any age from 8–50 who arouses the ire of the community. I think I have ample data to illustrate all these points. (Mead, 1926)

This concept of adolescence had come from the American culture, and what Mead was doing was simply testing it and seeking substantiating data to confirm the more universal application of the concept in another setting. Some would argue that this form of theory testing is inappropriate, running the risk of influencing findings, and that a more theory generating approach involving extensive exploration with no imposition of *a priori* researcher generated concepts would have been a better way to go and more in line with the traditional anthropological approach of extensive documentation and categorisation, allowing the data to speak for themselves. Yet despite strong direction from the concept of adolescence, Mead was able to come up with sufficient data to challenge the universality of the concept.

Theory generating

An example of theory generation within the ethnographic tradition can be seen in Laud Humphreys's (1970) exploration of impersonal sex between consenting males in public toilets. Here Humphreys, in taking the position of the 'watch queen' or lookout, was able to observe hundreds of acts of fellatio, writing up 53 in great detail in addition to reporting 30 further detailed records kept by one of the participants. This information was added to by the dozen respondents who consented to be interviewed, and by identification of other participants through car number plates, enabling the researcher to include 100 of them in a health survey interview. From all this Humphreys generated four major profiles: trade; ambisexuals; gay guys; and closet queens. The imposition of theory was limited to the micro level and the application of the concept 'deviance', as at that time such acts were illegal. He concluded that society had provided very few 'legitimate' sexual outlets for men so that turning to the 'tearooms' had become one of the few options available.

New ethnographic approaches

The move into postmodernism has resulted in an explicitly subjective orientation dominated by fragmentation and the rejection of grand theories as power-laden discourses. Extensive display of data rather than elaborate theorising is seen as the best way to bring your reader close to the experiences you wish to transmit.

However, many researchers draw on a range of theoretical perspectives usually at the micro level and with a strong focus on the transitional nature of any conclusions. Pamela Autry (1995) used autoethnography to study her own experiences as girl and woman, both as a student and as a teacher. She used feminist theory, the issues of gender and the cultural icon of 'Barbie' as well as the concepts of depression and adolescence to clarify her findings, ending up with a 'menopausal' theory of curriculum which focuses on the issues that teenage girls face in American society.

Some autoethnographic research tends to display the story first, then use particular concepts to lightly frame it. Shamla McLaurin (2003) positions herself and her view of self under the conceptual framework of 'recovering homophobe' after exposing how her bias against homosexuality can be connected to the context of her upbringing as poor, female, black and Baptist living in the southern United States. Cultural changes and several epiphanies changed her views in a roller coaster ride from supportive to aggressively attacking any mention of homosexuality and finally to a more accepting position, particularly with regard to lesbianism. In a similar manner, an impressionistic ethnography written by Jonathon Skinner (2003) presents a picture of the lifestyle on Montserrat, a British dependent territory in the eastern Caribbean, where the author was undertaking fieldwork. A volcanic eruption terminated his work, destroying the island and killing many of his participants. The documentation collected provides an insight into the lifestyle of the island people with whom the researcher came in contact. The tale is framed under 'paradise regained' and provides a reflection on the process of bringing the island and its characters – many now dead – back to life.

Grounded theory

Here the focus is your observation of the minutiae of interaction in the understanding of social patterns, social structures, social processes and social behaviours. The structure of data collection through the constant comparative process means that your theorising of data is put in place very early. You need to compare each data segment not only across the database with other segments but also with existing literature (if you have undertaken a review) and the concepts/ theories (theoretical sensitivity) which may shed light on what is emerging in terms of data groupings. This movement between data, literature and theories serves to consolidate data and theory in a theory generation process.

Glaser and Strauss (1967) indicated that the processes of comparison tend to clarify differences and patterns which can generate explanatory concepts and propositions to form part of a general discussion of the results gained. Two levels of theory can ultimately be generated. The first is *substantive theory* which is specific to a particular focus in the research: for example, teenage pregnancy, learning styles in school settings, or the care of the dying. The second is *formal theory* which develops out of this and concentrates on the further development of broader emerging explanatory concepts such as socialisation, gender roles, class structure etc. In order for a concept to move to the realms of formal theory, that concept will have to be linked to all like situations. For example, the concept of 'status passage' related to earlier work by the two researchers on transitions to dying. In order to elevate this concept to the level of formal theory, all kinds of transitions needed to be sought from a range of literature and research – e.g. transitions from adolescence to adulthood, from bachelorhood to marriage, from hidden homosexuality to overt homosexuality, from wellness to illness, from imprisonment to freedom, from marriage to singlehood – so that the concept could be widely substantiated and its properties identified. For example, the properties of status passage were that they were considered desirable/undesirable, inevitable, possibly reversible and repeatable/non-repeatable; they could be undertaken alone, in pairs or in groups, as well as in different styles such as calmness or anger; and they might involve situations where communication with others may or may not occur, where variable control over the situation may occur, where levels of choice and degree of control will vary, and where legitimation of entry may be needed and clarity of signs may vary (adapted from Glaser and Strauss, 1971).

In an example of substantive theory generation regarding corporate turnaround (Pandit, 1995), a number of concepts and categories were constructed during the processes of open and axial coding, and the development of core categories such as 'recovery strategy content' occurred during selective coding. These recovery strategies were found to be related to six contextual factors: the causes of decline; the severity of the crisis; the attitude of stakeholders; industry characteristics; changes in the macroeconomic environment; and the firm's historical strategy. The contents of recovery strategies were further divided into actions at operational and strategic levels and a process dimension was also uncovered. From this, actions for recovery were seen to be: management change; retrenchment; stabilisation; and growth. These findings led to the generation of 53 propositions linking the concepts and categories which were tested to identify levels of support within the database for the models of recovery strategies developed.

Phenomenology

Implicit assumptions do underpin this approach in that you as researcher have the capacity to access in depth the life experiences of the self and also of the other– through an assumption of interconnectedness and processes of intuition, exploration and thematic analysis. Another assumption is that people who have these experiences have particular ways of making sense of them within their own lives, and not only can they articulate this but it is acceptable that these meanings will differ. The findings have tended to be presented to readers by you as the final authority, with some theories/concepts generated to provide broader explanations. More recently, interview and observational data have been presented in different forms: poetry, drama, pastiche and narrative as well as other creative forms of display from within the postmodern tradition, where there is very little theorising.

An example of the former type of phenomenological study can be seen in the article by Anita Sinner (2004) of the lived experiences of three women with chronic pain who returned to learning. Their experiences are presented as three case studies in the participants' own voices to show the connections between chronic pain and returning to study. Mild conceptualisation occurs in the notion that contextualisation and politicisation of women's pain are important.

A more directed approach can be seen in a case study of educational leadership by van der Mescht (2004) where 17 education leaders answered a survey questionnaire and from this five leaders, chosen on the basis of colour and gender diversity, were interviewed in depth. The author imposes van den Berg's (1972) framework 'a different existence' on one of these detailed case studies to demonstrate the lack of coherence between this person's values and view of the world and the reality of the world which he has to face – a world where transformational leadership is required to bring about change.

Feminist research

Although the principles of feminist research can be applied to a range of approaches from ethnography through to poststructuralism, they tend to operate within the theory directed tradition. Feminist content analysis within the poststructuralist tradition can be seen in Patricia Leavy's (2000) textual, visual and audiovisual content analysis of America's social-cultural-political position in the 1990s as seen through the representative fictional character of Ally McBeal (played by Calista Flockhart). The issues to be explored included: feminism and female body image in the 1990s; reality versus fiction; and the (re)production and consumption of media images within postmodernity. Michel Foucault's ideas were used for investigation of the historical backdrop. The emphasis on feminist principles involved creating coding categories prior to analysis including: Ally as a feminist; eating disorders and Ally/Calista; and the physical appearance of Ally/Calista. Comparisons were undertaken using intertextual deconstruction as to how these are presented by different forms of the media. Leavy sought to uncover the processes by which Ally McBeal came to be labelled the 'poster girl for postmodern feminism' and how this symbolism clarifies the effects of patriarchalism and capitalism. Although theory generation is possible in this situation, the strong imposition of feminist ideas and other theories means that theory direction is likely to dominate.

Content analysis

The variety of theory directing and theory generating or data driven approaches which have been used in content analysis of personal construct psychology can be seen in Green (2004). Theory directed approaches have included: the imposition of limited categories defined *a priori* by the researcher, e.g. 'people', 'problems', 'time' (past present/future), 'degree' (high/low); word co-occurrence using cluster or factor analysis of word frequency matrices; and the use of psychological scales weighted for intensity or magnitude of anxiety, hostility, alienation etc. A theory generating approach can be seen in Burgess-Limerick and Burgess-Limerick (1998) who used grounded theory to clarify the content of interview data in order to understand the processes which need to be put in place to enable women who run their own businesses to also successfully manage a young family. The concept of 'processual being' – a person who was capable of adaptation, organisation and transformation – was generated by this study. Other theory generating approaches have involved thematic analysis to identify commonly recurring constructs in order to develop a coding schema, and either grid systems or cognitive maps to develop a hierarchy of constructs and linkages.

Conversation analysis: chatrooms

More than one approach within theory generation can be used on a data set. This is illustrated in computer mediated communication (Shi et al., 2006), where the primary purpose was to view the interaction patterns in online discussions using a grounded theory approach to generate a conceptual framework termed 'thread theory', which acted as a process for evaluating interactions and identifying turn taking. This framework was then used to undertake a discourse analysis of the content of the postings. The authors took the chaotic transcripts from online discussions and displayed them to show the actual order of interaction and identified ongoing themes such as 'course project' and ongoing 'noises off' which interrupted the flow of conversation. These threads (related messages on a particular topic) were then tabled and schematically visualised to show the non-linear, non-sequential appearance of the messages more clearly and to indicate where individuals are contributing simultaneously to particular threads, as well as the life, intensity and magnitude of a thread, where threads break and where new threads emerge.

Semiotic analysis of visual images

Within semiotic analysis, there is an assumption that visual codes will be able to be read (although perhaps not interpreted) in an almost identical manner by all observers from a particular culture. Paul Carter (2006) has explored front page photographs in three leading newspapers: *The Guardian* (a broadsheet with detailed news and articles), the *Daily Mail* (a more subjective tabloid) and *The Sun* (a peoples tabloid). On one particular day, the first two papers ran articles about the death of a white farmer in Zimbabwe, murdered by vigilantes over disputes about land, while *The Sun* ran a story about Madonna claiming that the sex of her unborn baby was male. The analysis covers the choice of news/

entertainment for the front page, and the size of the photo compared with the amount of type. *The Guardian* was 50/50 with the headline 'Death at dawn: the agony of Zimbabwe' and a photo of the body of the dead man and surrounds; the *Daily Mail* used under half for the same photo of the body only, but with a directional headline 'Have a happy birthday Mr Mugabe'; while *The Sun* used a sexual type photo of Madonna mid torso up to take up most of the page with a caption 'Madonna: it's a boy'. The signifiers of size of type, photo composition, lighting, visual depth and symmetry as well as headings are said to be used to direct the reader's attention. These help to clarify and generate the conceptualisation of each paper's ideological thrust: balanced and objective (*The Guardian*), judgemental (*Daily Mail*) or opinionated and populist (*The Sun*). Theoretical interpretation was at the micro (concept level) of generation only.

Theory direction more toward the middle range occurred in Davies (2006) where the theoretical concept of 'constructed femininity' formed the centre of interpretation for a semiotic analysis of teenage magazine covers. Two magazines, *19* and *More*, were analysed by their titles, fonts, layout, colours, paper texture and the language used as well as how these magazines target the readership sought, influence readings and feed desires. The presentations of female icons and role models were seen to influence young females into particular notions of femininity (beautiful and sexy, with perfect features, blond, tanned, tall, slim and attractive to males – who are represented only as sexual objects). To fulfil this notion of femininity, young women should also be interested in fashion and knowledgeable about the trivia of the lives of famous people. Thus through information reinforced by visual representation of these characteristics, subliminal education occurs and a particular form of femininity is constructed.

Hermeneutic approach

The general hermeneutic qualitative approach can also be theorised at any level. Isabel Brodie (2000) has provided an example of conceptual theorising in social work with regard to the exclusion from school of children who are looked after in residential accommodation (children in state care). She uses the concept 'exclusion' to build up a picture of 'exclusion by non-admission', 'exclusion on admission', 'graduated' and 'planned' exclusion to develop her interpretation of 'exclusion as a social process'.

Theory building through metaphor

Metaphor has also been used to build theory, via analogical mapping, to explore the nature of a school system. One example of this would be the application of the term 'teacher as nomad' (Aubusson, 2002) providing a possible comparison between the teacher and the nomad in terms of journey, gains and losses, obstacles to be overcome etc. and providing a link to another domain of knowledge which may serve to shed light on the life of the teacher and to provide another level of interpretation. The main metaphor used to provide comparison with the school system was that of an ecosystem. This term allowed the introduction of such terminology as: adaptation, complexity, homeostasis, succession, fitness, generation and regeneration, opportunism, reproductive maturity, fragility, evolution purpose and knowledge, which could be applied to generate new insights to the results.

Summary

From the above it should be clear that apart from situations where theory/ principle direction is occurring, the most usual forms of theorising in qualitative research occur along a spectrum ranging from the use of concepts in micro theorising, to the theory generation of middle range theory, and/or to the development of formal/grand theory as in grounded theorising. These processes are not exclusive and may shade into each other. Postmodernism lightly calls on multiple concepts or avoids theorising.

FURTHER READING

Becker, H. (1993) Theory: the necessary evil. Chapter originally published in D. Flinders and G. Mills (eds), *Theory and Concepts in Qualitative Research: Perspectives from the Field*, pp. 218–29. New York: Teachers' College Press. Also available from http://home.earthlink.net/~hsbecker/theory.html, accessed 1 May 2006. Becker insists that theorising is an essential part of undertaking qualitative research and presents a wide ranging argument for this position.

Flinders, D. and Mills, G. (eds). (1993) *Theory and Concepts in Qualitative Research: Perspectives from the Field.* New York: Teachers' College Press. This is one of the few texts that actually addresses the issues relating to theorising.

Kelle, U. (1997) Theory building in qualitative research and computer programs for the management of textual data. *Sociological Research Online* 2 (2), http://www.socresonline.org.uk/2/2/1.html, accessed 1 May 2006. This article looks at the processes of theory building and challenges the idea that the use of computer management of qualitative data will inhibit these processes.

http://www.csudh.edu/dearhabermas/theory.htm, accessed 1 May 2006. An eclectic website with a range of theory links, theory journals, theorists and various research articles using theory.

http://www.qualitative-research.net/fqs/fqs-eng.htm, accessed 1 May 2006. *Forum Qualitative Research (FQS)* is a peer-reviewed multilingual online journal for qualitative research. Established in 1999, it provides information and communication.

Incorporating Data from Multiple Sources

The mix of qualitative and quantitative data in terms of management and presentation will be dealt with in this chapter. The advantage of utilising an innovative mix of data sources is that, apart from providing a broader view of the research question, it allows the reader to view the phenomenon under study from different perspectives.

Key points

- The advantages of combining quantitative and qualitative data are that you can maximise the impact of both.
- For mixed methods to be successful, issues of sampling, design, data analysis and data presentation need careful attention.
- Three ways of mixing methods are: integration, triangulation and sequencing.

A brief history of qualitative and quantitative approaches

If we go back in time there appear to be three stages of debate relating to the possibility of combining quantitative and qualitative approaches.

Never the twain shall meet
Up to the mid 1980s the two approaches were polarised. They were seen as deriving from completely different theoretical underpinnings with very different methods and quite separate orientations: one toward objectivity and the other toward subjectivity. The outcome of this was that people argued fiercely for the superior capacities of one camp or the other and combinations were almost never to be seen.

Rapprochement
During the late 1970s philosophical and other differences gave way to a closer examination of possible complementarities between the two approaches and a realisation that although different they could well enhance each other, particularly when run in parallel. This led to a rash of studies within the quantitative tradition

where qualitative methods were used as an 'end on' approach. That is, before developing survey questions, a qualitative data set would be collected to identify the 'right' questions; or, after running a survey, some qualitative interviews would be carried out to clarify and expand on some of the statistical results gained. The dangers here lay in oversimplifying the complexities of data analysis and the rigours of theoretical interpretation in the qualitative data set in favour of a shallow identification of 'emerging issues' or 'recurring themes'.

Co-operation

During the last 25 years, as the limitations of both quantitative (in terms of detail) and qualitative (in terms of numbers) were recognised, designs to incorporate both equally or as part of a range of approaches (including the analysis of visual and other documentation) have emerged. When all data sets are properly designed and analysed, considerable enhancement occurs. Researchers from different research orientations who are seeking grant monies often find it useful to include multiple methods to enhance the breadth of exploration in a particular project.

What are the major differences between qualitative and quantitative?

These are usually distinguished by separate concepts. For example, *qualitative* tends to be seen primarily as an inductive approach using a research question and moving from instances gained in the data collection to some form of conclusion, often via comparison with existing concepts or theory. Questions tend to be exploratory and open ended and data are often in narrative form. Reality is a shifting feast, subjectivity is usually viewed as important, and power is seen as lying primarily with the participants who are the experts on the matter under investigation. Analysis is predominantly interpretive through thematic approaches and deals with meanings, descriptions, values and characteristics of people and things. The outcome sought is the development of explanatory concepts and models. Uniqueness is favoured and widespread generalisation (apart from logical generalisation, that is from similar instance to similar instance) is avoided.

In contrast, *quantitative* is generally viewed as deductive, where the conclusion drawn follows logically from certain premises – usually rule based – which are themselves often viewed as proven, valid or 'true'. Reality is seen as static and measurable, objectivity (distance, neutrality) is important, linearity (cause – effect) may be sought, outcomes are the major focus and prespecified hypotheses will dictate questions and approach. Researcher control of the total process is paramount, precision and predictability are important, and statistical approaches to identify numbers and to clarify relationships between variables will dominate data analysis. Theory testing is the key and generalisation and predictability are the desired outcomes. Survey and experimental research are the main design options.

Advantages of combining quantitative and qualitative results

Apart from improving the validity of your findings, providing more in-depth data, increasing the capacity to cross-check one data set against another, and providing other 'takes' on your data, other outcomes include the following.

Providing the detail of individual experiences behind the statistics

The intensive/extensive view. So, if for example 99% of survey respondents indicate that they are extremely dissatisfied with the resources offered to them by the government to support their role of carer for their child with a disability (Grbich and Sykes, 1989), then qualitative interviews can identify in detail what aspects of support the 1% were satisfied with as well as documenting the experiences of dissatisfaction of the remainder.

To help in the development of particular measures

To clarify in detail through the results of qualitative data what the major issues are and then to use the analysis of these responses to refine a survey questionnaire in order to gain results from a larger sample. For example, in the restructuring of a department it would be sensible to find out from all members what they considered to be the positive aspects of the current organisation and what were considered to be barriers to productivity. This detailed information could then be used to structure a focused questionnaire to suggest changes which might be rated for feasibility given departmental culture.

To track changes over time

A multistaged approach can clarify, from different perspectives, how a situation is progressing. For example, an initial qualitative interview might pick up on the range of stressors faced as couples with children separate following breakdown of relationships. Three months later an intervention might provide clarification of the long term roles and responsibilities which each parent needs to take into account regarding their children. The financial and emotional costs for each couple can then be calculated at a time which is less stressful than the initial separation period. At six months post separation a survey could explore the current situation and, for those who indicated that things were not working out as planned, further in-depth interviews could tease out their problems and seek solutions.

Maximising the impact of combining different data sets

Various forms of labelling and terminology have been used for combined approaches including synergy, triangulation or parallel methods and more recently merging, sequencing and concurrent use (Marsland et al., 2000). Combining this terminology produces three options as follows.

Integration or merging or synergy

This is a process where aspects of the usually separate approaches intermingle as follows.

Sampling and design

You can consider applying the tools which are generally used for one approach to the other as well. Take for example sampling strategies. When Grbich and Sykes (1989) were offered a total population of all people with intellectual disability who were registered with a particular state government authority, it made sense to consider a probability sample using simple random sampling of this population instead of using a snowball or convenience approach, or seeking quotas to enable maximum variation. This approach was able to mirror the total population in terms of the percentages of males and females and also matched the proportion of clients (10%) from different ethnic backgrounds. But, regardless of the type of population involved in qualitative data collection, probability sampling (be it random, systematic, stratified or cluster) could be considered (with justification) as a potentially useful technique for providing a representative sample, in particular when access to a large diverse group is available – even though statistical generalisation is not a possible outcome. In addition, and with regard to design, instead of running an open-ended survey to evaluate an intervention, a more radical approach might be to introduce an experimental design to measure outcomes in a more controlled environment and follow this with in-depth interviews.

Data analysis and presentation

Your application of statistics to qualitative data sets (categorical or naming data which have been sampled to encourage representativeness) and coding open-ended questions within an existing predesigned coding framework may well provide another perspective which could enhance traditional thematic analysis. Equally, displaying qualitative results graphically or in frequency tables can provide a concise snapshot of outcomes even though the results may not be 'statistically' generalisable to other settings. Also, teasing out the statistical results of a survey question by adding outcomes of related open-ended questions (properly investigated and analysed) can provide greater depth and enhanced comprehension of the complexity of the situation under investigation.

Another option is meta-analysis of the two forms of data sets which have been collected longitudinally, allowing the interrogation of each through the lens of the other by going backwards and forwards over time until the data start to coalesce into meaningful findings as key themes emerge. Secondary analysis of qualitative data can also be useful here.

Triangulation, concurrent usage or parallel methods

Here you would consider using multiple reference points where intact but separate data sets are collected concurrently. An example is to use dual sites with the same sampling approach but with different designs (one quantitative, one qualitative), then to use the synthesised results to build up a complex picture.

Research example

A triangulation approach can often be seen in multisite research. In an investigation of strategic scanning in organisations (Audet and d'Amboise, 2001) four organisations were selected for cross-case comparison along two polar dimensions: *performance of the firm* and *level of uncertainty in the firm's environment*. Two of the firms selected had high levels of uncertainty – one with a high and the other with a low performance level – and the remaining two had low levels of uncertainty and either a high or a low performance level. Data comprised semi-structured interviews in all sites with different levels of staff. Interview schedules comprised closed and open-ended questions relating to the variables which had been identified. Within-case analysis was followed by cross-case analysis of firms with similar performance levels.

Sequencing

You could undertake a qualitative study to explore a particular issue or phenomenon and you could create hypotheses from these results which you could test using a survey or an experimental design. Or, you could develop a short questionnaire survey to elicit key issues which can then be explored in depth using qualitative approaches of interviewing and observation. Synthesis of the two sets of results is needed to clarify the dual outcomes and to utilise the increased validity these two approaches provide.

You could also use the sequencing approach at a lower level within questionnaires to provide base data to enable movement into other data sets. For example, using both focused (limited response) quantitative and open-ended (qualitative) questions in a survey permits a more holistic view of the questions to be addressed and allows you to follow up responses:

Have you received any services from the government? Yes/No

If yes, could you name each service and provide a brief description of your experiences of this service.

These descriptions can then be fleshed out further in a follow-up face to face or telephone interview, the results of which can then be reincorporated in a more focused follow-up survey.

A typical sequencing design would involve:

1 representative survey of the population
2 exploratory qualitative interviews or focus groups to tease out the findings of the survey
3 hypotheses generated from stages 1 and 2 and tested by various interventions

4 participatory action research where the participants take control of the further development, implementation and evaluation of the most successful of these interventions.

Research examples of sequencing

An exploration of retail competition and consumer choice in Portsmouth (Clarke et al., 2004) used extensive quantitative surveys of shopping behaviour combined with qualitative interviews in a sequential approach to understand the variety of experiences of individual households with local retail provision and in particular the issue of consumer choice. Quantitative surveys were conducted with 2515 randomly sampled supermarket shoppers and a second postal survey question-naire went out to 2000 households of which 430 responded. Qualitative data comprised eight transcriptions of accompanied shopping trips (interview and observation) and eight transcriptions of kitchen visits to 10 participants in eight households in two different areas of Portsmouth.

Another example of a sequential approach can be seen in an examination of teachers' attitudes to educational change in England (Giannakaki, 2005). The study involved longitudinal data. Fifteen hundred teachers who teach adult literacy and numeracy were stratified across regions to represent different types of learning environments. Providers were to be followed over a three-year period from 2004 to 2007. Structured interviews for teachers (administered annually over three years) and closed questionnaires for senior managers (also adminis-tered annually) were combined with focus groups (for teachers and managers fol-lowing the collection of the quantitative data). In addition, semi-structured interviews were conducted to gauge their attitudes toward new policy initiatives, their personal experiences and their strategies for coping with change. This feed-back was then available on an annual basis over the three years and served to influence curriculum content, the development of learning materials and training programmes for teachers. Cluster analysis of the quantitative data allowed the identification of subgroups of teachers and managers whose characteristics were similar, such that a diverse mix of participants was able to be selected for group and individual interviews to provide cross-fertilisation of ideas. Classroom obser-vations of different instructional techniques also provided a way of identifying a more mixed group for further interviewing.

A further sequential study focusing on the potential contrast in student learn-ing between traditional classroom mode and distance education mode (Schoech and Helton, 2002) combined quantitative (pre-test and post-test comparative questionnaires) with qualitative and graphic techniques to address comparability issues and to identify which methods resulted in higher or lower student learning and satisfaction. The surveys indicated that students found the chatroom-based course more personal and more satisfying while the qualitative and graphic analysis of chatroom text helped to clarify why this was so, indicating through more detailed and probing questions that the focus on 'discussion' rather than on 'lecturing' was preferred and the anonymity of the chatroom encouraged shyer students to participate in a preferred non-verbal mode, although on the downside persistent technical problems appeared to impact negatively on learning.

Problems in attempting to combine data sets

The main danger is that the time consuming traditional methods of qualitative analysis may be bypassed or glossed over in favour of quicker but shallower approaches. This would lead to oversimplified results and to researcher directed rather than data derived results. Both the qualitative and quantitative data sets must be properly designed, collected and analysed. The quantitative data need to be systematic with clearly defined variables and a good sampling strategy to enable reliable predictions, while the qualitative data need clarification of process in terms of detailed and rich data properly collected and analysed with a theoretical interpretation which links closely to the data. When crossover techniques are used, transparency and justification are essential.

A further issue is that of equality in the weighting of the data. Is the study more qualitatively or more quantitatively focused, to the extent that the second approach operates more as an add-on or a minor data set? And is this important in the answering of the research question?

Questionnaires

In an attempt to ascertain the essential personal qualities of a computer educator, a three-phase sequential approach was used by Pieterse and Sonnekus (2003). First a survey questionnaire incorporated both quantitative and qualitative questions to build up a picture from a sample taken from one location. Then, during the second phase, the qualitative and quantitative results from the first phase were integrated to present a generic picture, and this was then presented to a national sample. In the third phase, quantitative and qualitative findings were integrated for an online questionnaire to an international sample of IT training groups, but with the additional option of a two-way e-mail contact. The researchers found that the difficulty in providing both qualitative and quantitative questions in the same survey, and in particular putting the closed questions earlier, was that the qualitative information did not appear to add very much in terms of new information, suggesting that the participants had become sensitised to the content and orientation of the earlier questions.

Design

Audet and d'Amboise (2001) found that although selecting cases on the basis of two dimensions seemed sound initially, in reality their dual-method questioning approach opened up unexpected information which really required another study to complete. They concluded that a simpler design with a focus on different performance levels only and omitting levels of uncertainty would have been easier to undertake and would have produced less complex findings.

Interpretation of results

Another issue is that of 'transformation' where the combining or homogenising of data requires a theoretical interpretation which includes both data sets when only one (qualitative) is usually treated in this manner – the quantitative set being viewed more as 'fact' reflecting 'reality' in the proving of a hypothesis. The tendency is for a low level conceptual interpretation to be undertaken.

Presentation of dual results

Separate data sets

Is it best to display each data set separately? The difficulties surrounding presentation of qualitative and quantitative approaches lie in their integration which leads to a very large results section with regular summaries, culminating in a final drawing together of the findings so that the reader can make sense of the diversity presented. An example of this is provided by Duncan and Edwards (1997) who interviewed 95 lone mothers in three countries (UK, USA and Sweden) and contextualised these within census data. The results are largely displayed in separate chapters (e.g. a chapter on social negotiation of understandings is followed by one on census data). This approach can leave the reader seesawing between the different data sets and integration may be difficult.

Combined data sets

In contrast to the separation of data sets, is it preferable to amalgamate the findings in such a way that a neat display of graphical information occurs, followed by a few carefully chosen qualitative quotes which serve to display the homogeneity (or diversity) of the data gathered? The use of matrices can serve to bring together variables, themes and cases, as can lists, network diagrams and graphical displays. Wajcman and Martin (2002) studied managers in six companies. A questionnaire was completed by a random sample of 470 managers together with interviews with 18–26 managers from each company. The data are presented equally: the quantitative survey results are displayed in an extensive single table, and the career narratives of 136 managers are divided into male and female responses and presented as substantial quotes and commentary. The totality of this approach may well be neater and more powerful in capturing the reader's attention through the different perspectives presented, but may also result in the complexity of the findings being 'dumbed down' and those findings which are not matched by the other data set somehow dropping off the radar screen.

Multiple data sets

Currently the majority of data collected are still within the survey/ interview/observation/document analysis framework in multiple data sets, with the documents traditionally being written communications. However, looking to the field of media images should alert us to what is being attempted there. Luciano Gamberini and Anna Spagnolli (2003) have brought together both qualitative and quantitative data sets under the heading of an exploration of human–computer interactions, looking at digital, physical, real and artificial aspects of this through three triangulated data sets. The first is the *split screen technique* which allows a synchronised visualisation of different environments on the same screen, in this case the real and the virtual environments in which a participant is involved. In this way individual interaction with a computer can be seen on one half of the screen while the other half details the depth view of what is actually happening in the screen as the individual interacts with the program. This process can be undertaken for one individual or multiple users by splitting the monitor into further blocks of two-screen displays. The second option is the *action indicator augmented display* which picks up the faster individual interactions with the computer interface, particularly quick hand movements on buttons, which are reflected in arrows at the bottom of the screen. The third is *the pentagram* which allows transcription of multiple sequences of events in its own timeline. Although these approaches can be used as tools to come to a single conclusion they can also serve to provide individual or multimedia displays in their own right, allowing the reader to observe all the data collected and come to their own conclusions. Qualitative discourse and interaction analysis are also used to analyse these human–computer interactions.

Summary

Mixed quantitative and qualitative data sets have the capacity to broaden and enrich research questions using styles of synthesis, triangulation and integration. Presentation can be via separate, combined or multiple data set display. The issue you need to be most careful about in combining methods is ensuring that your qualitative data have not been poorly designed, badly collected and shallowly analysed. Display techniques can now include the innovative technologies provided via computer and the internet.

FURTHER READING

Creswell, J., Fetters, M. and Ivankova, N. (2004) Designing a mixed methods study in primary care. *Annals of Family Medicine* 2: 7–12. This article evaluates five mixed methods studies in primary care and develops three models for designing such investigations. The authors recommend instrument building, triangulation, and data transformation models for mixed method designs.

De Vos, A. (ed.) (2000) *Research at Grass Roots: A Primer for the Caring Professions.* Pretoria: Van Schaik. The last section of this book deals with combining the basics of qualitative and quantitative perspectives.

Gorard, S. and Taylor, C. (2004) *Combining Methods in Educational and Social Research.* London: Open University Press. This book offers sound basic theorising and extensive practical illustrations of combined research methods. The combination of approaches encourages the development of diverse skills to combine different methods including complex interventions, triangulation, life histories and design studies.

Kelle, U. (2001) Sociological explanations between micro and macro and the integration of qualitative and quantitative methods. *Forum: Qualitative Social Research* 2 (1) February, http://www.qualitative-research.net/fqs-texte/1-01/1-01kelle-e.htm, accessed 1 May 2006. Kelle presents three versions of triangulation design: triangulation as mutual validation, triangulation as the integration of different perspectives on the investigated phenomenon, and triangulation in its original trigonometrical meaning.

Teddlie, C. and Tashakkori, A. (eds) (2003) *Handbook of Mixed Methods in Social and Behavioral Research.* Thousand Oaks, CA: Sage. This book covers issues and controversies, cultural issues, transformational and emancipatory research, research design, sampling and data collection strategies, analysing, writing and reading and their applications across such disciplines as organisational research, psychological research, the health sciences, sociology and nursing.

http://www.npi.ucla.edu/qualquant/, accessed 1 May 2006. This Qualitative Tools for Multimethod Research site was developed by members of the Division of Social Psychiatry at the University of California's Neuropsychiatric Institute. It includes an introduction which addresses the challenges for those who enter into qualitative inquiry. It also features extensive bibliographies.

16

Writing Up and Data Display

The display of your results is as important as consolidating the data into manageable forms. This chapter will demonstrate some of the older as well as the newer forms of display which are available for you to choose among.

Key points

- Your final writing up and display of data will be influenced by:
  - the audience to which the results are targeted
  - your position in your research study.

- Styles of display include:
  - graphic summaries
  - quotes
  - case studies
  - mixed methods (graphics and quotes)
  - interactive approaches
  - hyperlinks
  - vignettes
  - anecdotes
  - layers
  - pastiche
  - juxtaposition
  - parody and irony
  - fiction
  - poetry
  - narrative
  - drama
  - aural and visual displays.

- The type of research approach taken does not dictate or limit the form of data display, but if particular forms are preferred then the design and techniques of data collection need to reflect this so that you have adequate and appropriate data to work with.

Writing up

Your decisions regarding when to use which particular forms of writing up will depend largely on the following issues:

- the audience for whom you are writing
- the position you have taken as the researcher.

Audience

If you are writing for a particular research *journal* it is wise to familiarise yourself with the variety of styles which have appeared in issues over the past few years. If you are writing a *report for a government agency* then an executive summary of not more than four pages needs to include: the approach taken, the techniques employed, the analytical paths taken and a summary of results as well as recommendations for change where these are relevant. In other words, it should say what you have done, how you did this, what you found and what the authority needs to consider as a result of your findings.

If you are writing a *thesis* there is a general format which mirrors that of many journal articles:

Abstract

This is a summary of up to 200 words which should clearly identify your research question, how you undertook your study, what you found and the implications of this for the field.

Introduction

This is your opportunity to reveal (but only in a thesis) how you came to choose such a topic, your personal biases with regard to this topic (work/personal experiences or directions from previous research) and what the research journey has involved for you. For example, in my thesis on stay-at-home fathers I expected to find somewhat similar results to earlier researchers, which were that these men were prepared to stay in the home role with young children as a temporary measure for no more than two years, after which they would move fairly rapidly back into the workforce. I was quite surprised when I discovered that all the men in my group inhabited the role for at least five years and very few seemed in any hurry to rejoin the full-time workforce after this time, with most preferring to set up a part-time business to be run from home while they continued to contribute to the home role.

Literature review and theoretical/conceptual frames

A critical review of current literature (updated just prior to submission of the thesis) occurs here, allowing the researcher to identify, catalogue and even dismiss previous research in an effort to clear a space for his/her crucial (but previously missing) perspective on the field. Exposure of the theories and conceptual frames previously used by others as well as those that you as researcher plan to use, or think may be of relevance, should also occur here.

Study design/methods

What particular approach has been undertaken? Just naming one is not sufficient. Aspects which need to be discussed in this section include:

- Which approach was chosen or adapted? Why? And if adapted, how? And for what particular purpose? Did this adaptation work? What issues arose and had to be dealt with?
- Access to participants: how was this gained? What permissions were sought to tape? To video? To observe? To gain access to personal documents?
- What sampling approaches were used, and at what stage of the project? Why were these chosen? Were they effective?
- What ethical issues were addressed? And what ethics permissions were gained from which authorities?
- Were any political issues addressed?
- Were any agreements made with funding authorities or the major organisations which were accessed? If so, what was the outcome of such negotiations/agreements?
- Recording of information: how was this undertaken? How were data stored? And for how long will they be stored?
- What checks and balances were put in place to enhance design and data reliability?
- What forms of data analysis were undertaken?
- What forms of display were decided on, and why were these seen as the most appropriate?

Results

These are displayed in some appropriate or innovative manner depending on your position, that of the reader, and the extent to which you have decided to allow the participants to speak for themselves. The *discussion* section – which traditionally involves two things, a more abstract discussion of the results utilising the theoretical perspectives previously outlined or those generated by your data and the location of the findings within current literature – can often be intertwined within the results section (this is usual in grounded theory and in postmodern and poststructural research, where researcher interpretation is minimised in favour of reader interpretation) or it can be kept separate.

Conclusions and recommendations

The thesis ends with a final summary of findings, any recommendations and a brief discounting of the data – identifying its limitations (such as size of study, time available to do it etc.).

Researcher position

If the researcher has taken a more traditional position involving an authoritative researcher voice along the lines of 'I went', 'I saw', 'I found', then display will tend to be limited and will support conclusions already drawn. This display may well include thick ethnographic description (content, context and values) but the voices of participants are often limited to key quotes which illustrate the findings gained. This has been termed a 'realist' display (van Manen, 1988).

If the researcher has taken a subjective position, the 'I/eye' of his person will be heard/seen at some point in the text as he/she moves to upfront personal experiences or to address the audience directly before shifting offstage to enable the voices of participants to be heard. Author decentring allows the re-presentation of data in a range of formats from poetry to dramatic dialogue, fictionalised versions, polyphonic presentation and visual displays. The authoritative or subjective/decentred positions are two ends of a continuum along which a variety of mixes may occur.

Research approaches

Although some of the more established approaches such as grounded theory and classical ethnography have tended to use more conventional forms of data display (descriptive graphics, quotes and case studies) there are no rules which suggest that one form of display is more appropriate to any particular approach than another. The notion of a toolkit of possibilities with appropriate author justification is a better reflection of what is currently going on in the field, always bearing in mind the targeted audience. The type of data which are being collected should not limit the forms of display possible. For example an analysis of chatroom conversation could be displayed as any or all of the following: tables of ranked word frequencies and key words in context; individual case studies; illustrative quotes; a poetic form of one particular story; an author/participant voiced vignette; or a dramatic dialogue. The only limitations would lie in the lack of audio and visual data available to the researcher.

Despite this, in order to take, for example, a subjective approach which would require large chunks of personal data to be available for re-presentation, it would be necessary to design the study so that these data are collected either in the form of very detailed journal records or in the form of an autoethnography. Equally, if graphic displays are the preferred option then the data need to be more substantial than just a handful of people. If you have collected six in-depth case studies over time, constructed from a number of interviews, these data would be better used as a base for display using quotes, case histories, narratives, poetic form, pastiche, vignettes etc.

Display options

Graphic summaries

These include tables, bar graphs, pie charts, line graphs, matrices, hierarchical relationship indicators and flow charts. All of these provide a quick summary of considerable chunks of data, producing an overall snapshot which can then be

TABLE 16.1   *Example table showing percentages: 'Drugs discussed in the school program'*

Drug	% of schools ($n = 191$)
Tobacco	97
Alcohol	96
Marijuana	65
Analgesics (e.g. aspirin)	63
Prescribed drugs (e.g. sedatives)	59
Narcotics (e.g. heroin, morphine)	56
Stimulants (e.g. cocaine, amphetamines)	55
Inhalants (e.g. glue)	50
Hallucinogens (e.g. LSD)	49
Content not drug specific: general hazards	39

Source: Table 2.5 in Garrard et al. (1987: 25)

TABLE 16.2   *Example table showing interaction points: 'Patterns of association in downtown Jax'*

	Locals		Hippies			
	Men	Women	Men	Women	Children	Tourists
Grocery	•		•	•	•	•
Post office	•		•	•	•	
Café	•		•	•	•	•
Garage	•		•			•
Bar	•		•			•
Church	•	•				
School		•			•	
Laundry				•		•
Art centre		•				
Inn						•

Source: Figure 1 in Cavan (1974: 332), reprinted with permission

more fully explained and illustrated with other forms of qualitative display such as quotes or case studies.

Tables 16.1 and 16.2, and Figures 16.1, 16.2 and 16.3, show some examples.

Quotes

This is one of the most common approaches and usually involves the display of key quotes. For example, in the study on early career researchers, immediately under

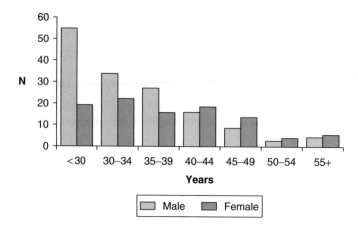

FIGURE 16.1 Example bar graph: 'Age of completion of PhD for a sample of male and female early career academic researchers' (Figure 4.1 in Bazeley et al., 1996: 99)

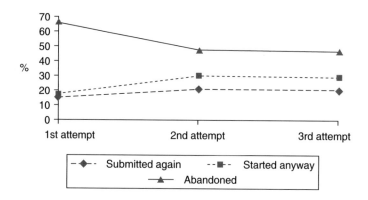

FIGURE 16.2 Example line graph: 'Changing pattern of response to successive funding failures, both internal and external' (Figure 3.1 in Bazeley et al., 1996: 81)

the heading 'Networking and becoming known' appears the quote from an interviewee:

> You can't afford to be introverted, in other words just stay in the four walls here, you have to get out there and particularly internationally. That would be the most important single key to success I believe ... it allows you to benchmark yourself. (Bazeley et al., 1996: 29)

And from a study on the experience of caring for a family member with terminal cancer, (Grbich et al., 2001) under the heading 'Positive emotions' come two

Minister knows the deceased

	Yes	**No**
Yes	**Cell A** Full- knowledge eulogy	**Cell B** Audience- knowledge eulogy
No	**Cell C** Particularised- knowledge eulogy	**Cell D** Depersonalised- knowledge eulogy

Minister knows the deceased's next-of-kin

FIGURE 16.3 Example matrix: 'An illustration of typology construction: types of eulogies' (Figure 11.5 in Minichiello et al., 1995: 267, reprinted with permission)

quotes. The first refers to the factor of time – the luxury of having time to say proper farewells – while the second refers to how one caregiver viewed herself in the caring process:

> You know this has been a gift, if you like, for us. The fact that he really now understands how much he is loved and how much people really think of him.

> I was like a duck – calm on top and paddling like mad underneath but he was so good. I couldn't sit down and show how I felt you know.

When more than one quote is displayed, the purpose is to demonstrate the variety in responses or to emphasise the concordance of a range of views on a particular issue. In both cases, the display acts as a starter for more detailed explanations or discussions.

Case studies

These tend to be either consolidated narratives in the voice of a participant; or author voiced summaries of typical or extreme situations or individual experiences; or, as in the following case study of a man excluded from the processes of decision making upon entry into a nursing home, a combination of author and participant voices.

Mr Barclay

Mr Barclay was 70 years old and had never married. A loner throughout his life, he drifted from one boarding house to another. He had few friends. Although he had two brothers and three sisters, he had not kept in touch with them 'for years'. He lost contact when his mother died twenty years ago. He said he feels close to no-one. For Mr Barclay, life after retirement was different from expectations. Without a job to go to, he no longer felt useful. With failing eyesight, he could not read the newspaper or watch television. Eye surgery was refused by his doctor unless Mr Barclay moved into a nursing home. Mr Barclay had never thought about living in a nursing home. In fact he held some very negative views about nursing homes:

> Some of them are like hovels. All they are interested in is taking old people's money. The government has closed some of them down because of abuses to patients, for ill treatment, neglect and all that ugly business. Well I was very wary of them.

Without consultation, the social worker announced the decision. Mr Barclay 'was not given a choice'. He was unhappy, had no knowledge of nursing homes, nor had he the opportunity to visit the home selected for him, prior to his admission.

> You just do not walk into places like this. You go to the doctor and he makes enquiries. It works just like going into a hospital. You just do not arrive at their doorsteps and say you want a bed. I did not choose to come here. They sent me here. If I had my way I'd still be living in a boarding house.

Source: Minichiello et al. (1990: 323–51), reprinted with permission

Mixed methods

Here survey results are presented in graphical forms and the findings are elaborated on through vignettes, quotes and case studies. An example is shown.

Interactive approaches

The introduction of techniques which can prompt an active response from the reader are only just starting to move into research from literature and films and can include feedback mechanisms – for example a questionnaire to gauge the reader's responses or experiences with regard to a particular display of data. The responses gained can become part of the ongoing collection and display of data from different phases in a research project. Another approach includes directions to the reader to go at a particular point in the text to a visual display – such as a video clip which has been supplied – or to a tape in order to listen to part of an interview of

---

Example of mixed methods: table and quotes

TABLE 16.3 *Satisfaction with the response of the police*

	Satisfied no.	%	Total answering
Time to attend	296	82.7	358
Details taken	429	88.1	487
Further action	305	64.2	475
Attitude towards the offence	397	81.5	487
Attitude towards the victim	424	87.8	483
Decide whether to proceed	121	78.1	155
Advise on preventing revictimisation	327	82.8	395
Information on available assistance	176	67.4	261

Although the majority were satisfied (64.2%) with further action taken by police, a quarter (24.4%) of victims were not satisfied. The main complaints were either 'nothing being done' (44.8%) or 'no feedback' (30.2%). Comments illustrating the latter view are as follows:

'Police said would follow it up and haven't,
would like to know what happened.' (assault victim)

'Don't know what's going on, not enough contact.
Expected them to get back.' (assault victim)

'Want to know what's gone on since then.'
(break and enter victim)

Source: Gardner (1990: 22), reprinted with permission

---

relevance to the conclusions being drawn. Paintings completed by researcher or researched can also be appended in hard copy or on CD to demonstrate emotions or experiences toward particular aspects of the research under study.

Another approach to prompting active reader interaction is the technique of leaving gaps in the narrative for the reader to fill from their own life experience or from common-sense expectations. Care needs to be taken here as this is difficult to do successfully and may just prompt reader frustration or at worst reviewer/examiner fury.

Hyperlinks

This involves the placing of raw data (interviews, observations and documents) at a hyperlinked point on the World Wide Web to allow the reader access to the complete transcript from which the quote has been drawn or the case study derived. The reader has now moved light years from the position where they are told what to think by the authoritative researcher. Processes of interpretation and representation thus become transparent. Hyperlinks can also be used to promote a multimedia experience (videos, photos, film clips, scanned documents, audio and digital media), allowing the reader to move from site to site and from textual to visual images. Aspects of design, analysis and ethics can become issues: for example when the borders between writing up and analysis become blurred, when issues of writing for a particular audience dominate, or when the ethics of displaying data to a broad audience where participants can never be anonymous is in question (Coffey et al., 2005; Dicks et al., 2005).

Vignettes

A vignette is like a photo with blurred edges, and it provides an example or small illustrative story which can clarify a particular point or perspective regarding some finding in the data. Vignettes can be author or participant voiced and tend to be formed either from compressed data or from consolidation of different data sources. Laud Humphreys's (1975) book on impersonal sex in public places has an initial scene setting vignette derived from his observation of these settings:

> At shortly after five o'clock on a weekday evening, four men enter a public restroom in a city park. One wears a well tailored business suit; another wears tennis shoes, shorts and teeshirt; the third man is still clad in the khaki uniform of his filling station; the last, a salesman, has loosened his tie and left his sports coat in the car. What has caused these men to leave the company of other homeward-bound commuters on the freeway? What common interest brings these men, with their divergent backgrounds, to this public facility?
>
> They have come here not for the obvious reason, but in a search for 'instant sex'. Many men – married and unmarried, those with heterosexual identities and those whose self-image is a homosexual one – seek such impersonal sex, shunning involvement, seeking kicks without commitment. (Copyright ©1975 by Aldine Publishers. Reprinted by permission of Aldine Transactions, a division of Transaction Publishers)

Susan Bell and Roberta Apfel (1995) have consolidated different sets of their data into three substantial vignettes to display very different participant voiced perspectives on the topic of women's experience of DES (diethylstilbestrol) related cancer which is triggered by a drug given to pregnant women in the 1950s to prevent miscarriage and which predisposed their female children to cervical cancer. The first vignette is a summarised transcript of a conference presentation given by a feminist health activist of the process of teaching women vaginal self-examination as part of an empowerment process. The second vignette likewise is a summary of an oncologist's conference presentation involving displaying a DES infected vagina to his medical colleagues. The third vignette is in the voice of a woman who has experienced

DES related cancer and who is sharing her experiences and clarifying the impact of this cancer on her sexual relationship. This last presentation is in poetic form and is derived from interview transcripts.

Anecdotes

An anecdote is a subjective story which is often used as a reflective tool to show a particular event in the data collection. Van Manen (1999: 20) has indicated that an anecdote is a very short and simple story usually relating to one incident which is close to the central idea of the research question. It includes important concrete detail, often contains several quotes, requires a punch line and closes quickly after the climax. In the following case, the anecdote illustrates the impact of one particular event on the prevailing view of the researcher:

> I had surveyed the literature on caregivers of family members/friends with a terminal illness and everything pointed to the 'burden' of care and its negative impact on carers' health and well-being. My first foray into data collection involved a focus group with a bereavement class almost a year after the death of their loved one. Much of the discussion did centre around issues of burden until one man said 'It was an absolute privilege to care for her and I am so pleased that I had the opportunity and that I was able to do it well.' This opened my eyes to other possibilities and we were ultimately able to gather sufficient data to challenge the 'burden of care' literature with a more positive perspective. (Grbich, diary record, 2001)

Layers

Presenting data in layers can help the reader to see more easily what you have sighted. These layers may involve the deliberate interweaving of different voices to juxtapose their views, for example sequential narratives on how an accident happened or how a marriage was broken or what was seen by whom in a particular incident or event. The following example comes from separate interviews with partners who had decided to reverse primary caregiving roles for their young children. The question asked was: *How did you come to change roles?*

> *Joe:* It springs from a desire to integrate more fully the different facets of my life – of our lives – a concept of the union of your personal and political lives. One of the things we have found is that if your work life does not reinforce your personal life and doesn't reinforce your interests, everything goes in a different direction. Your work life dominates and takes up too much time in your life thus leaving less time for your relationships, less time for other people, less time for the things you want to do, less time for yourself, less time for your family so everything goes against each other. We both had extremely high powered demanding jobs, our relationship was suffering and at that stage we had one child. We had both made the decision to leave work before we knew the second child was on the way.

215

> *Mary:* Well we started off with me staying home with the first child and him working and I found that very difficult to cope with because I'd been a very independent person with my own career and I really got stuck being at home and I had so many other things I wanted to do which I had tried to squeeze in at the same time. I was only on maternity leave, it was always intended that I would go back to work. So I stayed home for 10 months then I went back to work. Various people helped look after our child – that worked it made me feel as though I was getting back into life again. When I was at home I had the feeling that Joe was out doing all the vital and vibrant things and I was bogged down with the nappies and it made me feel awful, I just didn't cope with it at all. At least when we were both working it was equal; we both had exciting things to talk about. The more I stayed home the less he talked to me about his work. (Grbich, 1997)

Mary continues mirroring Joe's comments about the problems of both working and, although she agrees that both had decided to give up work and rear their children together, a preference for her workforce role sent her back to work as soon as their second child was born.

In these extracts it is clear that Jo rationalises the decision for both of them from an ideological perspective while Mary is clearly unhappy in the home situation and decides to stay in the workforce, leaving Jo with the home role.

In another version of layering, Mary's transcript could be displayed and different fonts used to tease out the different positions she takes. For example her dislike for the limitations of the home role could be highlighted one way, perhaps by using a different font, while her statements about the problems of family relationships when partners have high pressure jobs could be highlighted in another way to juxtapose two opposing views.

Pastiche

This more complicated version of layering involves 'quilting' or the display of many voices centring on a particular issue. A collage of fragments is presented which together help to build a more complete picture.

The example shows a pastiche of a number of comments which have been drawn from various interviews and from the researcher's own journal in order to build up a snapshot of the views of the family and friends of 'Tony' – a long term father at home caring for a young child. Tony's own voice is juxtaposed with these comments, and a separate collage of his views over the years he was in the role could also have been developed and displayed to show changes over time.

The use of different sized fonts and spacings, as well as emboldened information that you want to highlight, help focus the presentation of such information.

Juxtaposition

The placing of one set of information against another in an echoing manner in order to bring out the differences can be seen in the beginning of David Boje's

Responses by and to 'Tony' a home based father (Grbich, 2004)

Sue (wife)

I do think I missed out on a lot of the baby stuff. I still remember driving off the first day – he was standing at the front door with this little baby and I was feeling absolutely terrible and thinking 'how could I ever let this happen'... But because we're very different personalities I think Jane has gained immensely – in that he's much more willing to spend a lot of time with her – those things I'm not very good at doing, so she's got a lot more contact than if I'd stayed home. I think I probably would have come to the decision of going back to work ...

Sue's mother (Sue's report)

My mother never really encouraged us to be at home mothers, she wanted us to be professional women ... I think she was pleased that I was going to continue on with my career.

Tony's view of mothers at home

If you get talking to women at home at any length you often find that they hate it and they themselves wonder why anyone else would want to do it.

Female friends (to Sue)

Isn't he wonderful, I'd really like to have that opportunity.
How could you do it? How could you go back to work when she's so young?

Tony's parents (to Tony)

Mother. I think it's a great idea, but no doubt when Jane gets sick of working you'll go back to work. If you're not prepared to support your wife and child, I'll disown you. I have a brother-in-law who never worked from the day he got married, she (her sister) worked, and none of us thought much of him because of that.

Father. You don't mean you're going to go on and do this forever? You may find that when you want to go back to the workforce, you can't.

Women in community playgroup (to Tony)

Aren't you marvellous!

Tony

'It's the most demanding job I've ever had; isolated, unstructured. People tend to downplay it but after I've talked to them they realise there's a lot more to it than they thought. But being a man who feels a naturalness in that sort of role, you can be made to feel emasculated. From some men there's the attitude that I'm doing a female, lesser role.

Tony's parents to the researcher

Mother. Well our reactions were commonsense, that one or both or each of them were going to earn money. Sue was going to earn a lot more than Tony. Tony had the sort of temperament that I believe was capable of being a father. I think he was soft, he was quite – not quiet, he was softly spoken – he was intelligent and he had a deep love for that kid ... But I do wonder getting right back to the primitive thing of it – is it a natural thing – isn't it more of the woman having the nesting instinct, deep down – if she doesn't do it she is missing out. Aren't they going against the nature of things? A woman is a woman, that's their function – motherhood, and nothing, no matter what they do can take that away and if it's undeveloped, she's not much of a mother, if it is developed it's most rewarding. Although there's no doubt about it you get tired of being in the house all the time, you can't live for housework.

Male friends (to Tony)

How's the holiday? Getting lots of golf?

Parking attendant's response (to Tony)

At least I've got a job!

Tony's view of Sue

She feels she couldn't do this job at home, that she'd get too angry ... but she's also very sensitive to me being overwhelmed by it.

Researcher's journal

Tony moved into the father at home role at the age of 39. His most recent work force position was that of a real estate valuer – a job he didn't enjoy. When Tony and Sue had been married for some years, it became apparent they were unlikely to have children so Sue had decided to pursue medical qualifications and gain a career in medicine. At the end of her studies she became pregnant. It was decided that as Tony didn't like working and Sue had just spent a lot of time becoming a doctor (a job she liked), Tony would stay at home long term and Sue would share the early morning and evening childcare tasks.

Popular Mechanics Spectacle   **Nickerson Festival**

The noise of the city at day-break mixes with the sounds of the locking and loading of Heckler and Koch MP5 submachine guns and the slamming of double banana-clip magazines into CAR-15 assault rifles as nearly 60 cops mill about a rooftop in Los Angeles. They are preparing for urban combat. Lt. Tom Runyen, commander of the Los Angeles Police Department Special Weapons and Tactics (LAPD SWAT) platoon, walks confidently amid his men. Wearing grayish-blue fatigues, black Kevlar vests and Fritz helmets, they fill their Benelli automatic 12-gauge shotguns with 00-buckshot magnum shells, pack hand-toss flash-bang devices into the pouches of their body armor and recheck voice-activated helmet radios.

The noise of the community after school mixes with the sounds of size 24 clown shoes thumping and slamming on the sidewalk and the joyous chatter of Nickerson Gardens mothers, kids, and students from Loyola Marymount University as the festive parade of nearly 60 people wind their way through the streets and backyards of the gardens. Professor Boje, clown-professor of the College of Business and consultant to the Nickerson Gardens Resident Management Corporation (NGRMC) walks confidently amid his children. Wearing blue hair, red and white checkered jacket and a red clown's nose, he has filled his pockets with lolly pops, bubble gum, and a squirt gun disguised as a lapel flower. He does hand-tosses of the candies from his clown shorts pockets...

Source: Boje (2000), reprinted with permission

(2000) article. Here Boje uses the imagery of the 'tympan' – juxtaposition of texts in order to strike the ear 'obliquely ' from two perspectives with new ideas.

He presents two distinctly different views of the community of Nickerson Gardens. One is from *Popular Mechanics* by Samuel Katz (1997) called 'Felon Busters: when the cops are outgunned, LAPD SWAT breaks up the party' which sees Nickerson Gardens as a dangerous and drug ridden community inhabited by criminals. This is contrasted with a view drawn from David Boje's nine years of data collection in this community representing it as a strong cohesive group. The reader is instructed to move the cursor between the two texts and to read them in any way they prefer.

Parody and irony

Parody involves the mimicking of the work/roles of others for a particular effect, while irony can convey a meaning opposite to that to which the words actually refer. This technique has often been used to clarify what has been privileged and what has been marginalised in society. In written texts and films, male–female relations (typically portrayed as between couples of similar ages) are juxtaposed contrasted with young males (teenagers) in love with women who are octogenarian (Eco, 1993). In research, one example might be an article on men who stay home written in the heroic tradition with day to day father–child routines being presented as though they were major battles involving life threatening situations.

Fiction

The 'fictionalising' of qualitative data does not mean glancing at the data and then going off on a tangent which is only vaguely related. It generally means turning carefully collated data into a fictional form, as Caroline Ellis (1995) has done in her 'ethnographic short story' where she documents a subjective account of a meeting with a former colleague who was dying of AIDS.

Steven Banks (2000) has created what he terms a 'weak form of fiction' or 'accidental fiction' – a fictional story loosely based on the pseudo 'joyful' annual summer holiday letters which eventuate each year from holidaymakers, here constructed through the central character and 'writer' of these letters, a fictional wife and mother Ginny Balfour. In addition, Banks constructs and displays five of these letters, written over a period of six years, in order to share his understanding of the structural properties of such letters, their display of human struggles and values, and to create emotional responses in the reader.

Poetry

Gaining the essence of what is said in interview and maintaining the rhythm, tone and diction, pauses and repetition used by the interviewee is regarded as essential in turning transcripts into poetic form. These factors help to give the proper flavour of what might be a condensed form of many hours of interview. For example, from the following short interview two poems could be started:

> My primary concern in the role is looking after Jane and attempting to relate to her, and the rest is in my view quite an adjunct. I don't see this as having anything to do with housework, I object to the term 'housewife'. I came into it fairly worried because I figure that no-one is taught how to be a parent, we just don't do anything about that.
>
> Six weeks after the birth came, she [Sue, wife] drove off and it was just terrifying and I thought 'My god, what am I going to do when she [Jane, daughter] wakes up!' I think I managed to struggle on for the first few weeks. (Grbich, 1987)

Poetic form 1
> I came into it fairly worried
> No-one is taught how to be a parent
> It was just terrifying
> I think I managed to struggle along for the first few weeks

Poetic form 2
> My primary concern is looking after Jane
> The rest is quite an adjunct
> I object to the term 'housewife'

The orientation chosen will depend on whether the major focus of the poem is to be the experience of early stage caring or the father's view of the role.

Narrative

Moving beyond the editing of transcript data, the narrative poem often has the elements of a short story, with location, characters and situation around which the poem moves. It can be broadly 'fictional' (loosely based on data), factual, subjective or historical. The narrative as a story (with a beginning, a middle and an end) can be either participant or researcher voiced or can allow the 'I/eye' of the researcher to move in and out of the story, permitting other voices to speak in their own right and providing the reader with access to all players.

Margery Wolf (1992) has taken a set of data and presented different aspects in three juxtaposed narratives. The original data were collected 30 years previously and centred on an incident in a Taiwanese village where a woman appeared either to be experiencing madness or to have become a conduit for spiritual voices (a position of considerably higher status than the former). One narrative is taken from Wolf's own research journals, a confessional tale of heat, dust, precise observations minutely recorded but interspersed with frustration, ambiguity and the problems of interpreting the event under observation through barriers of language and culture.

The second story is constructed from the field notes of the Chinese research assistant and provides different cultural insights, while the third story is the authoritative author voiced article written about the event for an anthropological journal.

Drama

Dramatic performances of data can be seen in Caroline Ellis and Art Bochner's (1992) dialogue (gained from their own diary records) on this couple's separate experiences of Caroline's pregnancy and her abortion. Each speaker faces the audience, then turns his/her back so the other can speak without the expressions on their partner's face being visible.

In another mode, confrontational theatre performances based in research have been used for some time to bring about emotional catharsis in the audience. As we saw in Chapter 4 (p. 64), a dramatic performance of a beach party scene of a sole woman drinking and an attempted rape can provide potentially an emancipatory performance can be. These dramatic performances emancipatory in focus for both those who may have participated in heavy drinking as well as those who have had a professional role in dealing with this problem. The presence of counsellors and the addition of forums following the performance allow further interactions and discussions to occur.

Aural and visual displays

The inclusion of audiotapes and video clips can enhance the reader's understanding of a particular issue, story or experience.

The display of static visual data, be it from photographs or videos, can easily be incorporated into the paper-based text. However, additional CDs of synchronised audio tracked visual data can be presented as moving images as a two-way split screen, as a four-way split screen, as an action indicator augmented display (with graphical monitoring system visualised in a corner of the monitor and activated by participants' actions) or as a pentagram where multiple sequences of events are represented (Gamberini and Spagnolli, 2003).

Summary

Although the final writing up and display of data will be influenced both by the audience for which you are writing and by your own position, there are no hard and fast rules as to which particular form of data display should be attached to any given research approach. However if particular styles are preferred then it is wise to work out early whether the design you have developed will provide the kind of data that you can utilise for your favoured forms of display.

FURTHER READING

Coffey, A., Holbrook, B. and Atkinson, P. (1996) Qualitative data analysis: technologies and representations. *Sociological Research Online* 1(1), http://www.socresonline.org.uk/socresonline/1/1/4.html, accessed 1 May 2006. Traditional ethnographic presentation is the focus here, together with an exploration of the impact of computer assisted data and hypertext software.

Dicks, B., Mason, B., Coffey, A. and Atkinson, P. (2005) *Qualitative Research and Hypermedia: Ethnography for the Digital Age.* Thousand Oaks, CA: Sage. Explores the impact of digital technologies on qualitative research (the internet, e-mail, hypermedia etc.) and shows how this is reshaping how we research. The theoretical implications of writing and researching for the electronic screen are also discussed.

Ellis, C. and Bochner, A. (eds) (1996) *Composing Ethnography: Alternative Forms of Qualitative Writing.* Newbury Park, CA: Sage. Lots of good examples of innovative ways of displaying the newer forms of ethnography.

Ely, M., Vinz, R., Anzul, M. and Downing, M. (1997) *On Writing Qualitative Research: Living by Words.* Bristol, PA: Falmer. This very accessible and extremely practical book gives the reader a comprehensive, detailed and current overview of how to go about transforming collected words into qualitative research displays, covering the whole process of qualitative research writing from initial idea to final publication as well as how to create such forms as narrative turns, metaphors, drama and poetry. The examples in each chapter are drawn from many fields including sociology, psychology and education.

Wolcott, H. (1990) *Writing Up Qualitative Research*, 2nd edn. Newbury Park, CA: Sage. Lots of examples, reader friendly, with practical tips. Wolcott offers alternatives for handling questions of theory and method, how to proceed with the mechanics of preparing a manuscript from the table of contents to the index, and how to get published.

Wolf, Margery (1992) *A Thrice-Told Tale: Feminism, Postmodernism, and Ethnographic Responsibility.* Stanford, CA: Stanford University Press. An excellent and easy-to-read example of two pieces of data presented in three ways: the researcher's diary record, the research assistant's notes and an anthropological journal article derived from the two previous sources.

Part Five

Qualitative Computing Programs

This last part presents a brief overview of some of the many qualitative computing packages on the market. Computer packages for the management of qualitative data have been available in one form or another for the past 30 years. These have been of considerable help in organising and coding larger databases. However there are both advantages and disadvantages in utilising such packages and it is wise to be familiar with these before you assume this approach will be essential for your study.

This part will list some of the packages currently available while also critically assessing the impact of such tools on your data.

17

An Overview of Qualitative Computer Programs

This chapter will detail a brief history of the development of qualitative computing packages and will list a variety of currently available programs and their capacities while also providing a critical assessment of the impact of such packages on the qualitative analytical process.

Key Points

- Qualitative computing packages comprise three types:
    - those for coding and retrieving
    - those with a focus on theory generation
    - those for content analyses.
- These programs provide useful tools but you need to be aware of their pitfalls and limitations.

A brief history

Computing packages have undergone three distinct developmental eras since their emergence around 30 years ago:

- systematisation
- theory generation
- analysis of content.

Systematisation

The notion of systematic data emerged in the 1970s following an earlier push for more rigorous data which included moves toward quantification and justification of findings. The major focus of these earlier programs was the storage and retrieval of data and the provision of subviews of the data through the assigning of codes and categories (often termed 'code and retrieve' programs). Systematisation programs are usually single file systems and require the marking of text segments and the attaching of codes to segmented data (either on or off screen). This process tends to follow both preliminary and thematic data analysis which occurs off screen. The coded passages are then filed and stored with identification tags and sometimes memos are attached. These files can then be retrieved and printed out for further examination and consolidation. One of the more popular programs with researchers within this group is Ethnograph.

Theory generation

During the 1980s researchers at qualitative computing conferences recognised the benefits of the first generation of programs but pointed out their limitations, particularly the inability to address issues of 'validity', 'reliability' and 'generalisability' which some researchers still regarded as problematic. Another perceived limitation was the incapacity to facilitate combinations of qualitative and quantitative data and the lack of any capacity to undertake theory generation. These debates resulted in the development of a second generation of programs. These 'theory generation' programs comprise a two-file system (data and literature) and are often underpinned by the structural framework of grounded theory (in particular the constant comparative process which the researcher can operate between the two files). Relationships among coded categories in different folders within one file can be sought using the Boolean logic of 'and', 'or' and 'not' and conceptual and theoretical explanations for these can be sought in the other file. These processes can lead to hypothesis testing and the development of theoretical concepts. NUD*IST, NVivo and ATLAS.ti have been popular programs within this tradition.

The development of these more sophisticated programs prompted further discussion regarding the methodological and theoretical implications of the use of computers to manage qualitative data (Fielding and Lee, 1991). Initial concerns expressed included the possible impact on the 'craft' of qualitative research and the moves toward 'control' rather than 'diagnosis' and toward 'explanation' rather than 'interpretation' (Lyman, 1984: 86–7). The potential for minimising the gap between variable oriented (quantitative) and case oriented (qualitative) researchers was also noted with concern, as was the potential for method to define substance (Friedheim, 1984). Another concern was that computer managed data would encourage 'quick and dirty' research or research that is over-interpreted through the abuse of complex indexing systems (Fielding and Lee, 1991: 7–8).

Content analysis

These packages are useful tools for breaking into text. Most have the capacity to undertake *word frequencies* which can display how often each word occurs in a document; *category frequencies* where synonyms are grouped into categories and the program shows how many times each category occurs in the document; *key word in context* (KWIC) which displays, in alphabetical order, each word together with a number of words on either side to provide information on its context in the document; *cluster analysis* where groups of words can be identified as being utilised in similar contexts; and *co-occurrence of pairs* of words. The more sophisticated of these programs are developing the capacity to attempt semiotic analysis and often include cultural grammars.

Qualitative computing software

A brief summary of some of the many programs currently available is provided together with an address where further up-to-date information can be accessed.

Code and retrieve programs

CDC EZ–TEXT (PC) handles interview data and notes, allows database searches and can import and export data and codes. Further information at http://www.cdc.gov/hiv/software/ez-text.htm (accessed 1 May 2006).

Ethno 2 helps analyse sequential events. It can produce a hierarchical diagram showing the concrete links among events and illustrates how people, things and actions are linked by the events. Further information at http://www.indiana.edu/~socpsy/ESA/ (accessed 1 May 2006).

Ethnograph 5 (PC) is the most well developed of the cheaper code and retrieve programs. It can create and import data files, format the file and automatically save it as an 'ETH' file, import and number the file, and assign it to a project with no limit on the number of data files. It can also rename, move, merge, duplicate, delete or back up projects as desired. Further information at http://www.qualisresearch.com/ (accessed 1 May 2006).

SuperHyperQual (PC, Mac) handles structured and unstructured interviews, observations, documents and research memos. It can undertake manual, semi-automatic and automatic text tagging (coding) as well as flexible retagging of text chunks, editing of tag lists, management of multiple windows and the maintenance of a bibliographic database for literature reviews. Further information at http://home.satx.rr.com/hyperqual/ (accessed 1 May 2006).

Martin (PC) was developed for phenomenological data and operates as a basic filing system where documents and interviews, with memos attached, can be stored in files and then opened for further perusal. A graphics user interface is available for the display of a variety of texts simultaneously. Further information at http://homepages.vub.ac.be/~ncarpent/soft/soft_softsites.html (accessed 1 May 2006).

Theory generation programs

AQUAD 6 (PC) undertakes content analysis, and videos, audio recordings (including MPG) and pictures (JPG) can be coded directly on the screen.

Automatic coding from a master list, unlimited memos, three levels of criteria available for analysis, hypothesis testing and Boolean searching occur. More information at http://www.aquad.de/eng/index.html (accessed 1 May 2006).

ATLAS.ti 5 (PC) has an object oriented graphical user interface for processing of textual, graphical, audio and video data, on-screen coding (drag and drop), no fixed definition of data segments, simultaneous display of data segments in context, codes and memos, and virtually unlimited numbers of documents, segments, codes and memos. It integrates all relevant material – primary texts, codes, annotations and theories – into separate files. It also facilitates 'mind mapping' and graphical network editing, semi-automatic coding with multistring text search and pattern matching, theory building, hypertext links, Boolean logic, hypotheses, and end-on SPSS and networking. Further information at http://www.atlasti.com (accessed 1 May 2006).

Folio Views R (Mac, PC) is used for browsing and editing graphic, sound and video objects. Supports memo writing, hypertext linking of text segments and some theory building. Further information at http://www.thefiengroup.com/np-views.html (accessed 1 May 2006).

HyperRESEARCH 2.6 (Mac, PC) has advanced multimedia capabilities for text, graphic, audio and video data. Further information at http://www.researchware.com/ (accessed 1 May 2006).

MAXqda2 (PC) is the successor of the software package winMAX. It has a theory testing and theory generating capacity, is user friendly, can cope with large volumes of data and is stable and fast. It links to SPSS and content analysis packages as well as to MS Office and MS Internet Explorer. Further information at http://www.maxqda.com (accessed 1 May 2006).

NUD*IST N6 (Mac, PC) is a heavy duty program for large scale projects, allowing the import and export of data to and from statistical packages. It allows rapid coding, pattern seeking and hypothesis testing. Further information at http://www.qsr.com.au/ (accessed 1 May 2006).

NVivo 7 (Mac, PC), as yet not fully user tested, is designed for multimedia data and allows researchers to import and export data to and from statistical packages and to merge projects. It facilitates rich text, analysis, flexible interpretations, memos, development of matrices, modelling and framing. Early indications are that it is slow and doesn't cope with large data bases. Further information at http://www.qsr.com.au/ (accessed 1 May 2006).

Content analysis programs

askSam 6 TM imports word processing documents, e-mail, spreadsheets, web pages, PDF files. Sets up fields for key words, categories, subjects, dates etc. Undertakes wildcard, fuzzy and proximity searches. Further information at http://www.asksam.com/solutions/research.asp (accessed 1 May 2006).

PCAD 2000 (PC) undertakes Boolean and proximity searches, development of a dictionary tree, and key word frequency pages in and out of context. An unknown words finder allows quick identification of misspelled words, acronyms, technical words and proper nouns. Cluster analyses and proximity searches are available for two key words. Further information at http://www.gb-software.com/ (accessed 1 May 2006).

QDA Miner (PC) documents are stored and edited in rich text format. Cases can contain up to 2030 variables including multiple documents, numeric, nominal/ordinal, data and Boolean values. File importation can occur from Excel, Access, Paradox, dBase. Drag and drop assignment of codes with memos, some automatic coding and coding by variable can occur. An inter-coder agreement tool exists, and the WordStat program for data mining and SimStat for statistical analysis are both attached. It is available in English, French and Spanish with multi-user and merge features. Further information at http://www.provalisresearch.com/QDAMiner/QDAMinerDesc.html (accessed 1 May 2006).

TEXTPACK (PC) undertakes word frequencies, key word in context and key word out of context, cross-references and concordances, and word comparison of two texts. Further information at http://www.social-science-gesis.de/en/software/textpack/index.htm (accessed 1 May 2006).

WordCruncher for Windows (PC) multiple texts can be indexed up to 10 levels which can be either hierarchical (play, act, scene, line etc.) or non-hierarchical (speakers, themes etc.). Searches consist of words, phrases or multiple word searching using Boolean logic. An image library manager allows for the inclusion of graphics, and image maps with hyperlinks to other images can be created. Hyperlinks can also be created between graphics and text and for cross-referencing texts. Bookmarks and user notes allow for annotation. More information at http://users.ox.ac.uk/~ctitext2/resguide/resources/w125.html (accessed 1 May 2006).

WordStat 5.1 (PC) has Boolean and proximity searches, dictionary trees, options and frequencies, an unknown word finder and cluster analysis capacity. The document conversion wizard can extract text from PDF files. Further information at http://www.provalisresearch.com/wordstat/wordstat.html (accessed 1 May 2006).

ZyIndex (PC) provides a research tool for complete recall, appropriate in situations where any missing data could be catastrophic. Fast indexing of over 250 file formats, including HTML, PDF, Word, Excel, PowerPoint and Outlook, can occur. It integrates with ZyScan to make scanned documents searchable. Translated products for English, German, French, Dutch, Spanish, Italian, Danish, Swedish, Norwegian, Finnish, Portuguese, Turkish, Greek, Cyrillic and Arabic exist. More information at http://www.searchtools.com/tools/zyindex.html (accessed 1 May 2006).

Qualitative computing packages: continuing concerns

Despite their obvious usefulness in the management of large databases, the concerns which emerged in the 1980s regarding these packages have persisted. The following is a summary of the major issues.

The framing tools of computer programs

Interpretation which is undertaken by researchers without computing assistance utilises four complex interconnecting and overlapping framing processes: intertextual, extratextual, intratextual and circumtextual (McLachlan and Reid, 1994: 3–4). In non-computer managed research these are continually changing processes which occur from the initial stages of data collection to the final stages of data presentation. In placing a database into a computer package and separating it into program specific coded portions, these fluid and overlapping processes are necessarily truncated, omitted or made invisible by the specific requirements of data segmentation and the structured coding, categorising, relinking and reinterpreting performances required by the computer program.

Tools constructed for a particular program must inevitably impact upon the data. Technologies carry with them symbolic meanings and divisions of labour (Pfaffenberger, 1988: 11–24). They texture our ways of thinking, reading and writing (Idhe, 1990: 141–3, 182–3). In creating computer tools for the management of data, we cannot avoid shaping both the outcomes of our data interpretation and our perceptions of the outcomes. Each tool creates artifacts and metaphors (frames) which are not neutral in effect and which change our ways of thinking and seeing. 'Reality' has to be segmented, truncated and textured to prepare data to 'fit' a particular form of programming. These procedural aspects are fundamentally reductionist and affect our views of the data as they move from a complex, multifaceted reality of intersecting aspects embedded in rich contexts to a simplified, rational, decontextualised version which can be viewed as discrete groups of representations and subrepresentations.

These processes also promote procedural thinking (Rozak, 1994: 190) and high frequency logic, and have the capacity to enhance the distortion of time. The speed at which one can interact with data, atomising them and shifting them around, far exceeds the speed at which they were collected or at which they would be contemplated in a reflexive framing process off screen. Although speed and a capacity for logic may be advantageous in coping with computer technology, these may well foster superficial interpretations of qualitative data. The tendencies for decontextualisation and spurious theoretical conclusion abound (Laurie, 1992; Seidel, 1991).

The framing of knowledge

In the framing of knowledge, frames can be seen as storage systems bounding areas, while the framing process is seen as formal and restrictive or as active, dynamic and ongoing with flexible frame boundaries. Two of the theory generating programs, NUD*IST and ATLAS.ti, reflect these possibilities. The inverted tree framing structure of NUD*IST is very formal, bearing a close relationship with Metzing's (1980) cognitive frames for knowledge. Here, networks of 'nodes and relations' hang off a defined aspect or category. Adaptation of nodes and replacement of frames are part of the continuing process of gaining new knowledge through processes of matching and accommodation. More flexible and in a non-hierarchical fashion, ATLAS.ti uses a horizontal rhizomatic frame, the boundaries of which are constantly evolving. Despite this dynamic potential, one major limitation of any framing structure is its potential to gain a reified status, creating in the researcher a preference to confine and order rather than to allow for constant transformation and change. The sequential and procedural approaches which are intrinsic to individual programs must inevitably structure thought processes and texture the data in particular ways.

The act of enclosure within framing processes confines the data at an early stage within coded segments. Enclosure also serves to separate out the data from both the researcher and the context. Discovery then tends to be linear rather than chaotic and complex. It seems inevitable that these procedures must texture and simplify what we see, limiting the potential for change and transformation of both researcher and data in the research process (Grbich, 1998).

The texturing of reality

Currently, the programming languages which have been used as a basis for qualitative computing packages are either the very basic first- and second-generation languages with mechanical functions, or the third- to fifth-generation languages incorporating Boolean logic and true–false dichotomies. True–false dichotomies are based on the Boolean concept of minimisation that 'corresponds to the variable oriented experimental design' (Huber and Garcia, 1993: 145) in which single cases are compared. These rigorous mathematical approaches differentiate 'subjectivity' and foster the appearance of 'objectivity' (Guattari, 1984) through diagnosis and control. Units of data are treated as inert objects or 'input' (Murphy and Pardeck, 1988), further reinforcing the abstract model of segmentation, categorisation, comparison and relinking of data. Further, the rule-based approaches of computer programming have much in common with positivism. Views of reality are 'formal, discrete, reductionist, algorithmic, sequential, deterministic, mechanical, computational, atomised, digitalised, logical and rational' (Henman, 1992: 1). A close examination of qualitative computing packages supports this view. The separation of parts from the whole is a positivist rather than a qualitative approach.

The representations of 'reality' that are produced are based primarily on discrete objects, although fuzzy logic (where variables are less precise and can overlap) has been used in AQUAD (a program developed by a psychologist to access implicit theories of an individual's view of self). Fuzzy logic allows movement from the narrow true–false dichotomy based in probability to the wider 'possibility' of truth (Zadeh, 1988), but this possibility, found in overlapping boundaries, is still seen as quantifiable.

The generation of theory in qualitative research requires intact thick description for thick interpretation (Denzin, 1988: 432). Much of the more recent 'impressionist' work (Van Manen, 1988), done within postmodern ethnographic fieldwork and feminist approaches, requires minimally atomised data. Although re-presentations do occur, these are carefully reconstructed from rich, intact texts – a process that would not benefit from computer procedures.

Impact on knowledge

Computing programs are known for their capacity to texture reality. The gendering of technology through 'masculine' logic (Wajcman, 1991) is one area where texturing of reality has been identified as having the potential to distance women from involvement. The privileging of logic and rationality above lateral, multiperspective and creative thinking and the elevation of this form of information as authoritative (Nye, 1990) has led to a change in the nature of knowledge (Lyotard, 1984). The narrow focus on what stands as 'knowledge' has resulted in a silencing of female voices and a fragmentation of 'reality' (Bruhn and Lindberg, 1995; Henman, 1992). There is considerable potential for such minimal and decontextualised fragments to be hammered into a shape convenient to the purposes of the manipulator.

The capacity of programs to handle larger and larger data sets encourages more and more data to be collected. Although this may be advantageous in terms of allowing researchers access to both greater numbers and increased funding, it does beg the question of whether the collection of larger volumes of information will actually result in increased meaning. Jean Baudrillard has argued that more information does not produce more meaning, it simply wears itself out in staging it through a 'bombardment of signs' (1980: 140). The continual coding and counting of what may be becoming increasingly meaningless information (Henman, 1992) leads to the GIGO principle, 'garbage in, gospel out' (Rozak, 1994: 142). Baudrillard (1980: 139) has pointed to the danger of the development of the hyperreal. Here the elevation of a particular approach to interpreting data (such as one involving complex coding and subcoding) serves to disguise the loss of meaning which is also involved. The outcomes of the imposition of this new frame become more real than the original 'reality', which then becomes lost in the process.

Communication

Although networking facilities are available, especially for the more developed programs from the stables of NUD*IST/NVivo and ATLAS.ti, these structured forms of communication (person to computer, computer to computer) bear little resemblance to the more usual processes of collaborative research. Here, face to face processes comprise spontaneous verbal arguments, hands-on data interaction, and high level theoretical/conceptual discussions. These lose not only speed but flavour in the laborious type–send–wait–read–type–send–wait cycle of computer interaction.

Reification (or the glorification of the status of computer management)

The concept of reification emerges often within criticisms of qualitative computing packages. The first concern is the reification of the computer as a preferred way of defining the social world concisely and logically, where individuals become depersonalised and events neutralised (Dupuy, 1980). The second concern with reification is the relationship between the researcher and the data (Seidel, 1991). Once codes have been developed, they have a tendency to become objectified and treated as major explanatory foci. In addition, the reification of codes has led to them being regarded as variables to be looked at in terms of frequency of occurrence. This leads to inappropriate conclusions from the data (Laurie, 1992; Seidel, 1991).

Quantitative interfaces

The quantitative interface that has been developed in some programs through end-on statistical programs such as SPSS also imposes additional frames, especially in relation to the differing paradigms of origin. Where the same data set is involved in both quantitative analysis and qualitative interpretation, issues of different sampling techniques and lack of variable control become relevant (Hesse-Biber, 1995; Laurie, 1992). The emphasis in qualitative research on diversity, non-representativeness, small numbers, minimal stratification, self-selection, and thick ethnographic description suggests that drawing quantitative from qualitative data is contraindicated and that such a transformation produces unrealistic versions of the original. Where the quantitative data are from a separate data set with appropriate design and sampling strategies, these concerns do not apply.

Users' comments

Although many qualitative researchers have found computing packages essential in assisting with the management of larger databases, there is an ongoing discussion centring around users' concerns. The following issues have been highlighted:

- Many of the programs are idiosyncratic in nature, originally developed by individual academic researchers to help manage their own databases (Fielding and Lee, 1991). This poses the question as to how translocatable they really are to the different and equally idiosyncratic data sets of other researchers.
- Considerable time is required for the processes of setting up the data; the larger the sample, the more time will be required. One researcher compared the time she took interpreting qualitative data from a large British survey of household practices by hand and by using Ethnograph. She discovered that project analysis and interpretation took the same amount of time by hand as it did with

computer assistance (Laurie, 1992). This researcher also discovered that on-screen coding, which a number of programs now have, limits the researcher's view, encouraging and resulting in less complex coding patterns with fewer overlapping and nested codes (Laurie, 1992).

- Cutting up the text interrupts the chain of reasoning. Utterances have multiple actions and events embedded in them and segmentation disrupts the ethnographic process, tending to drive the research (Agar, 1991).
- Computing packages targeted at qualitative research tend to emphasise the common and shared properties of a large number, rather than variations in the minutiae of detail of small numbers (Agar, 1991). In addition, there is a likelihood of the loss of the 'untypeable' – the fleeting notes and doodles that often encapsulate insight (Richards and Richards, 1994).
- Particular program structures influence analytic results. The various processes of labelling, pattern making and synthesis, and pattern searching leading to thick description, must inevitably structure outcomes (Walker, 1993). In this manner, it seems likely that the etic (outsider, 'objective') rather than the emic (insider, 'subjective') approach to interpreting meaning will be fostered by the use of qualitative data management programs (Manwar et al., 1994).
- The dangerous ease with which one can move into quantitative mode in large databases, counting frequencies and undertaking variable analysis, is problematic (Bruhn and Lindberg, 1995). There is clearly an urgent need for a conversation regarding the theory of science within the processes of qualitative computing (Boy, 1992; Bruhn and Lindberg, 1995). Boy (1992) has suggested that computer aided qualitative research has lost its connection with the theoretical and methodological debates of the disciplines of sociology, psychology and philosophy, and that these links are in urgent need of reconstruction.

Summary

The way knowledge is constructed in our society is important, as is the hegemony of logic which determines which statements become knowledge. As human beings we have the capacity to create an inner representation of life which is multidimensional, complex and characterised by spontaneous reflexive actions. Processes involving segmenting and ordering data have the capacity to distance us as researchers, to limit perspectives, and to favour outcomes of homogenisation and standardisation. The tyranny of a system, however useful, which has the capacity to direct and simplify the construction of the views of researchers and ultimately those of readers, will thus always be problematic.

FURTHER READING

Ford, K., Oberski, I. and Higgin, S. (2000) Computer-aided qualitative analysis of interview data: some recommendations for collaborative working. *The Qualitative Report* 4 (3 and 4) March. This paper reports the use of the Mac-based software program NUD*IST to sort, code and index text units of interview data. The challenges of utilising such software in a collaborative context are explored.

Kelle, U. (ed.) (1995) *Computer Aided Qualitative Data Analysis: Theory, Methods and Practice.* London: Sage. The impact of computer-assisted analysis is discussed, and the author outlines strategies that capitalise on the computer's capacity to analyse large amounts of data in a short time. He offers new ways of integrating qualitative and quantitative analysis techniques as well as looking at the fundamental methodological and theoretical issues involved in using computers in qualitative research.

Ragin, C. and Becker, H. (1989) How the microcomputer is changing our analytic habits. In G. Blank, J. McCartney and E. Brent (eds), *New Technology in Sociology: Practical Applications in Research and Work*, pp. 47–55. New Brunswick, NJ: Transaction. An examination of the changes that computer technology has made upon social research.

There are other more detailed listings of computer programs available at the following sites, accessed 1 May 2006:

http://bama.ua.edu/~wevans/content/csoftware/software_menu.html
http://www.qualitativeresearch.uga.edu/QualPage/qda.html

Glossary

Analogical mapping
Use of analogy to map similarities between things that are dissimilar.

Basic hermeneutic approach
A method of data gathering and interpretation which seeks to understand the meanings of parts within a whole by going out into the field, collecting data, interpreting them and using this interpretation as a basis for further data collection and interpretation in an iterative cycle.

Centred
Where the researcher acts as the authoritative voice of the research, i.e. 'This is how the research was conducted', 'These are the findings.'

Decentred
The process of removing oneself from a central authority (as author/researcher) and allowing the views of others to be featured, often with minimal or no interpretation.

Différance
Jacques Derrida used this term to clarify the way in which all words (signs) create meanings in terms of their differences from other words or aspects and in terms of the constant deferral of meaning.

Discursive practices
Michel Foucault used this to describe the ways that particular discourses are maintained, e.g. the power of the doctor in hospitals is maintained by hierarchies of education and status, case notes, and the rituals of examination and prescribing which only doctors have control of.

Grand theory
Often called metanarratives; large bodies of authoritative thought which dominate belief systems, cultures or disciplines.

Hermeneutic
Hermeneutics is concerned with the interpretation of various forms of communication including speech, dramatic performances, written texts, art and events.

Matrix analysis
The development of a rectangular matrix, usually 2×2, to compare two different aspects discovered in the data.

Metaphor
A figure of speech in which a name or descriptive word is transferred to an object/objects to which it is not normally applied in order to provide a comparison.

Ontology
The study of reality through the conceptualisations of essences (models, interactions and things written about the nature of being) that underpin the particular domain under study, e.g. relationships.

Postpositivism
This follows and critiques positivism on the basis of issues regarding the problem of unity of all science; the separation between facts and theory; and the assertion that reality is partially a social construction such that measurement and variable control become problematic.

Quasi-statistical
Not quite but almost statistical, i.e. using descriptive (mean, median, mode and standard deviation) rather than inferential statistics.

Realism
The depiction of events and people as entities which exist independently of our conceptions.

Recursive spiral
A repeated spiral which enables the researcher to go backwards and forwards between the collection and interpretation of data in the development of a holistic view.

Transcendental realism
The belief that social phenomena exist in both the mind and the objective world and that the domains of the real (what exists), the actual (events) and the empirical (observable events) have reasonably stable relationships among them.

Typologies
The classification or grouping of common traits.

References

Chapter 1

Einstein, A. (1905/1923) *On the Electrodynamics of Moving Bodies in the Principle of Relativity*. London: Methuen.

Freud, S. (1900/1913) *The Interpretation of Dreams,* trans. A. Brill. New York: Macmillan.

Heisenberg, W. (1949) *The Physical Principles of the Quantum Theory,* trans. C. Eckart and F. Hoyt. New York: Dover.

Marx, K. and Engels, F. (1867/1999) *Das Kapital*. Washington, DC: Regnery.

Chapter 2

Bellavita, M. (1997: 181) quoted in Ely, M., Vinz, R., Downing, M. and Anzul, M. *On Writing Qualitative Research: Living by Words*. London: Falmer.

Couteau, R. (1990) Interview with Rae Bradbury. The complete version can be found at http://www.tygersofwrath.com/bradbury.htm, accessed 16 April 2006.

Dey, I. (1993) *Qualitative Data Analysis: A User-Friendly Guide*. London: Routledge.

Ellis, C. (1995) *Final Negotiations: A Story of Love, Loss and Chronic Illness*. Philadelphia: Temple University Press.

Ellis, C. (1997) Evocative ethnography: writing emotionally about our lives. In W. Tierney and Y. Lincoln (eds), *Representation and the Text: Reframing the Narrative Voice*. Albany, NY: State University of New York Press.

Goffman, E. (1974) *Frame Analysis: An Essay on the Organization of Experience*. New York: Harper and Row.

Grbich, C. and Sykes, S. (1989) *What About Us? Access to School and Work of Young People with Severe Intellectual Disabilities*. Victorian Department of Education, Melbourne and the Krongold Centre, Monash University, Australia.

Hepworth, J. (1999) *The Social Construction of Anorexia Nervosa*. London: Sage.

McLachlan, G. and Reid, I. (1994) *Framing and Interpretation*. Melbourne: Melbourne University Press.

Miles, Matthew B. and Huberman, A. Michael (1994) *Qualitative Data Analysis,* 2nd edn. London: Sage.

Seale, C. (2002) Cancer heroics: a study of news reports with particular reference to gender. *Sociology* 36 (1): 107–26.

Chapter 3

Bateson, G. (1972) *Steps to an Ecology of Mind. New York: Ballantine.*

Bennett, K. (1991) *Empowerment through Multicultural Education.* Chapter 1: Doing school in an urban Appalachian first-grade. Albany, NY: SUNY Press.

Bloom, B., Englehart, M., Furst, E. and Hill, W. (1994) Excerpts from *Taxonomy of Educational Objectives: The Classification of Education Goals. Handbook I: Cognitive Domain.* In L. Anderson and L. Sosniak (eds), *Bloom's Taxonomy: A Forty-Year Retrospective.* Chicago: University of Chicago Press.

Borgatti, S. (1999) Elicitation techniques for cultural domain analysis. In J. Schensul and M. Weeks (eds), *The Ethnographic Toolkit.* London: Sage.

Garrard, J. and Northfield, J. (1987) *Drug Education in Victorian Post Primary Schools.* Commonwealth of Australia, Canberra: National Campaign against Drug Abuse.

Goffman, E. (1974) *Frame Analysis: An Essay on the Organisation of Experience.* New York: Harper and Row.

Grbich, C. (1987) *Primary Caregiver Males: A Role Study.* Doctoral thesis, Monash University, Victoria, Australia.

Grbich, C. (1997) Male primary caregivers in Australia: the process of becoming and being. *Acta Sociologica* 40 (4): 335–55.

Spradley, J. (1980) *Participant Observation.* New York: Holt, Rinehart and Winston.

Whyte, W. (1955) *Street Corner Society.* Chicago: University of Chicago Press.

Whyte, W. (1984) *Learning from the Field: A Guide from Experience.* Newbury Park, CA: Sage.

Chapter 4

Barthes, R. (1977) *Image, Music, Text.* London: Fontana.

Behar, R. (1993) *Translated Woman: Crossing the Border with Esperanza's Story.* Boston: Beacon.

Brown, K. (1991) *Mama Lola: A Voodou Priestess in Brooklyn.* Berkeley, CA: University of California Press.

Chiu, J. (2004) 'I salute the spirit of my communities' I: autoethnographic innovations in Hmong American literature. *College Literature* 31 (3) Summer: 43–56.

Denzin, N. (2003) The call to performance. *Symbolic Interactionism* 26 (1): 187–207.

Denzin, N. (2001) The reflexive interview and performative social science. *Qualitative Research* 1 (1): 23–46.

Ellis, C. (1995a) The other side of the fence: seeing black and white in a small southern town. *Qualitative Inquiry* 1: 147–67. Newbury Park, CA: Sage.

Ellis, C. (1995b) *Final Negotiations: A Story of Love, Loss, and Chronic Illness.* Philadelphia: Temple University Press.

Ellis, C. (2003) Grave tending: with Mom at the cemetery. *Forum Qualitative Social Research* 4 (2), http://www.qualitative-research.net/fqs-texte/2-03/2-03ellis-e.htm, accessed 24 April 2006.

Ellis, C. and Bochner, A. (1992) Telling and performing personal stories: the constraints of choice in abortion. In C. Ellis and M. Flaherty (eds), *Investigating Subjectivity: Research on Lived Experience,* pp. 79–101. Newbury Park, CA: Sage.

Ellis, C. and Bochner, A. (2000) Autoethnography, personal narrative, reflexivity: researcher as a subject. In N. Denzin and Y. Lincoln (eds), *Handbook of Qualitative Research,* 2nd edn, pp. 733–68. Thousand Oaks, CA: Sage.

Ellis, C., Kiesinger, C. and Tillman-Healy, L. (1997) Interactive interviewing: talking about emotional experience. In R. Hertz (ed.), *Reflexivity and Voice.* Thousand Oaks, CA: Sage.

Gajjala, R. (2002) An interrupted postcolonial/feminist cyberethnography: complicity and resistance in the 'cyberfield'. *Feminist Media Studies* 2 (2): 1–16, http://www.cyberdiva. org/erniestuff/sanov.html, accessed 26 April 2006.

Holt, Nicholas L. (2003) Representation, legitimation, and autoethnography: an autoethnographic writing story. *International Journal of Qualitative Methods* 2 (1), article 2, http://www.ualberta.ca/~iiqm/backissues/2_1/pdf/holt.pdf, accessed 28 April 2006.

Kreiger, S. (1985) Beyond subjectivity: the use of the self in social science. *Qualitative Sociology* 8 (4): 309–24.

Mienczakowski, J. (1992) *Syncing Out Loud: A Journey into Illness.* Brisbane: Griffith University Reprographics.

Mienczakowski, J. and Morgan, S. (1993) *Busting: The Challenge of the Drought Spirit.* Brisbane: Griffith University Reprographics.

Mienczakowski, J., Smith, R. and Sinclair, M. (1996) On the road to catharsis: a theoretical framework for change. *Qualitative Inquiry* 2 (4): 439–62.

Mienczakowski, J. (1996) An ethnographic act the construction of consensual theatre. In C. Ellis and A. Bochner (eds), *Composing Ethnography: Alternative Forms of Qualitative Writing.* Ethnographic Alternatives. Book Series V 1. Walnut Creek CA: Alta Mira Press.

Mienczakowski, J. (1997) Theatre of change. *Research in Drama Education* 2 (2): 159–73.

Miller, D. and Slater, D. (2000) *The Internet: An Ethnographic Approach.* Oxford: Berg. Chapter 1, http://ethnonet.gold.ac.uk/, accessed 24 April 2006.

Olson, L. (2004) The role of voice in the (re) construction of a battered woman's identity: an autoethnography of one woman's experience of abuse. *Woman's Studies in Communication* 27 (1) Spring: 1–33.

Richardson, L. (2000) New writing practices in qualitative research. *Sociology of Sport Journal* 17: 5–20.

Ronai, C. (1992) The reflexive self through the narrative: a night in the life of an erotic dancer/researcher. In C. Ellis and M. Flaherty (eds), *Investigating Subjectivity: Research on Lived Experience.* Thousand Oaks, CA: Sage.

Sade-Beck, S. (2004) Internet ethnography: online and offline. *International Journal of Qualitative Methods,* http://www.google.com.au/search?q=cache:gVXDWpC20l0J: www.ualberta.ca/~iiqm/backissues/3_2/pdf/sadebeck.pdf+Internet+ethnography+online+ and+offline&hl=en, accessed 27 April 2006.

Saldana, J. and Woolcott, H. (2001) *Finding my Place: The Brad Trilogy.* A play adapted by Johnny Saldana from the works of and in collaboration with Harry Woolcott. Performance draft. Arizona State University Department of Theatre, Tempe, AZ.

Schreiber, R., Rodney, P., Brown, H. and Varcoe, C. (2001) Letters to the editor: reflections on deconstructing Harry, or when is good art bad science? *Qualitative Health Research* 11 (6) November: 723–4.

Tierney, W. and Lincoln, Y. (eds) (1997) *Representation and the Text: Re-framing the Narrative Voice.* Albany, NY: State University of New York Press.

Ward, K. (1999) Cyber-ethnography and the emergence of the virtually new community. *Journal of Information Technology* 14: 95–105.

Chapter 5

Baker, C., Wuest, J. and Stern, P. (1992) Method slurring: the grounded theory/ phenomenology example. *Journal of Advanced Nursing* 17: 1355–60.

Burgess, R. (ed.) (1982) *Field Research: A Sourcebook and Field Manual*. London: Allen and Unwin.

Dixon-Woods, M., Agarwal, S., Young, B., Jones, D. and Sutton, A. (2004) *Integrative Approaches to Qualitative and Quantitative Evidence*. London: National Health Service.

Glaser, B. (1978) *Theoretical Sensitivity: Advances in the Method of Grounded Theory*. Mill Valley, CA: Sociology Press.

Glaser, B. (1992) *Basics of Grounded Theory Analysis*. Mill Valley, CA: Sociology Press.

Glaser, B. (2002) Constructivist grounded theory? *Forum: Qualitative Social Research*, http://www.qualitative-research.net/fqs-texte/3-02/3-02glaser-e.htm, accessed 26 April 2006.

Glaser, B. and Strauss, A. (1967) *The Discovery of Grounded Theory*. New York: Aldine.

Glaser, B. and Strauss, A. (1971) *Status Passage*. London: Routledge and Kegan Paul.

McCallin, A. (2004) Pluralistic dialoguing: a theory of interdisciplinary teamworking. *The Grounded Theory Review*, http://www.extenza-eps.com/EMP/doi/abs/10.5555/conu. 2005.20.1.28, accessed 26 April 2006.

Schatzman, L. (1991) Dimensional analysis: notes on an alternative approach to the grounding of theory in qualitative research. In D. Maines (ed.), *Social Organization and Social Process: Essays in Honor of Anselm Strauss*. New York: Aldine de Gruyter.

Starr, S. (1991) The sociology of the invisible: the primacy of the work of Anselm Strauss. In D. Maines (ed.), *Social Organization and Social Process: Essays in Honor of Anselm Strauss*. New York: Aldine de Gruyter.

Strauss, A. (1987) *Qualitative Analysis for Social Scientists*. Cambridge: Cambridge University Press.

Strauss, A., Fagerhaugh, S., Suczek, B. and Weiner, C. (1985) *The Social Organisation of Medical Work*. Chicago: University of Chicago Press.

Van Loon, A. (1995) *What Constitutes Caring for the Human Spirit in Nursing?* Unpublished masters thesis, Flinders University, Australia.

West, G. and Glaser, B. (1993) New identities and family life: a study of mothers going to college. *Examples of Grounded Theory: A Reader*. Mill Valley, CA: Sociology Press.

Wilson, H. and Hutchinson, S. (1991) Triangulation of qualitative methods: Heideggerian hermeneutics and grounded theory. *Qualitative Health Research* 1: 263–76.

Wuest, J. (1995) Feminist grounded theory: an exploration of the congruence and tension between two traditions in knowledge discovery. *Qualitative Health Research* 5 (1): 125–37.

Chapter 6

Crotty, M. (1996) *Phenomenology and Nursing Research*. Melbourne: Churchill-Livingstone.

Devenish, S. (2002) An applied method for undertaking phenomenological explication of interview transcripts. *The Indo-Pacific Journal of Phenomenology* 2 (1) April.

Geelan, D. and Taylor, P. (2001) Writing our lived experience: beyond the (pale) hermeneutic? *Electronic Journal of Science Education* 5 (4) June, http://unr.edu/homepage/crowther/ejse/geelanetal.html, accessed 25 April 2006.

Giorgi, A. (1975) An application of phenomenological method in psychology. In A. Giorgi, C. Fischer and E. Murray (eds), *Duquesne Studies in Phenomenological Psychology*, pp. 82–103. Pittsburgh, PA: Duquesne University Press.

Grbich, C. (2004) *New Approaches in Social Research*. London: Sage.

Husserl, E. (1981) Inaugural Lecture at Freiburg im Breisgau. Pure phenomenology, its method and its field of investigation (1917), trans. Robert Welsh Jordan. In Peter McCormick and Frederick A. Elliston (eds), *Husserl: Shorter Works*. Notre Dame, IN: University of Notre Dame Press.

Husserl, E. (1982) (*Ideas 1*) *Ideas Pertaining to a Pure Phenomenology and to a Phenomenological Philosophy* (1913), trans. F. Kersten (1931). Dordrecht: Kluwer.

Knight, Z. and Bradfield, B. (2003) The experience of being diagnosed with a psychiatric disorder: living the label. *The Indo-Pacific Journal of Phenomenology* 3 (1), http://www.ipjp.org/back.html, accessed 28 April 2006.

Merleau-Ponty (1945) *Phenomenology of Perception,* trans. Colin Smith, NY: Humanities Press. Translation revised Forrest Williams (1981). London: Routledge and Kegan Paul. Reprinted 2002.

Moustakas, C. (1961) *Loneliness*. Englewood Cliffs, NJ: Prentice-Hall.

Moustakas, C. (1994) *Phenomenological Research Methods*. Thousand Oaks, CA: Sage.

Rabbets, F. and Edwards, S. (2001) Needs experienced by persons with late stage AIDS. *The Indo-Pacific Journal of Phenomenology* 1 (2) September: 1–9, http://www.ipjp.org/back. html, accessed 29 April 2006.

Trujillo, J. (2004) An existential phenomenology of crack cocaine abuse. *Janus Head* 7 (1) Summer: 167–87.

Willis, P. (2004) From 'the things themselves' to a 'feeling of understanding': finding different voices in phenomenological research. *The Indo-Pacific Journal of Phenomenology* 4 (1) August, http://www.ipjp.org/back.html, accessed 29 April 2006.

Chapter 7

Boucher, C. (1997) How women construct leadership in organisations: a study using memory work. *Gender, Work and Organisation* 4 (3): 149–58.

Crawford, J., Kippax, S., Onyx, J., Gault, U. and Benton, P. (1992) *Emotion and Gender: Constructing Meaning from Memory*. London: Sage.

Davies, B. (1990) Menstruation and women's subjectivity. Paper presented at the Australian Sociological Association (TASA), University of Queensland, Brisbane.

Davies, B. (2000) (*In*)*scribing Body/Landscape Relations*. Walnut Creek, CA: Alta Mira.

Farrer, P. (2000) *Relinquishment and Abjection: A Seminanalysis of the Meaning of Losing a Baby to Adoption*. Unpublished doctoral dissertation, University of Technology, Sydney, Australia.

Friend, L. (1997) *Understanding Consumer Satisfaction and Dissatisfaction of Clothing Retail Encounters*. Unpublished doctoral dissertation, Otago University, New Zealand.

Friend, L., Grant, B. and Gunson, L. (2000) Memories. *Australian Leisure Management* 20 April–June: 24–5.

Garrett, R. (1999) Feminist research dilemmas in *How Young Women Move*. Paper given at a conference of the Australian Association for Research in Education (AARE), http://www. aare.edu.au/99pap/gar99199.htm, accessed 29 April 2006.

Haug, F. (1987) *Female Sexualisation: A Collective Work of Memory*, trans. E. Carter. London: Verso.

Ingleton, C. (2000) Emotion in learning: a neglected dynamic. *Research and Development in Higher Education* 27: 86–9.

Kippax, S., Crawford, J., Benton, T., Gault, U. and Noesjirwan, J. (1988) Constructing emotions: weaving meaning from memories. *British Journal of Social Psychology* 27 (1): 19–33.

Kitzinger, C. (2000) Doing feminist conversation analysis. *Feminism and Psychology* 10 (2): 163–93.

Lather, P. (1996) Troubling clarity: the politics of accessible language. *Harvard Educational Review* 6 (3): 525–76.

Lather, P. and Smithies, C. (1995) *Troubling the Angels: Women Living with HIV/AIDS*. Columbus, OH: Greyden.

Leavy, P. (2000) Feminist content analysis and representative characters. *The Qualitative Report* 5 (1–2) May, http://www.nova.edu/ssss/QR/QR5-1/leavy.html, accessed 27 April 2006.

Magnusson, E. (2000) Positions, powers and hierarchies in feminist research: vicissitudes of egalitarian interviews. Paper presented at the 25th Annual Association for Women in Psychology Conference, 9–12 March.

Mitchell, P. (1993) *Bridesmaids Revisited: Health, Older Women and Memory Work*. Unpublished masters thesis, Flinders University, South Australia.

O'Conor, C. (1998) Assessment and us: a memory work project. *Literacy and Numeracy Exchange* 1: 53–70.

Onyx, J. and Small, J. (2001) Memory work: the method. *Qualitative Inquiry* 7 (6): 773–86.

Pease, B. (2000) Reconstructing heterosexual subjectivities and practices with white middle-class men. *Race, Gender and Class* 7 (1): 133–45.

Rummel, A. and Friend, L. (2000) Using memory work methodology to enhance student learning. Proceedings of the 25th International Conference, The University of the Future and the Future of Universities: Learner Centered Universities for the new Millennium, pp. 326–30, Frankfurt, Germany.

Shields, L. (1995) Women's experiences of the meaning of empowerment. *Qualitative Health Research* 5 (1): 25–35.

Small, J. (2003) Good and bad holiday experiences: women's perspectives. In M. Swain and J. Momsen (eds), *Gender, Tourism, Fun?* Elmsford, NY: Cognizant Communications Corp.

Stephenson, N. (2001) If parties are battles, what are we? Practising collectivity in memory work. In J. Small and J. Onyx (eds), *Memory Work: A Critique*. Working paper series, School of Management, University of Technology, Sydney, Australia.

Wadsworth, Y. (2001) What is feminist research? Paper presented at Bridging the Gap: Feminists and Participatory Action Research Conference, Boston, June, http://www.wnmu.org/gap/wadsworth.htm, accessed 13 April 2006.

Chapter 8

Altheide, D. (1987) Ethnographic content analysis. *Qualitative Sociology* 10 (1) Spring: 65–77.

Chandler, D. and Griffiths, M. (2000) Gender-differentiated production features in toy commercials. *Journal of Broadcasting and Electronic Media* 44 (3) Summer: 503–20, http://www.aber.ac.uk/media/Documents/short/toyads.html, accessed 28 April 2006.

Cohen, J. (1960) A coefficient of agreement for nominal scales. *Educational and Psychological Measurement* 20 (37): 46.

Vaughan, L., Gao, Y. and Kipp, M. (2005) Why are hyperlinks to business websites created? A content analysis. Faculty of Information and Media Studies, University of Western Ontario, London, Ontario, http://72.14.207.104/search?q=cache:6MOXPEd79HIJ: www.cais-acsi.ca/proceedings/2005/vaughan_2005.pdf, accessed 27 April 2006.

Chapter 9

Beech, N. (2000) Narrative styles of managers and workers: a tale of star crossed lovers. *Journal of Applied Behavioural Science* 39 (2) June: 210–28.

Eco, U. (1979) *The Role of the Reader: Explorations in the Semiotics of Texts.* Bloomington, IN: Indiana University Press.

Franzoni, R. (1998) Narrative analysis – or why (and how) sociologists should be interested in narrative. *Annual Review of Sociology* 24 August: 517–54.

Frye, N. (1957) *Anatomy of Criticism: Four Essays.* Princeton, NJ: Princeton University Press.

Grbich, C. (1987) *Fathers as Primary Caregivers: A Role Study.* Doctoral thesis, Monash University, Victoria, Australia.

Labov, W. (1972) *Language in the Inner City.* Philadelphia: University of Philadelphia Press.

Labov, W. (1997) Some further steps in narrative analysis. *The Journal of Narrative and Life History* 7 (1–4): 207–15, http://www.ling.upenn.edu/~wlabov/sfs.html, accessed 26 April 2006.

Labov, W. and Waletzky, J. (1967) Narrative analysis: oral versions of personal experience. In J. Helm (ed.), *Essays on the Verbal and Visual Arts.* Seattle, WA: University of Washington Press, pp. 12–44. Classic work focused on the importance of evaluative statements in first-person narratives, http://www.clarku.edu/~mbamberg/LabovWaletzky.htm, accessed 26 April 2006.

Personal Narratives Group (1989) *Interpreting Women's Lives: Feminist Theory and Personal Narratives.* Bloomington, IN: Indiana University Press.

Reissman, C. (2003) *Narrative Analysis.* Thousand Oaks, CA: Sage.

Stevens, P. and Doerr, B. (1997) Trauma of discovery: women's narratives of being informed they are HIV infected. *AIDS Care* 9 (5) October: 523–38, http://www.ncbi.nlm.nih. gov/entrez/query.fcgi?cmd=Retrieve&db=PubMed&list_uids=9404395&dopt=Abstract PubMed, accessed 26 April 2006.

Todorov, T. (1990) *Genres in Discourse.* Cambridge: Cambridge University Press.

Chapter 10

Antaki, C. (2002) Conversation analysis tutorial. Discourse and Rhetoric Groups, Loughborough University, http://www-staff.lboro.ac.uk/~ssca1/analysis1.htm, accessed 23 April 2006.

Jefferson, G. (1984a) On stepwise transition from talk about a trouble to inappropriately next-positioned matters. In J.M. Atkinson and J.C. Heritage (eds), *Structures of Social Action: Studies of Conversation Analysis*, pp. 191–222. Cambridge: Cambridge University Press.

Jefferson, G. (1984b) On the organization of laughter in talk about troubles. In J.M. Atkinson and J.C. Heritage (eds), *Structures of Social Action: Studies in Conversation Analysis*, pp. 346–69. Cambridge: Cambridge University Press.

Kalekin-Fishman, D. (2000) Constructing mundane culture: 'plain talk'. *Journal of Mundane Behaviour* 1 (1) February, http://mundanebehavior.org/index2.htm, accessed 28 April 2006.

Lynch, M. and Sharrock, W. (eds) (2004) *Harold Garfinkel*. London: Sage.

Parrish, R. (2006) Conversation analysis of internet chat rooms, http://www.polisci.wisc.edu/~rdparrish/Chat%20Rooms%20for%20Web%20Site.htm, accessed 23 April 2006.

Ten Have, P. (2006) Exemplary transcript excerpts, http://www2.fmg.uva.nl/emca/sample.htm, from the Ethno/CA News site, http://www2.fmg.uva.nl/emca/index.htm, accessed 23 April 2006.

Chapter 11

Foucault, M. (1970) *The Order of Things*. New York: Random House.

Foucault, M. (1972) *The Archaeology of Knowledge*, trans. A. Sheridan Smith. London: Tavistock.

Foucault, M. (1984a) Truth and method. In P. Rabinow (ed.), *A Foucault Reader*. Harmondsworth: Penguin.

Foucault, M. (1984b) Nietzsche, genealogy, history. In P. Rabinow (ed.), *A Foucault Reader*. Harmondsworth: Penguin.

Harley, T. (1855) *Moon Lore*. London: Swan Sonnenchein, Le Bas and Lowry.

Hepworth, J. (1999) *The Social Construction of Anorexia Nervosa*. London: Sage.

Hepworth, J. and Griffin, C. (1990) The 'discovery' of anorexia nervosa: discourses of the late nineteenth century. *Text* 10: 321–38.

Lupton, D. and Chapman, S. (1995) A healthy lifestyle might be the death of you: discourses on diet, cholesterol control and heart disease in the press and among the lay public. *Sociology of Health and Illness* 17 (4): 477–94.

Seale, C. (2002) Cancer heroics: a study of news reports with particular reference to gender. *Sociology* 36 (1): 107–26, http://soc.sagepub.com/cgi/content/abstract/36/1/107, accessed 29 April 2006.

Chapter 12

Apollodorus (1921) English translation by Sir James Frazer, 2 vols. Cambridge, MA: Harvard University Press. London: Heinemann.

Crinall, K. (1999) My aunt, our mother, their face: sharing identity in a family photograph. *Visual Anthropology Forum*, http://cc.joensuu.fi/sights/karenc.htm, accessed 26 April 2006.

Levers, L. (2001) Representations of psychiatric disability in 50 years of Hollywood films. *Theory and Science,* http://theoryandscience.icaap.org/content/vol002.002/lopezlevers. html, accessed 26 April 2006.

Moriarty, S. (1995) Visual semiotics and the production of meaning in advertising. Paper presented at the Visual Communication Division of Education in Journalism and Mass Communication Conference, Washington, http://spot.colorado.edu/~moriarts/vissemi-otics.html, accessed 26 April 2006.

O'Neill, R. (2006) Iconology of the tower cards. Association for Tarot Studies, *Newsletter Archive* no. 6, http://association.tarotstudies.org/news6.htm, accessed 26 April 2006.

Panofsky, E. (1974) *Meaning in the Visual Arts: Views from the Outside. A Centennial Commemoration of Erwin Panofsky (1892–1968).* Princeton, NJ: Princeton University Press.

Saxl, F. (1957) *A Heritage of Images: A Selection of Lectures by Fritz Saxl.* London: Penguin.

Chapter 13

Aycock, A. (1993) Derrida/Fort-da deconstructing play. *Postmodern Culture* 3 (2) January, http://www.iath.virginia.edu/pmc/text-only/issue.193/aycock.193, accessed 1 May 2006.

Barthes, R. (1977) Death of the author: structuralist analysis of narratives. In *Image, Music, Text.* London: Fontana.

Baudrillard, J. (1993) Simulacra and simulations. In M. Poster (ed.), *Jean Baudrillard: Selected Writings.* Stanford, CA: Stanford University Press.

Boje, D. (2000) Postmodern detournement analysis of the *Popular Mechanics* spectacle using stories and photos of the festive community life of Nickerson Gardens. *EJ-ROT Electronic Journal of Radical Organization Theory* 6 (1), http://web.nmsu.edu/~dboje/pmdecon9705.htm, accessed 1 May 2006.

Deleuze, G. and Guattari, F. (1987) *Thousand Plateaus: Capitalism and Schizophrenia,* trans. B. Massumi. Minneapolis: University of Minnesota Press.

Derrida, J. (1972/1982) *Margins of Philosophy,* trans. A. Bass. Brighton: Harvester.

Derrida, J. (1976) *Of Grammatology,* trans. G. Spivak. Baltimore: Johns Hopkins University Press.

Derrida, J. (1978) Structure, sign and play in the discourse of the human sciences. In *Writing and Difference,* trans. A. Bass. Chicago: University of Chicago Press.

Derrida, J. (1984) Living on borderlines. In H. Bloom, P. de Mann, J. Derrida, G. Hartman and J. Hills Miller (eds), *Deconstruction and Criticism.* London: Routledge and Kegan Paul.

Derrida, J. (1985) Letter to a Japanese friend, 10 July 1983. In D. Wood and R. Bernasconi (eds), *Derrida and Difference.* Warwick: Parousia.

Derrida, J. (1987) *The Post Card: From Socrates to Freud and Beyond.* Chicago: University of Chicago Press.

Derrida, J. (1992) Psyche: invention of the Other. In D. Attridge (ed.), *Acts of Literature.* London: Routledge.

Fox, K. (1996) Silent voices. In C. Ellis and A. Bochner (eds), *Composing Ethnography: Alternative Forms of Qualitative Writing.* Thousand Oaks, CA: Sage.

Habermas, J. (1987) *The Philosophical Discourse of Modernity.* Boston: MIT Press.

Irigaray, L. (1985) *The Sex Which Is Not One,* trans. C. Porter. Ithaca, NY: Cornell University Press.

Nietzsche, F. (1911/1954) On truth and lies in an extra-moral sense. Fragment from the *Nachlas* (1873) 1. In *The Viking Portable Nietzsche*, trans. W. Kaufmann. New York: Vintage.

Roseneau, P. (1992) *Postmodernism and the Social Sciences: Insights, Inroads and Intrusion.* Princeton, NJ: Princeton University Press.

Saussure, F. de (1907–11/1916/1983) *Course in General Linguistics*, trans. R. Harris. La Salle, IL: Open Court.

Chapter 14

Aubusson, P. (2002) Using metaphor to make sense and build theory in qualitative analysis. *The Qualitative Report* 7 (4) December, http://www.nova.edu/ssss/QR/QR7-4/aubusson. html, accessed 1 May 2006.

Autry, P. (1995) *The Trouble with Girls: Autoethnography and the Classroom.* Doctoral dissertation, Louisiana State University.

Brodie, I. (2000) Theory generation and qualitative research: school exclusion and children looked after. *Theorising Social Work Seminar Series*, London: ESRC.

Burgess-Limerick, T. and Burgess-Limerick, R. (1998) Conversational interviews and multiple-case research in psychology. *Australian Journal of Psychology* 50 (2): 63–70.

Carter, P. (2006) A semiotic analysis of newspaper front-page photographs, http://www.aber. ac.uk/media/Students/pmc9601.html, accessed 2 May 2006.

Davies, S. (2006) Semiotic analysis of teenage magazine front covers, http://www.aber. ac.uk/media/Students/sid9901.html, accessed 2 May 2006.

Glaser, B. and Strauss, A. (1967) *The Discovery of Grounded Theory.* New York: Aldine.

Glaser, B. and Strauss, A. (1971) *Status Passage: A Formal Theory.* Chicago: Aldine-Atherton.

Green, B. (2004) Personal construct psychology and content analysis. *Personal Construct Theory and Practice* 1: 82–91.

Humphreys, L. (1970) *Tearoom Trade: Impersonal Sex in Public Places.* Chicago: Aldine. http://www.angelfire.com/or/sociologyshop/SOCIOLOGY.html, accessed 1 May 2006.

Leavy, P. (2000) Feminist content analysis and representative characters. *The Qualitative Report* 5 (1 and 2) May.

McLaurin, S. (2003) Homophobia: an autoethnographic study. *The Qualitative Report* 8 (3): 481–6, http://www.nova.edu/ssss/QR/QR8-3/abstract.html, accessed 1 May 2006.

Mead, M. (1926) Letter from Margaret Mead to Franz Boas, her supervisor, 14 March 1926, http://www.ssc.uwo.ca/sociology/mead/March14.1926.htm, accessed 5 May 2006.

Mead, M. (1931) Life as a Samoan girl. In *ALL TRUE! The Record of Actual Adventures That Have Happened to Ten Women of Today.* New York: Brewer, Warren & Putnam.

Pandit, N. (1995) *Towards a Grounded Theory of Corporate Turnaround: A Case Study Approach.* Doctoral thesis, University of Manchester, United Kingdom.

Shi, S., Mishra, P., Bonk, C., Tan, S. and Zhao, Y. (2006) Thread theory: a framework applied to content analysis of synchronous computer mediated communication, http://www.itdl. org/Journal/Mar_06/article02.htm, accessed 1 May 2006.

Sinner, A. (2004) Chronic pain and returning to learning: exploring the lived experiences of 3 women. *The Indo-Pacific Journal of Phenomenology* 4 (1), http://www.ipjp.org/ back.html#v4e1, accessed 1 May 2006.

Skinner, J. (2003) Montserrat place and Mons'rat neagra: an example of impressionistic autoethnography. *The Qualitative Report* 8 (3): 513–29.

Van den Berg, J. (1972) *A Different Existence: Principles of Phenomenological Psychopathology*. Pittsburg: Duguesne University Press.

Van der Mescht, H. (2004) Phenomenology in education: a case study in educational leadership. *The Indo-Pacific Journal of Phenomenology* 4 (1), http://www.ipjp.org/back. html#v4e1, accessed 1 May 2006.

Chapter 15

Audet, J. and d'Amboise, G. (2001) The multi-site study: an innovative research methodology. *The Qualitative Report* 6 (2) June, http://www.nova.edu/ssss/QR/QR6-2/index.html, accessed 1 May 2006.

Clarke, I., Jackson, P. and Hailsworth, A. (2004) Retail competition and consumer choice, 2002–2004. UK data archive, University of Essex, http://www.data-archive.ac.uk/finding Data/snDescription.asp?sn=5049, accessed 1 May 2006.

Duncan, S. and Edwards, R. (1997) Lone mothers and paid work: rational economic man or gendered moral rationalities? *Feminist Economics* 3 (2): 29–61.

Gamberini, L. and Spagnolli, A. (2003) Display techniques and methods for cross-medial data analysis. *PsycNology Journal* 1 (2): 131–40, http://www.psychology.org/File/ PSYCHNOLOGY_JOURNAL_1_2_GAMBERINI.pdf, accessed 1 May 2006.

Giannakaki, M. (2005) Using quantitative and qualitative research methods to examine teachers' attitudes to educational change: the case of the skills for life strategy for improving adult literacy and numeracy skills in England. *Educational Research and Evaluation* 11 (4): 323–48.

Grbich, C. and Sykes, S. (1989) *What About Us! A Study of Access to School and Work for Young People with Severe Intellectual Disability*. Ministry of Education, Victoria.

Marsland, N., Wilson, I.M., Abeyasekera, S. and Kleih, U. (2000) *A Methodological Framework for Combining Quantitative and Qualitative Survey Methods*. Statistical Services Centre, University of Reading, http://www.eldis.org/static/DOC13680.htm, accessed 1 May 2006.

Pieterse, V. and Sonnekus, I. (2003) Rising to the challenges of combining qualitative and quantitative research. Paper presented to Sixth World Congress on Action Learning, Action Research and Process Management (ALARPM) in conjunction with the Tenth Congress on Participatory Action Research (PAR). ALARPM, pp. 1–12, http:// 66.102.7.104/search?q=cache:Mkq-Qla2cuoJ:www.education.up.ac.za/alarpm/ PRP_pdf/Pieterse%26Sonnekus.pdf+pieterse+and+sonnekus&hl=en, accessed 1 May 2006.

Schoech, D. and Helton, D. (2002) Qualitative and quantitative analysis of a course taught via classroom and internet chatroom. *Qualitative Social Work* 1 (1): 111–24.

Wacjman, J. and Martin, B. (2002) Narratives of identity in modern management: the corrosion of gender difference? *Sociology* 36 (4): 985–1002, http://soc.sagepub.com/cgi/ content/abstract/36/4/985, accessed 1 May 2006.

Chapter 16

Banks, S. (2000) Five holiday letters: a fiction. *Qualitative Inquiry* 6 (6) September: 392–405.

Bazeley, P., Kemp, L., Stevens, K., Asmar, C., Grbich, C., Marsh, H. and Bhathal, R. (1996) *Waiting in the Wings: A Study of Early Career Academic Researchers in Australia*. Canberra: Australian Government Publishing Service. Commissioned Report no. 50.

Bell, S. and Apfel, R. (1995) Looking at bodies: insights and inquiries about DES-related cancer. *Qualitative Sociology* 18 (1): 3–19.

Boje, B. (2000) Postmodern detournement analysis of the *Popular Mechanics* spectacle using stories and photos of the festive community life of Nickerson Gardens. In *EJ-ROT Electronic Journal of Radical Organisation Theory* 6 (1), http://web.nmsu.edu/~dboje/pmdecon9705.htm, accessed 1 May, 2006.

Cavan, S. (1974) Seeing social structure in a rural setting. *Urban Life and Culture* 3 (3): 329–46.

Coffey, A., Dicks, B., Mason, B., Renold, E., Soyinka, B. and Williams, M. (2005) Methods Briefing 8. Ethnography for the digital age, http://64.233.179.104/search?q=cache:c_c-C41tGJIJ:www.ccsr.ac.uk/methods/publications/documents/coffey.pdf+interactive+qualitative+data&hl=enon, accessed 1 May 2006.

Dicks, B., Mason, B., Coffey, A. and Atkinson, P. (2005) *Qualitative Research and Hypermedia: Ethnography in the Digital Age*. London: Sage.

Eco, U. (1993) *Misreadings*. Florida: Harcourt.

Ellis, C. (1995) Speaking of dying: an ethnographic short story. *Symbolic Interaction* 18 (1): 73–81.

Ellis, C. and Bochner, A. (1992) Telling and performing personal stories: the constraints of choice in abortion. *Investigating Subjectivity: Research on Lived Experience*. Thousand Oaks, CA: Sage.

Gamberini, L. and Spagnolli, A. (2003) Display techniques and methods for cross-medial data analysis. *PsychNology Journal* 1 (2): 131–40.

Gardner, J. (1990) *Victims and Criminal Justice*. Adelaide: Office of Crime Statistics, South Australian Attorney General's Department.

Garrard, J., Northfield, J., Slattery, M., Polowski, M. and Grbich, C. (1987) *Drug Education in Victorian Post Primary Schools*. Monash University, Faculty of Education.

Grbich, C. (1987) *Primary Caregiving Males: a Role Study*. Doctoral thesis, Melbourne, Monash University.

Grbich, C. (1997) Primary caregiving males: workforce or ideological change. *Acta Sociologica Scandinavica* 40 (4): 335–56.

Grbich, C. (2004) *New Approaches in Social Research*. London: Sage.

Grbich, C., Parker, D. and Maddocks, I. (2001) The emotions and coping strategies of caregivers of family members with a terminal cancer. *Journal of Palliative Care (Canada)* 17 (1): 30–46.

Humphreys, L. (1975) *Tearoom Trade: Impersonal Sex in Public Places*. Chicago: Aldine. http://www.angelfire.com/or/sociologyshop/SOCIOLOGY.html, accessed 1 May 2006.

Katz, S. (1997) Felon Busters: when the cops are outgunned, LAPD SWAT breaks up the party. *Popular Mechanics* May, http://www.popularmechanics.com/science/law_enforcement/1280896.html, accessed 1 May 2006.

Mienczakowski, J. (1996) An ethnographic act: the construction of consensual theatre. In C. Ellis and A. Bochner (eds), *Composing Ethnography: Alternative Forms of Qualitative Writing*. Thousand Oaks, CA: Sage.

Mienczakowski, J. and Morgan, S. (1993) *Busting: The Challenge of the Drought Spirit*. Brisbane: Griffith University Reprographics.

Minichiello, V., Alexander, L. and Jones, D. (1990) A typology of decision-making situations for entry into nursing homes. In *In Depth Interviewing: Researching People*. Melbourne: Longman Cheshire.

Minichiello, V., Aroni, R., Timewell, E. and Alexander, L. (1995) *In Depth Interviewing*, 2nd edn. Melbourne: Longman.

Van Manen, M. (1988) *On Writing Ethnography*. Chicago: University of Chicago Press.

Van Manen, M. (1999) The practice of practice. In M. Lange, J. Olsen, H. Henning and W. Bynder (eds), *Changing Schools/Changing Practices: Perspectives on Education Reform and Teacher Professionalism*. Luvain, Belgium: Garant.

Wolf, Margery (1992) *A Thrice-Told Tale: Feminism, Postmodernism, and Ethnographic Responsibility*. Stanford, CA: Stanford University Press.

Chapter 17

Agar, M. (1991) The right brain strikes back. In N. Fielding and R. Lee (eds), *Using Computers in Qualitative Research,* pp. 181–94. London: Sage.

Baudrillard, J. (1980) The implosion of meaning in the media and the implosion of the social in the masses. In K. Woodward (ed.), *The Myths of Information Technology and Post Industrial Culture*, pp. 137–48. New York: Coda.

Boy, P. (1992) Introductory remarks: current trends in computer-aided qualitative analysis. Paper presented at the Qualitative Research Process and Computing Conference, Bremen, Germany.

Bruhn, A. and Lindberg, O. (1995) Computer-aided qualitative data analysis: some issues from a Swedish perspective. Paper presented at the Australian Association of Social Research Conference, Victoria, Australia.

Denzin, N. (1988) Review of the book *Qualitative Analysis for Social Scientists*. *Contemporary Sociology* 17 (3): 430–2.

Dupuy, J. (1980) Myths of the informational society. In K. Woodward (ed.), *Myths of Information: Technology and Postindustrial Culture*, pp. 3–17. New York: Coda.

Fielding, N. and Lee, R. (1991) *Using Computers in Qualitative Research*. London: Sage.

Friedheim, E. (1984) Field research and word processor files: a technical note. *Qualitative Sociology* 7 (1–2): 90–7.

Grbich, C. (1998) Computing packages for qualitative data measurement: what is their real impact? *Australian Journal of Primary Health – Interchange* 4 (3): 98–104.

Guattari, F. (1984) *Molecular Revolution*. Harmondsworth: Penguin.

Henman, P. (1992) Grounding social critiques of computers: the world-view embodied in computers. Paper presented at the Australian Sociological Association Conference, Adelaide, South Australia.

Hesse-Biber, S. (1995) Unleashing Frankenstein's monster? The use of computers in qualitative research. In R. Burgess (ed.), *Studies in Qualitative Methodology: Computing and Qualitative Research*, pp. 25–41. London: JAI Press.

Huber, G. and Garcia, C. (1993) Voices of beginning teachers: computer assisted listening to their common experiences. In M. Schratz (ed.), *Qualitative Voices in Educational Research*, pp. 131–56. London: Falmer.

Idhe, D. (1990) *Technology and the Life World: From Garden to Earth*. Bloomington, IN: Indiana University Press.

Laurie, H. (1992) Using the ETHNOGRAPH: practical and methodological implications. Paper presented at the International Conference on the Qualitative Research Process and Computing, Bremen, Germany.

Lyman, P. (1984) Reading, writing and word processing: towards a phenomenology of the computer age. *Qualitative Sociology* 7 (1–2): 75–89.

Lyotard, J. (1984) *The Postmodern Condition: A Report on Knowledge*. Minneapolis: University of Minnesota Press.

McLachlan, G. and Reid, I. (1994) *Framing and Interpretation*. Melbourne: Melbourne University Press.

Manwar, A., Johnson, B. and Dunlap, E. (1994) Qualitative data analysis with hypertext: a case of New York City crack dealers. *Qualitative Sociology* 17 (3): 283–92.

Metzing, D. (ed.) (1980) *Frame Conceptions and Text Understanding*. Berlin: de Gruyter.

Murphy, J. and Pardeck, J. (1988) The computer micro-world, knowledge and social planning. *Computers in Human Services* 3 (1): 127–41.

Nye, A. (1990) *Words of Power: A Feminist Reading of the History of Logic*. London: Routledge.

Pfaffenberger, B. (1988) *Microcomputer Applications in Qualitative Research*. Newbury Park, CA: Sage.

Richards, T. and Richards, L. (1994) Using computers in qualitative research. In N. Denzin and Y. Lincoln (eds), *Handbook of Qualitative Research*, pp. 445–62. Thousand Oaks, CA: Sage.

Rozak, T. (1994) *The Cult of Information: The Folklore of Computers and the True Art of Thinking*. Berkeley, CA: University of California Press.

Seidel, J. (1991) Method and madness in the application of computer technology to qualitative data analysis. In N. Fielding and R. Lee (eds), *Using Computers in Qualitative Research*, pp. 107–16. London: Sage.

Van Manen, J. (1988) *Tales of the Field: On Writing Ethnography*. Chicago: University of Chicago Press.

Wacjman, J. (1991) *Feminism Confronts Technology*. University Park, PA: Pennsylvania State University Press.

Walker, B. (1993) Computer analysis of qualitative data: a comparison of three packages. *Qualitative Health Research* 3 (1): 91–101.

Zadeh, L. (1988) Fuzzy logic. *Computer* 21 (4): 83–93.

Author Index

Subject Index